Happy Father's & Mother's Day!! 6/14/86

With love,

John

The Savage's Romance
The Poetry of Marianne Moore

THE SAVAGE'S ROMANCE
The Poetry of Marianne Moore

John M. Slatin

The Pennsylvania State University Press
University Park and London

To my parents, Myles and Diana Slatin

I am grateful to the editors and publishers of the *Marianne Moore Newsletter* and *Twentieth Century Literature* for permission to reprint portions of this book which first appeared in the pages of those journals.

Permission to quote from the following works by Marianne Moore is hereby acknowledged: *Collected Poems*, copyright 1935, 1941 by Marianne Moore; renewed 1963 by Marianne Moore and T.S. Eliot; and renewed 1969 by Marianne Moore. Reprinted with permission of Macmillan Publishing Company, Inc. *What Are Years?* copyright 1941, and renewed 1969, by Marianne Moore. Reprinted with permission of Macmillan Publishing Company, Inc.

Excerpts from *Collected Poems 1909–1962* by T.S. Eliot, copyright 1936 by Harcourt Brace Jovanovich, Inc.; copyright 1963, 1964 by T.S. Eliot. Reprinted by permission of the publisher.

Previously unpublished material by Marianne Moore, copyright 1986 by Clive E. Driver, Literary Executor of the Estate of Marianne C. Moore. Used by permission.

Library of Congress Cataloging-in-Publication Data

Slatin, John M.
The savage's romance.
Includes index.
1. Moore, Marianne, 1887–1972—
Criticism and interpretation. I. Title.
PS3525.05616Z827 1986 811'.52 85–43250
ISBN 0–271–00425–8

Contents

Acknowledgments

I have incurred many debts. The first is to Arthur Bennett, a teaching assistant in the Great Books course at the Honors College of the University of Michigan in 1970, who early one morning set my mind spinning with Moore's phrase "imaginary gardens with real toads in them." Professor Herbert C. Barrows' course on Modern Poetry provided the first opportunity to read Moore. The first chance to write about her came in 1975, in a graduate seminar on American poetry taught by the late Laurence B. Holland, whose exemplary devotion to literature and criticism has continued to inspire me; I hope this book would have gone some way toward repaying him for his continuing interest in my work on Moore.

It was Hugh Kenner who suggested that that seminar paper might be the seed of a dissertation, and who provided the opportunity to develop my ideas more fully. As patient as he was generous, Kenner was all that one could have asked for in a dissertation director.

I owe a great deal to friends and colleagues who have read and commented on various versions of this manuscript: to Hugh Kenner, again; and to Marcus Klein, of SUNY Buffalo, who was likewise kind enough to read an entire draft and offer some invaluable suggestions for its improvement. Helen Hennessy Vendler read and responded to an early version of chapter 2, which I had sent to her unsolicited. Patricia C. Willis of the Rosenbach Museum and Library has not only read various versions of various parts of the book; she has also placed her tremendous knowledge of Moore and the Moore Archive at my disposal, answering questions, tracking information without stint. I am deeply grateful to her, as I am to John P. McWilliams, Jr., and Stephen Donadio, both of Middlebury College, for their responses to my writing. I have also benefited greatly from William P. Nemir's careful reading of the manuscript.

This book was completed with the aid of generous grants from the Faculty Research Council of Middlebury College, and from the University Research Institute of the University of Texas at Austin.

The continuing support of my friends and colleagues at the University of Texas has made this project a pleasure and an adventure. Joseph Malof provided crucial and timely advice. Alan Warren Friedman and Elizabeth Cullingford have offered helpful criticism and moral support all along, as has Susan Heinzelman. I have been talking for ten years with Evan Carton about American literature, and about writing: those conversations have shaped this book in ways no less crucial than his comments in the margins of my manuscript. And I owe more than I can say to Kurt Heinzelman, who listened to and read and minutely criticized innumerable drafts, urging me toward an economy I never quite achieved.

I have been nudged still closer to clarity by the scrupulous copyediting of Patricia Coryell at the Pennsylvania State University Press; her task was made easier by the careful typing of Mrs. Sarah Williams. Philip Winsor has been the best and most supportive of editors.

Without the help of these generous people this book would be much less than it is; but it would never have been finished without the help and steady support of my wife, Deborah Anne Carroll-Slatin. To her, and to Ledia and Mason, thanks from the bottom of my heart.

A NOTE ON THE TEXTS OF MOORE'S POEMS

If it were up to me, all of Marianne Moore's work would still be in print. But it isn't up to me, and everything except the recently reissued *Complete Poems* has been out of print for years. I ask the reader to bear this in mind upon discovering that the texts of the poems discussed in this book differ —often quite substantially—from the texts of the "same" poems as they appear in *Complete Poems.* As I shall explain in the introduction, *Complete Poems* does not provide a reliable basis for discussing the first two decades of Moore's career. For the sake of historical accuracy, therefore, I have based my argument on the first published text of each poem discussed, except where stated otherwise.

Introduction

I

This is a book about the poems Marianne Moore produced between 1915, when she first got into print, and 1936, the year after her *Selected Poems,* edited and introduced by T.S. Eliot, was published in New York and London.[1] The usual justification for studying the early stages of a poet's career is that it facilitates understanding of the writer's later, maturer, and more important work. The grounds are different in this case, however. I have given full attention to the poems Moore wrote during the first twenty-one years of her long career (she went on writing until 1970, two years before her death) because I believe that they, and not the later poems, afford the basis for Moore's claim to status as a significant poet.

Many of the poems under consideration here are extremely difficult; they can be read, however, despite—or perhaps even because of—their difficulty. Ironically, Moore's poems are difficult precisely because, in their apparently almost total lack of reference either to poetic tradition or to anything we might agree to call the real world, they seem to have achieved something very close to the perfect autonomy which the New Criticism attributed to the poetic object. Of course there is no such thing as perfect autonomy, and Moore's poems do not achieve it. This failure is insignificant unless we allow the possibility that the impression of autonomy is not an accident. And that is the premise upon which this book rests.

My goal has been to demonstrate, by means of detailed explications, *à la* New Criticism, not only how Moore's poems attempt to secure autonomy for themselves, but also how their repeated, necessary failures create the disruptions upon which explication depends for its clues. Thus explication destroys the autonomous status which the New Criticism claimed for the poetic object and which Moore tries to claim for herself, by binding Moore and her poems within an increasingly complex network of literary relationships.

Many of these relationships have so far gone unrecognized or undiscussed, and the ways in which Moore conducted her poetic relations have been little understood. Moore must bear the lion's share of the blame for this neglect, since she could not or would not explain her relationships with other writers in any full way; indeed, when opportunity for explanation presented itself, as it did every time Moore was asked about her quotations, she became thoroughly evasive. But criticism has so far allowed those evasions to go unquestioned.

Our vision of Moore's earlier poems, and of the earlier part of her career as a whole, continues to be refracted through the lens of her later and slighter verse, and is thus significantly distorted. Since the first book-length study of Moore—Bernard F. Engle's *Marianne Moore*—appeared more than twenty years ago, critical discussion has been based almost exclusively on either the *Collected Poems* of 1951 or its successor, the misnamed *Complete Poems* of 1967 (revised 1981).[2] But the *Complete Poems* is not complete (it omits roughly half of the poems Moore had published before 1925, for instance). Moreover, its early pages are dominated by late and often quite radical revisions which frequently alter difficult early work to make it accord more comfortably with the simpler, more recent, and far more numerous poems which won Moore a considerable public following. Taken together, these omissions and revisions make the *Complete Poems* completely unreliable as the basis for any discussion of Moore's early years.

Laurence Stapleton, who argues that Moore reached the height of her powers in *What Are Years?* (1941) and *Nevertheless* (1944), avoids some of these problems by basing the argument of *Marianne Moore: The Poet's Advance* on successive collections of Moore's verse.[3] This is a step in the right direction, but it does not go far enough. The collections on which Stapleton relies are already marked by revisions. These revisions are of course part of the development I am trying to trace, but they must be treated in context—that is, *as revisions.* My argument, therefore, revolves around the texts of the poems as published in the magazines where they originally appeared; subsequent revisions are treated as Moore's critical responses to her own work and taken into account when they help to expose the issues more clearly.

This approach involves the discussion of some unfamiliar texts. These may be unfamiliar early versions of familiar poems, or they may be poems which do not belong to the Moore "canon" defined by the *Complete Poems.* ("Black Earth" and "Roses Only," both discussed at length in chapter 2, are examples of poems in the latter category; "Virginia Britannia," treated in chapter 7, falls into the former.) The contours of Moore's development are likewise unfamiliar.

In assembling the early texts and subsequent revisions of Moore's work, I found that the twenty-one-year period with which this book is concerned may be subdivided into three distinct phases. The terminal dates for each phase correspond nearly to the publication dates of Moore's first three books: *Poems* (1921), *Observations* (1924; 2d ed., 1925), and *Selected Poems* (1935).[4] But the correspondence is not quite exact, and the differences matter. The first phase extends from 1915 to 1920, the second from 1921 to 1925, and the third from 1932 to 1936. (Moore produced no new poems between January 1925 and June 1932. She served as acting editor and then editor of *The Dial* from 1925 to 1929, and had no time to write; but she remained silent for another three years after moving from Greenwich Village to Brooklyn in the fall of 1929: see chapter 6.)

The distinctive poetics of each phase is most clearly displayed in the formal characteristics which divide them from one another. The poems of the first phase, written between 1915 and 1920, and discussed in chapters 1 and 2, are all composed in syllabic verse. Most of them appeared either in *The Egoist* or *Others.* The poems of the second phase, published between 1921 and 1925, appear as free verse. Becoming gradually longer as time goes on, they incorporate many more quotations than the poems of any other phase; these poems are treated in chapters 3, 4, and 5. With a few exceptions, they were first published in *The Dial,* which became Moore's chief outlet from 1920 on.

As we shall see in chapters 6 and 7, Moore returns to syllabic verse during the third phase of her career, from 1932 to 1936. The poems of this period appeared in such magazines as *Poetry, Hound and Horn, Life and Letters Today, The New Republic,* and *The Criterion.* These poems are generally quite a bit longer and formally more complex than the earlier syllabic poems of the period 1915 to 1920; unlike the earlier syllabic poems, many of the new ones are conceived as belonging to coherent sequences.

These formal differences are also thematic differences. Each of these phases involves a different conception on Moore's part of her relationships with her predecessors and contemporaries, and a correspondingly different strategy or set of strategies for negotiating those relationships—and thus a different conception of poetic form. Each phase, then, involves a different relationship between Moore and her audience, and represents a different stage in Moore's definition of her identity as a poet who is also an American woman. That developing identity, together with the different forms in which it appears and the literary relationships which threaten or enable it, is my principal subject in this book. It was Moore's as well.

II

Virtually everything Moore wrote between 1915 and 1920 responds (or contributes) in some way to the profound sense of isolation at the core of her sense of self. The first task facing the young poet was to find some way of reconciling her interest in radically innovative young writers like Ezra Pound and the other Imagistes, with the gentility which was and remained a fundamental aspect of her sensibility. The effort to forge a coherent poetics is inseparable from the attempt to construct a distinctive identity; it would not be overstatement to say that the principal aim of Moore's poetics during the initial stage of her career is the creation of a self and a poetry (and for her there is no real difference between the two) capable of withstanding the pressure to conform.

Moore was raised in a devoutly Presbyterian household by her mother, Mary Warner Moore, the daughter of a St. Louis minister who was acquainted with T.S. Eliot's grandfather; her brother, John Warner, was ordained in 1914 and spent most of his life as a Navy chaplain.[5] From the time of her birth in November 1887 until 1894, Marianne lived in the home of her maternal grandfather in Kirkwood, Missouri.[6] Then, after Reverend Warner's death, Mrs. Moore took her two children to Carlisle, Pennsylvania, an industrial town of about 10,000 people.[7] She taught English at the Metzger Institute for Girls, where Marianne went to school, and, so far as her daughter was concerned, she retained considerable literary authority throughout her life; she died in 1947, when Moore was almost sixty. They had never lived apart, except during the four years Moore spent at Bryn Mawr College between 1905 and 1909. After graduation Moore went back to Carlisle, where publications like *The Literary Digest* and the Boston *Evening Transcript* were the major sources of news about the latest literary trends—which, of course, they reported disapprovingly. Perhaps there was never any real doubt that gentility would win out in the end; but the struggle lasted twenty years, and what concerns us here is Moore's on-going effort to maintain an uneasy balance between opposing forces. For it is in that balance that the power of her work inheres.

What Moore does is to develop a poetic style of her own which is radically innovative almost in spite of itself. It combines both conservative and radical aesthetics without aligning itself (or Moore) fully with either. For the sort of conventionally prettified poetic diction preferred by *The Literary Digest*'s anonymous reviewers, Moore substitutes the conventionally prosaic diction in which the same reviewers composed their defense of convention; for conventional rhyme she substitutes rhyme so light and unobtrusive as to be virtually undetectable; for conventional English meters she substitutes an elaborate syllable-count which is even more difficult to recognize than her rhymes. And for conventionally "poetic" subject-matter Moore substitutes one of more urgent concern: the nature of poetry itself, and of her own relationship to it. Like her identity, Moore's poetics is worked out in her poems.

It emerges very early on, however, that she does not believe poetry can or should be explicitly defined. In fact, she doesn't really believe it can be *written* any longer—certainly not by her, and perhaps not by anyone. Even in what is clearly a poem of definition, like "Poetry,"[8] Moore refuses to offer a definition. Instead we get the negative assertion that "the result is not poetry" when things have been "dragged into prominence by half poets." Then comes the prediction that we "shall . . . have / it [poetry]" only when the unnamed "autocrats" who are now busy making dogmatic pronouncements about what poetry is have become "'literalists of / the imagination,'" capable of presenting for our "inspection, imaginary gardens with real toads in them"—which is to say, never. As I shall argue at length in chapter 1, it is not the apparent metaphorical equation of "poetry" with "imaginary gardens" and "real toads" that counts. What counts is the necessity for and the difficulty of the metaphor. Our inability to understand it is in fact a measure of the distance at which we stand from poetry itself. For poetry—so I think Moore believes, though she nowhere says so explicitly—is originality, truth, absolute clarity.

This must seem a wildly implausible claim. After all, Moore herself says that "complexity is not a crime,"[9] and even the most cursory glance at her work leaves an impression of formidable complexity, both formal and rhetorical—an impression, indeed, of an obscurity so profound as to amount nearly to impenetrability. As early as 1923, Williams was scratching his head over "the incomprehensibility" of Moore's poems,[10] and two years later the *New York Times* was editorializing against "the New Euphues."[11] Eliot wrote in 1935 that "It would be very difficult to say what exactly is the 'subject-matter' of 'The Jerboa'" (he was introducing Moore's *Selected Poems* at the time!),[12] and Auden bore him out, admitting in *The Dyer's Hand* that he had found it impossible to "make head or tail" of the *Selected Poems.*[13] So it is a little hard to see what Moore's poems have to do with clarity. The answer is: "Everything, and not much."

Clarity—poetry—is the ideal Moore holds up not only to herself but to her contemporaries as well; like Paradise, though, it is impossible to attain. (The association is made explicit in "In the Days of Prismatic Colour" and "When I Buy Pictures," among others, and most importantly in "An Octopus."[14]) All is not lost, however. It may be impossible to *write* true poetry, but "in the meantime" it remains possible for those who are "interested in poetry" to approximate or imitate it.

This would require major changes in the character of Moore's art. As I argue in chapter 2, poetic form is for Moore an expression of identity, and at this stage of her career Moore's identity depends on resistance. Her syllabics are supposed to guarantee distinctiveness; they are in effect designed, therefore, to prevent the sort of mimetic effort I have just mentioned. They also work to minimize quotation, which is equally a threat to distinctiveness. The net result, however, is what Moore thinks of as a loss of clarity—though considered from another vantage point, nothing could be clearer than what Moore is trying to do.

There are certain words which recur in poem after poem—keywords which reveal some of the most fundamental aspects of Moore's enterprise. Their significance and explanatory power depend upon their recurrence from poem to poem, and in my own argument as well. Persuaded as I am that readings of Moore's poems must be "performed" rather than simply recounted,[15] I have re-employed her phrases in my own prose as I think she uses them in her verse, in a manner which allows their significance to reveal itself incrementally.

Expediency signifies both the purposiveness and the inadequacy of *form*; and just as "form . . . is a matter of expediency," so the importance of a thing is a matter of whether or not it is *useful. Opaque,* and related words like *dark, black,* and *hard,* are in effect Moore's code words for the *complexity* and *obliqueness* of form she associates with her own work (as distinct from the clarity and *perpendicularity* that belong to the original work of others and to *truth,* which is obscured by Moore's complexity).

Like the elephant which speaks "Black Earth," Moore's early poems take a certain ambivalent pride in their impenetrability, which is directly associated with their efforts to resist what they call *experience* or *light* or *electricity*—all synonyms, in Moore's vocabulary, for the influence of other writers. Syllabic verse is the most expedient means of defense against such powerful forces. It is thus the burden of form to preserve the opacity on which Moore bases her claim to *superiority*. Moore wants above all to appear *self-dependent,* to use the phrase she borrows from Emerson's "The Transcendentalist,"[16] but finally she has to acknowledge that all her efforts have only isolated her from other writers—and from potential readers as well.

In fact, Moore's verse is not nearly so opaque, nor so impervious to the presence of other writers, as she would like to pretend. She is constantly, though furtively, measuring the degrees of difference and affinity between herself and others. Thus contact is not so much prevented as disguised, and Moore is left in the awkward position of having to disavow the debts she has incurred. My account of the early poetry and poetics amounts to a description of the various expedients by which Moore keeps herself in touch with poetry even as she seeks to sustain the illusion of what "Poetry" calls "a perfect contempt." My readings expose the multiplicity of the poems' affiliations and reveal the extent to which they are indeed (in Emerson's phrase) "luminous with manifold allusion."[17]

The multiplicity of those affiliations is what finally makes it impossible for Moore to sustain what I have chosen to call "the savage's romance." The phrase comes from the opening line of "New York" (1921), where it stands for all that must be swept away to make room for the "commerce" (a new keyword for the second phase of the career) on which Moore's work will more or less openly depend.[18]

III

The second phase of Moore's career began in July 1921, when she published the first of her free verse poems, "When I Buy Pictures" and "A Graveyard" (later retitled "A Grave"); significantly, both texts were achieved by converting earlier syllabic drafts into free verse. During this phase of her career, Moore reverses herself in virtually every respect.

The change to free verse is part of a deliberate effort on Moore's part to clarify her work and get "closer to the truth."[19] It proceeds from Moore's conviction that her previous efforts to establish her "native superiority" by insisting on formal perfection had been motivated by an unchristian pride which must be subdued. That conviction, in turn, proceeds in part from Moore's reading of T.S. Eliot's poetry and criticism.

Thus the poetics of resistance that had dominated Moore's work for the first five years of her career is replaced by what Moore calls "the principle of accommodation."[20] She now actively tries to admit into her poems the *light* she had formerly sought to "turn aside"; to acknowledge the extent to which she has been "devastated" by the *electricity* of "creative power," despite or even because of the "remoteness" of which she had boasted. Similarly, she makes a virtue of her newfound accessibility to the *experience* she had tried so hard to resist as she had earlier made a virtue of her isolation—by making it the basis of her work.

These changes in attitude are revealed most clearly by the increasing reliance on quotation, which is made formally possible by the shift to free verse. Criticism has so far concentrated on pointing out the differences between quotation in Moore and in Eliot and Pound. Almost everyone knows, for instance, that instead of borrowing from literary figures like Dante or Milton or Virgil or Shakespeare, Moore tends to quote directly from the popular press of the day—from magazines like *Vogue* and the *Illustrated London News* and *The Literary Digest,* to name only a few—and she tends to quote rather unprepossessing phrases, too. Nor does she make extravagant claims for the phrases thus appropriated. Asked again and again to account for their presence in her work, she repeatedly described them as phrases she liked and wished to preserve—like flies in amber—and for which she felt obliged to thank the authors by appending notes to each volume of her verse. (And then, in the *Complete Poems,* she suggested that people bothered by the notes could go ahead and ignore them—as if she would have put them there and called attention to their presence if she'd wanted them ignored. Even at eighty she was capable of irony.[21])

Critic after critic has noted these things and concluded—reasonably enough but quite incorrectly—that quotation in Moore serves a much more limited function than it does in Eliot or Pound.[22] But such arguments cannot even begin to make sense of poems like "An Octopus," which consists almost entirely of quoted material, as do the closing lines of the slightly earlier "Novices" (discussed at length in chapter 3). This is not to say, either, that Moore's growing dependence on quotation is merely quantitative. Her handling of quotations becomes more sophisticated with each new poem. And I shall demonstrate that this is a direct consequence of an increasingly complex engagement with Eliot's critical and poetic precepts.

Quotation finally becomes the principal means by which Moore constructs her approximations of texts whose originality she cannot claim for herself (although I am not saying, of course, that each poem of Moore's is, in its entirety, an "approximation" of one other text). Moore's quotations thus bear at least as great a burden as those of Eliot or Pound, and indeed I think they carry an even greater weight. Eliot and Pound depend on (or hope for) instant recognition of their borrowings, at least some of the time. When Eliot borrows a line from Dante or Tennyson, for example, he fully expects that at least some of his readers will recognize the source. Furthermore, he counts on their knowing the literary *value* of that source, and assumes that that knowledge will inform the reader's valuation of his (Eliot's) own poem as well. By contrast, Moore tends to deprive herself and her readers of such landmarks and signposts, and this is one reason we find so much of her poetry so difficult. Her sources are almost invariably both obscure and "non-literary"; even when she identifies them in her published notes, most readers find them charmingly but meaninglessly eccentric.

There is a sense in which the very recognizability of Eliot's borrowings, or Pound's, operates as a limit on the uses to which they may be put. A phrase derived from *Paradise Lost* is after all a phrase from *Paradise Lost,* with (for Eliot in 1922) a 250-year tradition of commentary behind it; that line refers resolutely to *Paradise Lost.* But when Moore borrows an anonymous sentence from an anonymous government pamphlet, she can make it allude to almost anything—even *Paradise Lost*—because she is not bound by either the reader's expectations or her own ingrained respect for the cultural status of the text she quotes.

I have in mind a passage near the end of "An Octopus" (1924), one of Moore's longest and most difficult poems. "An Octopus" is set on a glacial mountain, Mt. Rainier in Washington State, and takes us on a very unsettling tour of the mountain's scenery. For more than two hundred lines, which incorporate fifty-eight separately marked quotations, the poem presents a series of dazzling images, offering virtually no explanation as to the relationships between them and no commentary on their significance. After struggling with the poem for several years I one day found myself concentrating on a passage I had never paid any special attention to before:

> . . . upon this game preserve
> where "guns, nets, seines, traps, and explosives,
> hired vehicles, gambling, and intoxicants are prohibited,
> disobedient persons being summarily removed
> and not allowed to return without permission in writing."

The lines are quoted from a National Parks Service pamphlet given to visitors to the park where Mt. Rainier stands. Their relevance, and that of their unlikely source, began to appear to me when I realized that these lines, with their list of forbidden things and their statement of the consequences of disobedience, occur in a sentence immediately following an attempt to define happiness—an attempt cut short when the poet declares that it cannot be done without "such power as Adam had and we are still devoid of." Some thirty-five lines later the poem ends "in a curtain of powdered snow launched like a waterfall," an avalanche which expels poet and reader alike from the coldly ironic and very American Paradise which the poem has been slowly reconstructing—as the lines quoted above reveal in their indirect allusion to *Paradise Lost.* According to Christian doctrine, we are all "disobedient persons," like Adam; and in the closing lines we are "summarily removed" from Paradise. We cannot stay any longer because, like Adam, "we are devoid of" the "power" to give things their proper names. We cannot decide whether this place should be called Mt. Rainier (the name does not appear in the poem), or "Mount Takoma," or "Big Snow Mountain," and indeed we do not even know until too late that its true name is Paradise. And because the poet, like us, has lost the power of naming, she can only approximate the grandeur of *Paradise Lost.* In "An Octopus," therefore, the Law is handed down not by God and his angels, but rather by "these odd oracles of cool official sarcasm"—pamphlets issued under the imprimatur of the supreme secular authority, the government of the United States.

We have to learn Moore's allusive techniques, as we have already learned those of Eliot and Pound and Joyce. It is a question of training oneself to hear or see, in the specific words quoted in the specific context in which they occur in Moore, and in the specific context from which they are taken in the first place, a clear relationship to a text which does not "appear" in Moore's text at all. But even more than that, it is a matter of persuading ourselves that her quotations do have meaning. They are taken from sources no more unsuitable than those out of which Joyce reconstructs the *Odyssey*—as he and his commentators would have us believe—in the form of the modern novel, with a Dublin Jew for Ulysses and an arrogant Catholic aesthete cast as Telemachus, or perhaps as Hamlet; with Blazes Boylan doing duty for all Penelope's hundred suitors and Molly playing her many parts as best she can given her total ignorance of the script. Moore's materials are no less likely, either, than those out of which Pound carves the Malatesta Cantos. Indeed, as R.P. Blackmur suggested in 1935,[23]

Pound's method may have been derived in part from his reading of Moore, who also led Williams to the triumphant poetic discoveries of *Spring and All* and the compositional method of his own superb attempt to recover America as Paradise, *In the American Grain.*[24]

Criticism has spent sixty years learning to read Eliot and Pound, thirty years reading Williams, twenty years reading Stevens. Now it is Moore's turn. The goal is to discover and describe her affinities, first, with contemporaries like Williams and Pound and Eliot (Eliot above all); second, with the Anglo-American poetic tradition from which she seems to stand aloof; and finally, and perhaps most importantly, with the specifically American tradition that stems from the Puritans and runs through Emerson and Henry James (and Williams, and Pound, and Eliot) and which Moore tries to reconstruct.

IV

The third phase of Moore's career—and the last one with which this book is concerned—is best understood under the rubric of *reconstruction.* It is marked, first of all, by a return to the syllabic verse which had characterized her early work, and to the sense of isolation which had informed it. That feeling of isolation is not entirely unwelcome, however, as Moore's decision to leave her Greenwich Village apartment for a quieter neighborhood in Brooklyn attests. On the contrary, Moore's relatively isolated position in Brooklyn becomes the base from which she continues her search for community. Now, however, her interest extends to matters of civil as well as literary import.

Moore's civic concerns begin to be evident in "The Steeple-Jack," "The Student," and "The Hero," published together in 1932 under the collective heading "Part of a Novel, Part of a Poem, Part of a Play."[25] As I argue in chapter 6, the shared burden of these poems is that the ideal American community must be forged, or rather re-forged, like the Paradise of "An Octopus," from existing materials. Moore remains acutely conscious, however, that the community thus reconstructed is in some fundamental sense a fiction, as the collective title suggests.

"The Steeple-Jack," for instance, seems to describe a New England village in minute detail. But this village is a composite that Moore created by incorporating details garnered from visits up and down the Eastern seaboard, and it is in fact a representation of Brooklyn as, apparently, the idyllic and quintessentially American community. Moreover, its apparent ideality is a function of the subtlety with which Moore mediates her vision through the darker visions of artists like Albrecht Dürer and Nathaniel Hawthorne. It is, in short, a fiction from first to last.

The aim of that fiction is to represent the community to itself in such a way as to expose the internal corruption which threatens the integrity on which the community depends for its survival. But the fiction is dangerous precisely to the extent that the belief it compels is powerful enough to overwhelm recognition of its fictionality. Thus Moore discovers the paradox of her position as an artist in the course of her attempt to define the nature of her citizenship. On the one hand, she struggles to save the community, seeking heroically to awaken her readers to the danger that "could not be" at the center of American life but is there just the same. On the other hand, she must re-create the very danger she would avert in order to persuade us that it is real and present. The artist corrupts in order to preserve.

Moore can no longer sustain the illusion of her own innocence. As she now realizes, she is implicated not only in the current predicament of her elected community, but in its history as well. Just as "The Steeple-Jack" seems to describe a New England village, so the poems of "The Old Dominion" sequence—"Virginia Britannia," "Bird Witted," "Half Deity," and "Smooth Gnarled Crape Myrtle!" published individually in 1935–36 and as a sequence in 1936—seem to describe the landscape of colonial Virginia.[26] Like "The Steeple-Jack," though, they do not so much describe that landscape as reconstruct it.

Of course that landscape is already a reconstruction. The colonists' nostalgic re-creation of "an almost-English" scene turns Tidewater Virginia into an inadvertent parody of both England and Paradise, and casts the mold for the future. American history becomes a long series of repeated Falls, of imitations gone more or less humorously, more or less grotesquely, more or less finely wrong. The only way to correct and redeem that history is self-consciously and guiltily to accept it and its circular logic, to take personal responsibility for perpetuating it.

In reconstructing the Virginia landscape, then, Moore's poems reconstruct the history of America itself. At the same time, the sequence as a whole presents a mythologized version of Moore's own history—a reenactment of her own loss of innocence which implicates her directly in the historical process and makes her what she calls Henry James: "a Characteristic American."[27]

In these poems, Moore implies that imitation and parody may be the most distinctively "American" features of American art and American history. Acknowledging at last that "one must overcome one's reluctance to be unoriginal" (as she later put it), in "Virginia Britannia" she flagrantly adopts the language and less obviously parodies the form of Wordsworth's Immortality Ode, while "Bird Witted" and "Half Deity" parodically mime the movements of Keats's "Ode on a Grecian Urn" and the "Ode to Psyche." She thus gives to the decidedly "unEnglish" ground of her art "an almost-English" form of its own. That form is capable of sustaining a rapid, subtle interplay between opposing forces—domestic and foreign, natural and artificial, self and history: but not for long.

V

To the extent that there is a debate about Marianne Moore, the issue is whether she did her best work in the 1930s or the 1940s; there is no question at all about the work of the 1950s and 1960s, whose slightness is conceded universally.[28] My own conviction is that Moore's work begins to decline in 1940, following a three-year poetic silence which indicates a profound crisis. The decline is evident in the radically simplified style of poems like "Rigorists" and "What Are Years" and "Light Is Speech" (all 1940 or 1941), and it has become still more pronounced by 1943 and 1944 in such poems as "In Distrust of Merits" and "Propriety" and "Nevertheless."[29]

At the most general level, it may be that Moore's decline is only one symptom of the crisis under which modernism in general is suffering. Pound's energies are devoted to propaganda, not poetics; Eliot's attention is slowly turning away from the writing of poetry to the writing of verse drama and cultural criticism. Their withdrawal—and especially Eliot's—leaves a vacuum; a crucial stimulus is gone, and Moore's work suffers for it. But the failure of Moore's work needs explaining specifically in terms of her own poetry and poetics; and I believe that the history of Moore's career as I have described it makes it possible to account for the remainder, if only to suggest in a very general and summary way why I have limited discussion of it to a brief afterword.

The subtle parodies and multiple imitations which characterize the poems of the middle 1930s devolve, subsequently, into more straightforward and unitary efforts at literary mimesis. Moore's adaptation of Maria Edgeworth's eighteenth-century novel, *The Absentee,* for the stage, is a late and minor instance of this trend;[30] her translations are its most significant products. These translations lie beyond the scope of this study for the simple reason that they *are* translations, and thus they pose a number of special problems, both theoretical and practical, which have no particular bearing on the concerns I have tried to address here.

It is worth pointing out, however, that the simplifying, moralizing tendency which mars so much of Moore's work after 1940 is evident in the texts she chooses to translate. Her career as a translator begins in 1945 with a rendition of Adalbert Stifter's *Rock Crystal: A Christmas Tale,* made in collaboration with Elizabeth Mayer. It ends, not quite twenty years later, with the publication of *Puss in Boots, The Sleeping Beauty, and Cinderella: A Retelling of Three Classic Fairy Tales Based on the French of Charles Perrault* (1963). Perrault was a contemporary of Jean de La Fontaine, whose courtly, elegantly formed *Fables* provide the original for Moore's greatest achievement as a translator: the monumental *Fables of La Fontaine,* begun in 1946 after W.H. Auden suggested to a publisher that Moore would be ideally suited to such an undertaking, and completed eight years and seven entire revisions later, in 1954.[31]

Moore's work as a translator has been overshadowed by the poems she was writing and publishing while she worked on her translations. The later poems, too, may be seen to emerge from the great work of the middle 1930s and to depend upon Moore's having defined herself and her community as participating in the larger processes of American history.

Having defined her citizenship, having ceased to think of herself as an outsider, a "pariah" (as she told Donald Hall she had once felt herself to be),[32] Moore has a stake in the preservation of the status quo, from which her own identity can no longer be disentangled. With the advent of World War II, the acceptance of history which had cost Moore so much in the 1930s becomes, by a strange irony, an urgent imperative to keep things as they are, or rather to keep them *as they were before the war*: an imperative to resist the chaotic, even demonic forces which had been let loose upon the world in 1939 to threaten civilization itself, and which the formal end of the war in 1945 did little to abate. And so Moore comes to see herself as having been appointed—and here, as in her earliest work, she models her sense of mission on the biblical prophets—to rescue us from what increasingly appears to be "our decay," as she puts it in "A Carriage from Sweden" in 1944.[33]

This is the poem in which, for the first time in her career, Moore discovers something "that makes [her] feel at home"—discovers it, moreover, right in Brooklyn, "this city of freckled / integrity" which she has come to love so much since 1929. Ironically, though by no means incidentally, the object in question was made in the eighteenth century, in "Sweden's once-opposed-to- / compromise archipelago / of rocks. Washington and Gustavus Adolphus," Moore apostrophizes, "forgive our decay." But she herself cannot "forgive" that "decay."

Having finally found a "home" for herself—at almost sixty—she has from this point forward to defend that home against whatever threatens to change it, for to change it is to destroy it. As the pace of social and technological change accelerates in the years after the war, Moore becomes increasingly desperate to discover objects like the carriage. The once villagelike landscape of Brooklyn is beginning to change, and New York's landmarks, too, are threatened.

Once Moore had been able to recombine the disparate fragments of an apparently random and disorderly universe so as to reveal and re-create within the form of her poems the order she had perceived as being immanent in all things. (Thus she had been able to find material for poetry almost anywhere: in "business documents and / school-books," in book reviews and newspaper articles, in advertisements.) But now that order itself is vanishing into mere history. It is discernible only in a few objects like the carriage, which are virtually invisible to everyone save the poet herself (the carriage, for instance, is in storage in a museum); in sacred landmarks threatened with demolition, like Carnegie Hall,[34] or otherwise doomed, like "The Camperdown Elm"[35]—or in sacred places whose sacredness consists precisely in the fact that they are no longer there at all, like the "Old Amusement Park," which has been torn down to make room for LaGuardia Airport.[36] These are the elements of the lost Paradise Moore spent the first twenty years of her career trying to reconstruct. Like Pound, she was unable to make it cohere; but unlike Pound, she stopped trying and settled instead for reminding her readers that the world had once been different, and better. "Stand for truth," she says wearily in the closing lines of one of her last poems. "It's enough."[37] But it's not enough. The very poems in which she tries so desperately to hold up a few precious objects as amulets against our decay are themselves virtually lost as soon as they appear. They get buried, as things so often do in *Vogue* and *Harper's Bazaar* and even the *New Yorker,* between feature articles and glossy photographs and the advertisements she had once been able to transform into the stuff of art.

They have been overshadowed, too, by the figure of the poet herself. Perhaps Moore's greatest achievement during the last quarter-century of her career was to create herself as a highly visible public character. There is a photograph, in black and white, which reveals a diminutive, elderly woman wrapped in a long black opera cape and wearing a black tricorne hat—a tiny, faintly smiling, female General Washington who has crossed the Delaware to find herself in an urban setting.[38] Behind her, cutting diagonally across the picture plane, the sweeping lines of a great bridge set her clearly off against the less sharply focused blocks of modern apartments lining the riverbank in the background, emphasizing her smallness and frailty, and strengthening, too, the impression that we are looking at a figure out of America's legendary past, a living relic.

The bridge is the Brooklyn Bridge, and the year is 1958; but the careful composition of blacks and grays, with its strong horizontals and diagonals, its clear foreground and slightly blurred background, actually works to divide the poet from the contemporary moment in which it appears to place her. To reach the contemporary world from the poet's position in the middle of the picture plane, we would have to cross the bridge, moving backward across the river to the apartments in the background—but those buildings are out of focus, and the photograph reveals no means of access to the bridge.

This is a photograph of the character Moore presented to the public late in her career, both in her person and in her poems. This character is far more dynamic than the poems for which it is supposed to have been responsible, but it is nonetheless a caricature, partly self-created and self-sustaining, partly the product of what Moore's audience wanted to see and hear and believe—and like the *Complete Poems* of 1967, it is sadly incomplete.

Like any caricature, it seizes upon the more obvious features of its subject and exaggerates them at the expense of subtler and more complicated details, so as to make itself instantly recognizable as the image of a type—the type, in this case, ironically being that of the highly idiosyncratic and individualistic verging upon and shading into eccentricity. A drastically simplified and pared-down version of Moore's former self, this public character is part of her protective apparatus, part of the armor she wrote about with increasing frequency as she grew older. I do not mean to suggest, however, that that armor can be stripped away to reveal the "self" as something entirely separate from it: as Moore knew very well, "armor" only "*seems* extra" (my emphasis).[39] The character works like one of her poems, simultaneously revealing and concealing the identity of its creator, and partly creating that identity as well.

It is time we stopped confusing this character or caricature with the author of all Moore's work. The poems which form the principal subject of this book were not written, and could not have been written, by the character I have just been describing. The woman who wrote them was much younger and more severe than the kindly old lady in the photograph, intellectually more rigorous and emotionally a good deal less generous, inclined rather to irony and satire than to celebration and nostalgia. She was by turns aggressive and shy, confident and uncertain, compliant and unyielding, angry, rebellious, frightened, proud, humble, and—where her own work was concerned—devastatingly and sometimes disastrously critical.

She was also fiercely ambitious. The young Marianne Moore was stubbornly determined to make a place for herself within the literary community. This book is an attempt to describe how she went about doing that and to suggest the consequences of her success. Here we have less to do with the evidently considerable charm of Moore's personality than with the power of her poems, singly and collectively, to engage and persuade not just our own belated attention but the attention of her contemporaries as well.

1

Ecstasy, Expediency, and Contempt: The Problem of Definition

I

Originally published in *Others* in December 1915, the slight poem now known as "The Past Is the Present" affords a convenient point of departure. Here we see the outlines of the strategy by which Moore defines her own position in the on-going debate about the nature of poetry and thus in the literary community. Both in this poem and in the much better known "Poetry" (which we shall consider in the last section of this chapter), Moore is explicitly concerned with competing definitions of poetry, and both poems place special emphasis on the relationship between poetry and prose. In both poems, too, she uses what amounts to an allusive code as a means of defining her relationship to at least one literary predecessor as well as to other, more contemporary figures such as Eliot and Pound. Ultimately, however, she represents herself as standing apart from the literary community.[1]

The earlier poem represents the poet's isolation as being essentially historical. To say that "The Past Is the Present" is to assert an absolute identity between the two, and to imply an indifference to the movement of time. The poem's original title, however, suggests a radical disjunction, not between past and present but between present and future:

So far as the future is concerned,
"Shall not one say, with the Russian philosopher,
'How is one to know what one doesn't know?'"
So far as the present is concerned. . . .

The original title leaves the speaker isolated in the present, out of phase, and apparently quite nervous. The future is unknowable, and the present is hardly more stable; the poem is an effort on Moore's part to guarantee her own survival by removing herself as far as possible from the temporal flux—a strategy which serves ultimately to deepen the anxiety it is supposed to alleviate.

> If external action is effete,
> And rhyme is outmoded,
> I shall revert to you,
> Habakkuk, as on a recent occasion I was goaded
> Into doing, by XY, who was speaking of unrhymed verse.
>
> This man said—I think that I repeat
> His identical words:
> "Hebrew poetry is
> Prose with a sort of heightened consciousness. 'Ecstasy affords
> The occasion and expediency determines the form.'"

As in a great many of Moore's poems, the title (or at least the introductory clause of its second sentence) is part of the poem's opening sentence; it takes us straight from the unforeseeable future into the grammatically parallel and equally uncertain present. It may be a while, however, before we realize just how uncertain the present is. The poem begins with an apparently unexceptionable pair of propositions about poetry; these furnish the criteria by which the poet may determine her future course of action: "If external action is effete, / And rhyme is outmoded, / I shall revert to you, / Habakkuk. . . ." But we already know that the future cannot be determined; furthermore, this is 1915, and the status of rhyme, like everything else having to do with poetry, is very much open to dispute.

Not only are the propositions controversial; it is difficult to say what exactly is being proposed, and even more difficult to determine the poet's position. It is not immediately clear what the phrase "external action" means here, so we cannot say what it would mean to call it "effete." We do not know, either, the precise nature of the relationship between "external action" and "rhyme"—an important question, since the reversion to Habakkuk will evidently take place only if both propositions are held to be true. It would be tempting to stop at this point, satisfied that the poem is incoherent. But the questions it raises do in fact make sense, and they can be answered; and in the effort to answer them, we shall make some crucial discoveries about Moore's poetics.

We may begin to answer our questions about "external action" by working backward and eliminating certain possibilities. To begin with the most obvious, we frequently associate "action" with narrative; but "So far as the future is concerned" contains at most the germ of an anecdote. The poem tells us nothing about when, where, by whom, or in what context the all-important remark about Hebrew poetry was made. This makes it impossible to tell whether the reversion to Habakkuk into which the poet "was goaded" by that remark implies a positive or negative reaction on her part. Except in the trivial sense that such a reversion might literally entail opening the Bible to the appropriate pages, moreover, it can hardly be said to constitute an "external action," and it seems to be further internalized because it is being both remembered and projected as a possibility for the future; apparently it is not going on now. Habakkuk's significance to the poet is also unstated; therefore the significance that would attach to any reversion on her part remains implicit as well. This is entirely in keeping with the apparent burden of the closing lines, where the poet's insistence that "expediency determines the form" leads us to presume that the correspondence between internal states like "Ecstasy" (which "affords / The occasion" for utterance) and their "external" manifestations in "action" (in specific utterances) will be somewhat less than perfect.

The appearance of words like "expediency" in conjunction with such privileged terms as "Ecstasy" is typical of the daring violations of the conventional boundaries between poetry and prose which scandalize Moore's early critics and delight early admirers like Eliot and Williams and Pound. Poetry is supposed to be a very serious affair, but it is not supposed to be serious in practical ways—at least so far as the more conventional critics are concerned—and it is decidedly not supposed to be self-conscious. (In 1911 Moore picked up a copy of Pound's *Canzoni,* which contained excerpts from various reviews of *Personae* and *Exultations*; one, from the London *Morning Post,* said that Pound "immediately compels admiration by his lack of self-consciousness." Moore responded incredulously, underlining the last phrase and placing a large exclamation point beside it.[2]) Conventional criticism during this period places a very high premium on poetic ecstasy, an inspired state of self-forgetfulness in which utterance takes the appropriate rhythmical form by natural—that is, magical—means. A word like "expediency" implies, however, a self-consciously practical concern with form; but it also implies, and at the same time, what the title of another poem, dated 1916, says explicitly: that "In This Age of Hard Trying Nonchalance Is Good. . . ."[3]

As Moore uses the word "expediency," it seems to imply a certain self-conscious casualness where form is concerned; it suggests that the poet does not take form quite seriously, and that she is willing to settle for what is near at hand so long as it will do the job. We might make the further presumption, then, that Moore's apparent willingness to take the line of least resistance must be a function of her conviction that "external action" is indeed "effete," that there is nothing to be gained from a long, drawn-out search for the perfect form. But Moore's nonchalance is more apparent than real. In speaking of "expediency," she displays what "In This Age of Hard Trying" calls "a feigned inconsequence of manner," and gives us our first glimpse of the way she wields "that weapon, self-protectiveness."

Since rhyme is an aspect of poetic form, it must have something to do with "expediency" as well—though the relationship is not clear. Like XY, the poet is "speaking of unrhymed verse," and it is likely to appear to any reader not well acquainted with Moore's work (there was no other kind of reader in 1915) that she is speaking in "unrhymed verse" as well. The rhymes are there, however. They come at strange but regular intervals (*a b x b x / a c x c x*) at the ends of lines whose lengths seem completely unpredictable. But line-length only seems irregular, for even here there is a definite pattern. As in the vast majority of Moore's poems, the determining factor is not the ratio of stressed to unstressed syllables but rather the total number of syllables per line, regardless of stress (9, 6, 6, 15, 15 / 9, 6, 6, 15, 15).

There is nothing casual, then, about the form of "So far as the future is concerned." On the contrary, it now appears that rhyme is not so much "outmoded" as it is hidden—by diction, by syntax, and by the apparent lack of meter. Conventional rhyme schemes and meters often seem to require or even to produce certain syntactical forms, like the inversions of word-order that bothered Pound so much early in his career.[4] By contrast, Moore's rhymes seem to be discovered by her syllabic patterns, which are in turn generated by syntactical structures that accommodate diction conventionally associated with prose (this is one reason "expediency" shocks the reader) and obey the principles by which prose is conventionally ordered. We might say, then, that in conventional English verse rhyme works like an exoskeleton, supporting the sentence from the "outside" and audibly articulating its constituent parts. Moore's rhymes also help to support and articulate the sentences by which they seem to have been found, but they do so from the "inside," as it were, like an endoskeleton.

I do not mean that Moore actively tries to hide her rhymes; she simply does nothing formally to call attention to them. The first of the three rhyme-pairs, *effete/repeat,* is likely to go unnoticed unless one is looking for it; this is partly because the rhyming words are so widely spaced, and partly because we do not expect a line in one stanza to rhyme with the corresponding line in the next. And since we usually treat rhyme as having both aural and semantic functions, the apparent lack of any significant semantic link between "effete" and "repeat" puts another obstacle in the way of our perception. Besides, the rhyme is not completed until after the intervention of the second rhyme-pair; if we miss the latter, as we are more than likely to do since the third and fifth lines do not rhyme at all, the first rhyme-pair is all the more likely to escape our notice. The members of the second and third pairs, *outmoded/goaded* and *words/affords,* are only two lines apart, instead of five; but they show no obvious semantic relationship either, nor are they metrically equivalent, as we usually expect rhymes to be and as the members of the first pair are. The final syllable of each word in the second pair is unstressed, too; this makes the rhyme even harder to hear and distinguishes it as well from the stressed rhymes of the first and third pairs. The rhymes are obscured in part, then, by their differences from one another; syntax and enjambment play their parts, too. In both stanzas, an on-going sentence carries us through all or part of a fifteen-syllable line, past the second member of the rhyme-pair, and into another fifteen-syllable line without interruption.

It is precisely because the rhymes are so obscure that Moore calls attention to their presence rhetorically and forces us to consider the place of rhyme within this poem. I have said that there seem to be no significant semantic links between the members of the poem's three rhyme-pairs, but a closer reading discloses considerably more play between them than the discussion so far has allowed. We must therefore consider that while the presence of rhyme in this poem is evidently a matter of simple "expediency," it is not on that account trivial or inert. For this poem, rhyme may be the most expedient means of effecting the linkages on which its "action" depends.

Rhyme, like quotation, is one form of the repetition with which the poem is concerned. But repetition wears things out; and a given "external action" becomes "effete," loses its vitality, when it is too often or too precisely "repeat[ed]." (In "Poetry" we read that certain things may "become so derivative as to become unintelligible"—a variation on the same theme.) The differences between the various rhyme-pairs are crucial, then, for the entire poem is built on repetitions.

The poet is "goaded" into thinking of Habakkuk by the suggestion that "rhyme is outmoded"—just as, on some unspecified but still-"recent occasion" she had been "goaded / Into doing, by XY, who was speaking of unrhymed verse," and whose "identical words" she now "repeat[s]" (or so she "think[s]") in a manner which helps to reveal how his statement "affords" part of the poem's occasion." But if Moore repeats XY's "identical words," she repeats them in such a way as to avoid effeteness. By quoting him in a poem that rhymes, she endows his "unrhymed" and therefore prosaic remarks with "'the sort of heightened consciousness'" XY himself attributes to Hebrew poetry. Similarly, the repeated and crucial word "occasion" escapes being "effete" because it is used in two different ways. In the first stanza, it refers to the time and place when XY "was speaking"; in the second stanza, it refers to the way in which his "words" have caused the poem itself to be written.

Rhyme expresses the internal logic of the poem by forcing its component terms into active "external" relationships among themselves. And so rhyme becomes the most expedient way of allowing the poem to participate as well in the "external action" of the on-going debate about the nature of poetry, in which young radicals like Pound and Eliot pitted themselves against the conservative guardians of the decaying genteel tradition. The presence of rhyme in a poem which explicitly wonders about the status of rhyme must be construed as an active entry into that debate; but we must be careful in describing Moore's position.

Moore regularly read the new little magazines devoted to the publication and discussion of the radical "new verse"—magazines like *Poetry, The Egoist, Others,* and *Blast,* to name only a few. But she was also a regular, and not entirely unsympathetic, reader of magazines like the weekly *Literary Digest,* which voiced a far more hostile opinion of current literary trends. The following is an excerpt from an anonymous review of the anthology *Des Imagistes* (1914), edited by Ezra Pound; Moore clipped it from *The Literary Digest* and pasted it into her scrapbook:

> "Imagisme" is the latest poetic fashion—its devotees would give it a more dignified name. The writers of this school (many of whom, like Ezra Pound, are Americans living in London) share with the Futurists a dislike for rime and the other established conventions of poetry. They are concerned chiefly, it seems, with the presentation of beautiful images, and, for some reason not readily understood, they believe in only the homeopathic use of capital letters.[5]

The fact that Moore saved this passage should not necessarily be construed as indicating agreement on her part; but neither should her use of rhyme be construed as necessarily implying her belief that rhyme is still *à la* mode. Indeed, she must be willing to concede not only that "external action is effete," but that "rhyme is outmoded," too, for she does in fact "revert" to Habakkuk in the present moment of the poem, addressing him directly in the second person to tell him that she "shall revert" to him "If external action is effete, / And rhyme is outmoded. . . ." Perhaps it simply does not matter to her whether or not these propositions are true.

Moore appears, then, to dissociate herself firmly from "the latest poetic fashion" as scornfully described by *The Literary Digest,* for of course her poem rhymes as those in *Des Imagistes* do not. Nor is it concerned "with the presentation of beautiful images": it is utterly devoid of imagery. At the same time, though, Moore seems to separate herself with equal sharpness from the anonymous reviewer's passionate defense of "the established conventions of poetry." First she acknowledges that rhyme may indeed be "outmoded," thereby placing herself on the side of the new; then she employs a set of rhymes so subtle, so unconventional, and so apparently arbitrary as to constitute a kind of private joke at the expense of both convention and innovation. And for that joke Moore offers no justification other than the strikingly unpoetic "expediency." Neither in her rhyming, nor in her diction, nor in her syntax, nor in her syllabic patterns, nor in her avoidance of imagery, does Moore adhere to "the established conventions of poetry"; but she seems just as far from obeying the dictates of the "fashion" which is now in the process of displacing those "established conventions" with conventions of its own. Reverting to Habakkuk and Hebrew poetry, Moore situates herself instead with respect to a tradition of even greater durability and enormous moral and literary authority.

But the relation thus established is by no means a simple one. Moore's poem would be rendered "effete" by any merely mechanical repetition either of her own previous actions or of Habakkuk's original words. But Moore avoids the danger by reverting in rhymed verse to the example of a poet whose work, like most ancient Hebrew poetry, is "unrhymed." This is the same strategy she employs in repeating XY's "identical words," and indeed it now appears that she repeats those words in place of Habakkuk's.

Nowhere in "So far as the future is concerned" does Moore say explicitly that Hebrew poetry ought to be taken as a model for poetry in English, but she follows Hebrew practice from the outset. Hebrew poetry does not rhyme words; it rhymes grammatical structures, as Christian poetry rhymes temporal and narrative structures in typology. Moore rhymes both grammatically and temporally in titling her poem ("So far as the future is concerned . . . So far as the present is concerned"), and her consciously "prosaic" diction offers additional confirmation of the extent to which she identifies her own practice with XY's definition of Hebrew poetry as "Prose with a sort of heightened consciousness. . . ." Most striking of all, however, is the evidence afforded by a letter to Pound dated 9 January 1919, where Moore explains how "expediency determines the form" of her poems:

> Any verse that I have written has been an arrangement of stanzas, each stanza being an exact duplicate of every other stanza. I have occasionally been at pains to make an arrangement of lines and rhymes that I liked, repeat itself, but the *form* of the original stanza of anything I have written has been a matter of *expediency,* hit upon as being approximately suitable to the subject.[6]

It is very unlikely that the repetition of terms here is anything more than coincidence. The letter postdates "So far as the future is concerned" by more than three years, and it involves a fairly detailed technical discussion of two quite recent poems which Moore had sent to Pound. But this makes the coincidence even more interesting. One wants to know what triggers it after so long, and what it signifies. It is triggered, I think, precisely by the fact that Moore is writing to Pound. With characteristic obliqueness it points to a direct relationship between her reversion to Hebrew poetry and Pound's work.

I have said that Moore employs what amounts to an allusive code. Her allusions work by a kind of algebraic system in which direct quotation often serves as an allusion, not to the writer being quoted at the time but rather to another figure: thus XY's "identical words" take the place of Habakkuk's words while at the same time retaining their own identity. Names, too, may enter into these equations. The letters "XY" stand for a specific individual whose name would be meaningless to the reader; similarly, the name "Habakkuk" itself may stand for the name Pound.

"So far as the future is concerned" was published in December 1915, eight months after the first appearance of Pound's *Cathay* (April 1915), the translations from the Chinese classics which Pound had developed from the notebooks of Ernest Fenollosa.[7] *Cathay* is not just a collection of translated poems: it is a demonstration of the way the ancient poetic language of one culture may become an active model for the modern poetic language of an entirely different culture, and it is meant to catalyze new reactions in American and English poetry.[8]

Moore was already aware of Pound's interest in Chinese by the time *Cathay* appeared. Early in March 1915—a month before *Cathay* came out—she sent the following poem (quoted here in its entirety) to the recently established *Little Review* (whose editors understandably rejected it):

Ezra Pound:

"'Frae bank to bank, frae wood to wood I rin.'"

The rinning that you do,
Is not so new
    As it is admirable.
        "Vigor informs your
        Shape" and ardor knits it.

Bless Meditatio
And bless Li Po;
    Bless that page of Blast, on which
        Small boats ply to and
        Fro in bee lines. Bless Blast.[9]

This is mere enumeration, a catalogue of fragments held together by the poet's "ardor" and nothing more; but the fragments are important. "Meditatio" and "Li Po" are the titles Pound gave to two small poems printed on consecutive pages of the June 1914 issue of the Vorticist magazine *Blast,* which Moore read in the Library of Congress on 2 March 1915. The epigraph, the first line of a sonnet by the sixteenth-century Scottish poet Mark Alexander Boyd, is quoted not from Boyd himself but from the first part of Pound's long essay, "The Renaissance"; subtitled "The Palette," this section was published independently in *Poetry* in February 1915.[10] Moore's quotation of Pound's quotation from Boyd is a perfect example of her allusive technique: she takes a line at which Pound himself merely glances in passing and uses it to define the context of her own collection of Poundiana. The paragraph in which Pound's quotation from Boyd occurs is not otherwise significant for our present purposes; the crucial passages come later in the essay.

The first is a single sentence: "It is possible," Pound declares, "that this century may find a new Greece in China."[11] The second is the final paragraph of "The Palette," which amplifies the remark just quoted. Throughout the essay, Pound says, he has "tried . . . to set forth a color-sense" for would-be poets: just as the painter must find "good color," so the poet needs to know which poets "'are pure red'" and which are "'pure green.'" He concludes:

> Undoubtedly pure color is to be found in Chinese poetry, when we begin to know enough about it; indeed, a shadow of this perfection is already at hand in translations. Liu Ch'e, Chu Yuan, Chia I, and the great *vers libre* writers before the Petrarchan age of Li Po, are a treasury to which the next century may look for as great a stimulus as the renaissance had from the Greeks.[12]

Like Moore's XY, Pound is "speaking of unrhymed verse" here; his deliberately anachronistic use of the term *vers libre* to characterize poets working in China "before the Petrarchan age of Li Po" enforces the historical analogy between latter-day China and present-day Europe, implying that the *vers libre* of the past few years is a harbinger of the new "renaissance" Pound is now trying to bring about.

Chinese and Hebrew are of course very different languages, but for the purposes of this discussion the differences between them do not greatly matter. What matters is that they are neither English nor European, that neither of them employs the Roman alphabet, and that neither of them reads from left to right across the page. They are visibly alien, and for both Moore and Pound this is at least part of their value. The obvious strangeness of these languages as written makes the poets receptive to ideas they might otherwise reject: knowing from the outset that they lack the necessary competence to read Chinese or Hebrew on their own, they know, too, that they must turn for guidance to those who present themselves as authorities on the subject. Pound, of course, has Fenollosa's notebooks, from which he draws not only the poems gathered in *Cathay* but also material on Japanese Noh drama and the *Essay on the Chinese Written Character as a Medium for Poetry*. Moore has, first, her notes on a series of lectures on the Bible given in 1914–15 by the Reverend E.H. Kellogg of Carlisle, Pennsylvania—the "XY" of "So far as the future is concerned," and a Presbyterian minister. She also relies on A.R. Gordon's *Poets of the Old Testament* and on the four volumes contributed by George Adam Smith to a series called *The Expositor's Bible*—a two-volume translation, with commentary, of *The Book of the Twelve Prophets, Commonly Called the Minor,* and a similar two-volume treatment of *The Book of Isaiah.*[13]

The linguistic principles Moore derives from these sources are remarkably similar to the principles Pound takes from his study of Fenollosa's notebooks, although there can be no question of direct influence. Pound did not publish Fenollosa's *Essay* until 1919, four years after Moore had attended Kellogg's course of lectures, so the *Essay* can only have prompted Moore to take a fresh look at her sources (there are several new entries on Hebrew, taken primarily from Smith, in her reading notebooks for 1920 and 1921). (The similarities may be traced to the indirect influence of Ralph Waldo Emerson. Fenollosa was deeply indebted to Emerson's theories of language, and Emerson may have exerted some influence within the nineteenth-century tradition of biblical commentary upon which Moore relies.[14]) "The Chinese written character," says Fenollosa, "has not only absorbed the poetic substance of nature and built with it a second world of metaphor, but has through its very pictorial visibility, been able to retain its original creative poetry with far more vigor and vividness than any phonetic tongue."[15]

Hebrew is a "phonetic tongue," but Moore's notes on Kellogg's Bible lectures record a description of Hebrew whose terms are very similar to Fenollosa's. Hebrew, Kellogg tells his audience (he is quoting A.R. Gordon), is a "'lang[uage] of action and picture—very little inflection[.] Every word has in it a picture and often a picture of action'—'movies.'"[16] This entry was made in 1914. The following note, jotted down in 1915, comes even closer to Fenollosa: Kellogg is quoted as saying that "There is an image in the heart of every Hebrew word."[17]

In addition to their emphasis on the pictorial quality of Hebrew, Moore's sources share with Fenollosa a conviction of the primacy of verbs. According to Fenollosa, the transitive verb is the basic unit of language; one of the major flaws of modern English, he contends, is that the primitive force of its verbs has been greatly attenuated by a mistaken concentration on nouns, with the ironic result that the relationship of words to things has been severed and language cut off from its origins in nature. Chinese stands as a therapeutic model, for Chinese has never forgotten the importance of its verbs; furthermore, since English once depended on verbs in much the same way, it may recover something like its original force by reverting to what Fenollosa regards as its proper structure:

> The form of the Chinese transitive sentence, and of the English (omitting particles [*sic*]), exactly corresponds to this universal form of action in nature [that is, that "all truth is the *transference of power*"]. This brings language close to things, and in its strong reliance on verbs it erects all language into a kind of dramatic poetry. . . .[18]

A.R. Gordon, too, emphasizes the power of the verb and its centrality to poetry. Moore transcribed the following passage—again this is Kellogg quoting Gordon—in June 1914: "The essence of poetry—and action best (of speech w[hich] depicts action) expressed by the verb—Often we have a very abyss of verbs a sea of words where action ever rolls surging into action."[19] Six years later, in "England," Moore stresses the "dramatic poetry" which inheres in the Hebrew verb and makes an explicit link between "The sublimated wisdom / of China" and "the cataclysmic torrent of emotion compressed / in the verbs of the Hebrew language."[20]

It seems clear that Moore was well aware by 1920 of the relationship between her own interest in Hebrew and Pound's interest in Chinese, and that she was aware of that relationship when she wrote "So far as the future is concerned." It is thoroughly in keeping with Moore's conception of rhyme as a form of "action" (which derives ultimately from Emerson's notion that "words are also actions"[21]) that her use of Habakkuk's name should constitute an "action" by which she rhymes herself with Pound. Habakkuk mediates the relation between the two poets; the presence of his name is an indication both of what unites them and of what keeps them apart.

Moore explained to Pound in January 1919 that "the minor prophets" were among "the direct influences bearing on [her] work."[22] We must bear in mind, however, that her reading of all the prophets, major and minor, is mediated through explicators like George Adam Smith. What concerns us here is primarily Habakkuk's *name* and the significance of his example. For, as Smith writes, "we know nothing [of Habakkuk] that is personal save his name—to our ears his somewhat odd name."[23] Moore copied Smith's remark from *The Expositor's Bible* into her reading notebook in February or March 1915, at about the same time that she was reading "The Renaissance" and *Blast*; like "Marianne Moore," "Habakkuk" is only a name appended to a few pages, and Pound is hardly more.

This is 1915: Ezra Pound is no giant, but a young man whose great work has not begun. A number of people have heard of him in London, and a few know his work and admire it—Ford Madox Hueffer, Yeats, Richard Aldington and H.D., Eliot (Joyce is in Trieste); of these, only Yeats, and possibly Hueffer, are names to conjure with in 1915. And the American audience Pound is addressing in essays like "The Renaissance" can hardly be said to exist at all; it is doubtful that many but Marianne Moore knows so much as Pound's name in Carlisle, Pennsylvania, and even more doubtful that anyone but Moore cares to hear that "The first step of a renaissance, or awakening, is the importation of models." Pound goes on to enumerate:

> Let us choose: Homer, Sappho, Ibycus, Theocritus' idyl of the woman spinning with charmed wheel: Catullus, especially the *Collis O Heliconii.* Not Virgil, especially not the Aeneid . . . [though] Dante was right to respect him, for Dante had no Greek, and the Aeneid would have stood out nobly against such literature as was available in the year 1300.
>
> I should wish, for myself at least. . . .[24]

One hears him wishing for others to join him on the ground he is defining with such care, and that is what makes it possible for Moore to see in Pound's "admirable" "rinning" an effort comparable to the one George Adam Smith sees in Habakkuk. Through the prophet's "chosen words," Smith writes,

> there breathes a noble sense of responsibility. The prophet feels he has a post to hold, a rampart to guard. He knows the heritage of truth won by the great minds of the past, and in a world seething with disorder, he will take his stand upon that and see what more his God will send him. At the very least, he will not indolently drift, but feel that he has a standpoint, however narrow, and bravely hold it. . . . Men who drift never discover, never grasp aught. They are only dazzled by shifting gleams of broken truth, only fretted and broken by experience.[25]

Like Habakkuk, Pound has clearly taken his stand upon as much of "the heritage won by the great minds of the past" as he is able to discover. He writes in *The Spirit of Romance* that "The history of an art is the history of masterwork, not of failures, or mediocrity," and that the "study of literature is hero-worship."[26] In his insistence on the importance of the past he becomes, in effect, what Moore would have recognized as a secular prophet.

In her notes on the Bible lectures, Moore quotes Kellogg as warning his pupils to "avoid the idea of prophecy as *pre*-diction,"[27] advice he qualifies two and a half weeks later when he says that "Prediction is an element of prophecy but not the essence of prophecy."[28] The prophet's central concern, says George Adam Smith, is for the significance of "events" in the real world. "These form either the subject-matter or the proof or the execution of every oracle [the prophet] utters."[29] Thus, prophecy is concerned no less with the past and the present than with the future; in an entry made six months earlier, Moore quotes Kellogg (who is quoting Smith) as saying that "All those passages called prophetic—are rivers but are tidal rivers. They flow back" into the past, not forward into the future, and their real force is in bringing the past to bear on the present moment and on the future.[30]

Moore, too, has "a standpoint, however narrow," and she is determined to "hold it" with every means at her disposal as she contemplates the present state of poetry. Thus she represents herself as an unknown figure joining forces with Habakkuk, an almost equally anonymous figure out of the distant past, and through Habakkuk she works to link herself with Pound as well—another nonentity, to be sure, but one who may yet achieve a certain historical significance. We must not forget, however, that in reverting to Habakkuk Moore chooses a model other than those Pound recommends so strongly in "The Renaissance" and *The Spirit of Romance,* just as she makes formal decisions which set her work clearly apart from his. The effort to establish connections has intensified the sense of isolation under which she had been working since graduating from college in 1909.

Moore is always associated with New York City, but when she wrote "So far as the future is concerned" she had not yet been there. Back with her mother in Carlisle after graduating from Bryn Mawr, Moore followed what was being published and discussed elsewhere as well as she could, but it wasn't easy. The state of the town library may be gauged by the fact that Moore had to travel to Harrisburg or Philadelphia or Washington, D.C., in order to find the magazines in which the "new verse" was appearing. And then she had no one except her mother with whom she could discuss the new work that was being done, whether her own or someone else's, and her mother's aesthetic conservatism (she was an English teacher of the old school) created problems, as we shall see.

Poetry began publication in October 1912; in March 1913, Pound's Imagiste manifesto, "A Few Don'ts by an Imagiste," appeared in the same magazine;[31] *The Glebe,* predecessor to *Others* (1915) and likewise under the direction of Alfred Kreymborg, brought out *Des Imagistes* a year later, after a series of delays.[32] We have already seen how *The Literary Digest* responded to that event; and though Moore told Donald Hall in 1960 that she had wondered at the time "why anyone would adopt the term" (a statement which helps to explain why she pasted *The Literary Digest*'s remarks into her scrap album),[33] the advent of Imagisme must also have forced her to measure her own solitude against the fresh sense of group activity the new magazines revealed and helped to foster. There were movements going on, collaborative efforts involving numbers of people apparently in close, regular contact with one another, working toward common goals; and though Moore did not share their objectives, she could "recall," as she told Howard Nemerov in 1963, "feeling oversolitary occasionally (say in 1912)—in feeling no 'influences'; in not being able to be called an 'Imagist.' . . ."[34] Three years earlier she had reported to Hall her feeling that she was "a pariah, or at least that [she] had no connection with anything."[35]

She was not far from being wrong. By 1914 she was submitting poems regularly to numerous magazines, but they all came back, rejected by both conservative periodicals like the *Atlantic* and more radical ones like *The Masses* or *The Smart Set* or *The New Republic.*[36] She was keenly aware of pressure to conform with the standards upheld by those whom she called the "scarecrows / Of aesthetic procedure";[37] and one such "scarecrow" was her mother. Evidently Moore contemplated putting a book together in 1915, but her mother said, in a conversation Moore transcribed, that she ought to change her "style" before trying to place a book. "Huh!" Moore responded. "Then you would omit all these things I prize so much?" Her mother's reply is characteristically uncompromising: "Yes, theyre [*sic*] ephemeral."[38]

But Moore had no intention of changing her "style" to please anyone. Sometime in 1915, she began a short poem (never quite finished) which shows her resistance to external pressure, whatever the source:

To a Tiger in a Bamboo Thicket
Advocating that Conformity be Made the Vogue

Mimetic colouring
Is an imaginary thing,
Yet you are illustrating
    An aesthetic principle. Tiger,

The human panther, pard
And ocelot will disregard
Pleas for conformity—guard
    Psychic frauds, and purr till they're extinct.[39]

It is not clear who is supposed to "guard / Psychic frauds"; what is clear enough, however, is Moore's determination to "disregard / Pleas for conformity." Rather than put on "Mimetic colouring," she will lie still, catlike, purring until "Psychic frauds" become "extinct."

Evidently dissatisfied with this effort, Moore set out once more to refute the charge that her poems are mere "ephemera." On the contrary, she claims in "Diligence Is to Magic as Progress Is to Flight," they are "prosaic necessities, not curios," and they are "tough-grained" and durable, like the hide of the elephant on which she rides so "laboriously."[40] But this poem, too, is slight, and it fails because it tries too hard to make light of a problem Moore took very much to heart.

Both "To a Tiger" and "Diligence Is to Magic" date from the same period as the more successful "To a Steamroller"—a poem whose title reveals how intensely Moore felt the pressure of those "Pleas for conformity," and whose opening lines reveal how intensely furious they made her:

> The illustration
> Is nothing to you without the application.
> You lack half wit. You crush all the particles down
> Into close conformity, and then walk back and forth on them.
>
> Sparkling chips of rock
> Are crushed down to the level of the parent block . . .[41]

That last phrase makes one wonder: perhaps the poem is directed, not altogether consciously, at the poet's mother, the "parent block" to whose "level" the poet refuses to be "crushed down." The second stanza is perfectly apt as a characterization of Mrs. Moore's response to "all those things" her daughter "prize[s] so much," but Moore is on very dangerous emotional ground here, and the danger increases as her anger builds. Elizabeth Bishop tells the story of a "well known" writer who was never invited to the Moores' apartment, though he had known Moore for a long time and admired her very much; asked why, Moore said in all seriousness that "He *contradicted* Mother."[42] If Moore is to avoid open confrontation, then, she has to prevent herself going too far—hence the abrupt shift in the second line of the final stanza and the grudging, metaphoric acknowledgment that perhaps Mrs. Moore is not completely soulless after all:

> . . . Were not "impersonal judgment in aesthetic
> Matters, a metaphysical impossibility," you
>
> Might fairly achieve
> It. As for butterflies, I can hardly conceive
> Of one's attending upon you, but to question
> The congruence of the complement is vain, if it exists.

The "congruence" of these lines with the rest of the poem is not at all obvious, but "it exists" here as it does not in "To a Tiger." And there is another difference between these three poems which may be even more crucial from Moore's point of view: "To a Steamroller" and "Diligence Is to Magic" were published. For her "Diligence" had worked its "Magic": Richard Aldington, one of the original Imagistes, now married to H.D. and associate editor of *The Egoist,* had accepted two unsolicited poems for publication on 1 April 1915;[43] Harriet Monroe printed five poems—at least one of which had been submitted as early as 10 July 1914—in the May 1915 issue of *Poetry.*[44] *The Egoist* printed two more of Moore's poems in May, two more in August, and yet another pair in October; finally, to cap the year properly, Alfred Kreymborg ran five of her poems, including "So far as the future is concerned," in *Others* for December.[45]

At about the time her poems appeared in *Others,* Moore made a week-long pilgrimage to New York City in the company of a friend from Carlisle. The Armory Show, an earlier fascination of hers, was gone, but she went almost immediately to Stieglitz's gallery, 291, which she later described as "an American Acropolis," and apparently returned more than once; she also spent a good deal of time with Alfred Kreymborg and his wife.[46] At last she was meeting other writers—some of them at the "bohemian parties" she attended over her friend's objections. "I was fearless about that," she told Donald Hall in 1960. "In the first place, I didn't think anyone would try to harm me, but if they did I felt impervious. It never occurred to me that chaperones were important."[47]

She may have been fearless when it came to walking the streets of New York or going alone to "bohemian parties," but the city posed threats of an entirely different order as well, and Moore was less "impervious" to these. Her first poetic allusion to New York occurs in a short poem called "Is Your Town Nineveh?" which was probably composed the following year and is most likely addressed to her brother, Warner—and though the poem is primarily concerned with a family dispute, the allusion to New York is quite revealing.

In the late summer of 1916, Moore and her mother moved from Carlisle to Chatham, New Jersey, to keep house for Warner, who had recently been named pastor of the Ogden Memorial Presbyterian Church there. Warner had no inclination to settle in Chatham, however; he had received his commission as a naval ensign in March 1916, discovered that he liked the work, and expressed a desire to stay on. Mrs. Moore opposed him vehemently on this issue, as she later opposed his plans to marry,[48] and the argument evidently disturbed her daughter very much. In "Is Your Town Nineveh?" Moore seems at first to be taking her mother's side, implicitly comparing

Warner's refusal to accede to Mrs. Moore's instructions with Jonah's refusal of the Lord's command that he go to Nineveh. The second stanza, however, reveals a certain ambivalence, for it suggests a similar desire for freedom on the sister's part; as in "To a Steamroller," however, she is finally unwilling or unable to break with her mother. In an image which enforces the contrast between her brother's unruly rejection of Mrs. Moore's authority and the poet's own reluctant acquiescence, the closing lines show her as standing still, poised between a symbol of imprisonment on one side and a symbol of freedom on the other. I quote the poem in its entirety, as it appears in *Poems* (1921), where it was first published:

Why so desolate?
And why multiply
in phantasmagoria about fishes,
what disgusts you? Could
not all personal upheaval in
the name of freedom, be tabooed?

Is it Nineveh
and are you Jonah
in the sweltering east wind of your wishes?
I, myself have stood
there by the aquarium, looking
at the Statue of Liberty.[49]

New York, then, is the site of both imprisonment and an equally dangerous potential liberty; by 1917 it is clear that New York, not Chatham, is the modern Babylon—and it is equally clear that Moore wants very badly to go there. "Sojourn in the Whale" (1917) is a far more complicated poem than "Is Your Town Nineveh?" and it is not explicitly concerned with New York; it takes its title, however, from the heading of a letter written from New York in December 1915, in which Moore tells Warner what she has been doing during the visit above.

Two extended analogies reinforce and complicate each other here. The first, implied only in the title, refers again to Jonah, but this time Moore herself is the "pariah" who fears being "swallowed up"; the second is an allusion to the Easter Rising in Ireland (1916), which England put down. These two references combine to form an implicit metaphor for Moore's own situation: she is Jonah trying to escape the whale; but she is also an explicitly feminine Ireland trying, not willfully but automatically, to win her freedom from English and specifically masculine oppression. She has been condemned to drudgery, but she wants to do her real work, which requires that she enter Babylon:

Trying to open locked doors with a sword, threading
The points of needles, planting shade trees
Upside down; swallowed by the opaqueness of one whom the seas
Love better than they love you, Ireland—

You have lived and lived on every kind of shortage.
You have been compelled by hags to spin
Gold thread from straw and have heard men say: "There is a feminine
Temperament in direct contrast to

Ours which makes her do these things. Circumscribed by a
Heritage of blindness and native
Incompetence, she will become wise and will be forced to give
In. Compelled by experience, she

Will turn back; water seeks its own level": and you
Have smiled. "Water in motion is far
From level." You have seen it, when obstacles happened to bar
The path—rise automatically.[50]

The earlier letter headed "Sojourn in the Whale" is an exuberant, detailed account of Moore's visits to 291 and to the Kreymborgs' home, a record of thrilling discovery. The poem, however, tells a very different story, that of a woman who, like Ireland (and the Moores were Irish), has "lived and lived on every kind of shortage" for many years, during which she has been "compelled by hags"—another potentially dangerous allusion to her mother, perhaps—to perform an endless series of menial tasks supposed to produce miraculous results despite the lack of good materials—and with no hope of rescue by Rumpelstiltskin. She has received not help but condescension from those around her: told by "men" that this is no place for a woman, assured that she will be "Compelled by experience" to "turn back," the poet "rise[s]" up in anger, as Ireland has done, confident that though she may be put down now, she cannot be kept down forever. "Personal upheaval in / the name of freedom" is no longer "tabooed": it is automatic, instinctive, fueled by an anger powerful enough to overcome any "obstacles" that might "bar / The path. . . . " But she is still "Trying to open locked doors with a sword."

For all the intensity of Moore's desire to escape the "opaqueness" that imprisons her, so that she may carry her message into the heart of the modern Babylon, New York poses a threat to her identity, and her awareness of that threat persists for some time after she and her mother take up residence there in December 1918. As we shall see in chapter 3, "New York" (1921) replaces the comparative safety of "the savage's romance," the "wilderness" of isolation, with a new "wilderness" of "commerce" which offers an "accessibility to experience" so frighteningly compelling that Moore does indeed contemplate turning back, as the mocking male voice of "Sojourn in the Whale" promises she will: "one must stand outside and laugh / since to go in is to be lost."[51]

Moore is fighting hard here to maintain an "imperviousness" that will in the end be overwhelmed by "experience," for by this point she has come to depend upon her isolation and she is reluctant to give it up, for reasons which will be discussed in some detail in the next chapter. But the sense of isolation that comes through so strongly in the image of "locked doors" and in the remarks quoted earlier—the regret at "not being able to be called an 'Imagist,'" the sense of having "no connection with anything," of being "a pariah"—is far less willful.

In "So far as the future is concerned"—to return once more to our starting point—Moore is trying as hard to conceal her fear of isolation as she is trying in "New York" to conceal her fear of "experience"; but the title of the earlier poem gives her away.

Consider again the way Moore phrases her inability to predict the future:

So far as the future is concerned,
"Shall not one say, with the Russian philosopher,
'How is one to know what one doesn't know?'"
So far as the present is concerned. . . .

Like the poem as a whole, the title is built around a quotation, this one from a novella by Ivan Turgenev. *The Diary of a Superfluous Man* is narrated by a man of thirty who is dying of an unnamed disease (obviously tuberculosis) in a decaying village which is all that remains of his father's estate. He says that he is writing "for [his] own amusement,"[52] but as the novella progresses his thoughts focus more narrowly on his unrequited love for a seventeen-year-old girl named Liza; the history of the abortive affair dominates the book. The episode from which Moore draws her title occurs approximately two weeks after the narrator's first meeting with Liza; the two are walking in the woods outside a small provincial town, alone for the first time. The narrator is full of his love for her, and he senses in the girl's obvious agitation a similar feeling on her part. He is quite right—but her emotion is not for him, and as he brings the story of that day to an end, the narrator reflects bitterly upon the futility of it all:

> If someone had whispered in my ear then: "You're raving, my dear chap! that's not a bit what's in store for you. What's in store for you is to die all alone, in a wretched little cottage, amid the insufferable grumbling of an old hag who will await your death with impatience to sell your boots for a few coopers . . . !"
>
> Yes, one can't help saying with the Russian philosopher—"How's one to know what one doesn't know?"
>
> Enough for today.[53]

Like Turgenev's narrator, Moore registers a painful awareness that in retrospect the future that "'one doesn't know'" may turn out to have been a nasty joke at one's own expense. It is neither possible to predict it nor desirable to try—hence the anxiety which infuses her contemplation of the present.

The joke is, of course, that one may find oneself, as the narrator has done, to have been "utterly superfluous. . . . A supernumerary, that's all."[54] Moore's effort to dissociate herself simultaneously from "the established poetic conventions" and from "the latest poetic fashion" is an attempt to avoid the fate of the Superfluous Man—to avoid becoming "outmoded"—by removing herself as far as possible from the world in which fashions change and by appropriating to herself a measure of Habakkuk's durability. But it is not quite so simple, for in order truly to avoid superfluity one must be willing to risk it—as Moore does here. Like Turgenev's narrator, Moore cannot speak without "the appearance of painful constraint,"[55] and so she cannot say explicitly that what "affords / The occasion" for this poem is not the joy we conventionally associate with "Ecstasy": it is a different sort of ecstasy altogether, for Moore is beside herself with fear lest she end like the narrator, dying "all alone" in a provincial village with no one for company but her mother, an impatient "old hag" who calls her work "ephemeral." Similarly, the effort to make contact with Pound is inhibited by a "painful constraint" which makes it virtually incomprehensible to anyone but the poet herself. Taken simply at face value, as an "external action," the allusion to Habakkuk does not unite Moore with Pound but separates her from him, just as her rhymes separate her from Habakkuk, so that she is left more isolated than ever.

She is, it seems, simply an obscure writer joining forces with one of the lesser biblical figures in an extremely tentative way, for reasons she does not specify. But it is not by any means an empty gesture. By reverting to

Habakkuk, Moore indicates her awareness—or rather her hope—that she may come to play a significant part in the history of poetry, just as Habakkuk plays a small but essential part in the history of prophecy. An innovator, like Pound, Habakkuk initiates a "transition to speculation."[56] According to George Adam Smith, Habakkuk marks

> . . . the beginning of speculation in Israel. It does not go far: it is satisfied with stating questions *to* God; it does not, directly at least, state questions *against* Him. But Habakkuk at least feels that revelation is baffled by experience. . . . As in Zephaniah prophecy begins to exhibit traces of apocalypse, so in Habakkuk we find it developing the first impulses of speculation.[57]

For modern American poetry, that "transition to speculation" begins with Moore. She is only beginning to discover her own "standpoint," but it is too "narrow" as yet and she must go on to define it more carefully, to broaden it to the fullest possible extent. This is a protracted effort involving a great deal of speculation about the nature of poetry and her own relationship to its traditions—speculations to which Moore herself has no final answers, and which constitute the basis of her claim to poetic authority.

II

By the summer of 1919, when "Poetry" appears in *Others,* the isolated position Moore had begun to define for herself as she sought to escape the fate of Turgenev's Superfluous Man has become a position of some authority as well. It is a strange authority, though, because it does not depend on Moore's having sided with Pound, Eliot, and other exponents of the "new" in their struggle against the "established conventions of poetry." On the contrary, Moore's authority depends precisely on her continuing refusal to take sides, on her ability to transform her sense of isolation into something closely analogous to Hawthorne's "neutral territory"—a ground, that is, where the radical poetics of modernism, of *The Egoist* and *Others,* may meet and fuse with the conservative aesthetic espoused by *The Literary Digest* and by the poet's mother. In Moore's work generally, and in "Poetry" in particular, apparently irreconcilable positions are brought into combination, with the result that each position "imbues itself with the nature of the other," as Hawthorne says "the Actual and the Imaginary may" do under the right conditions[58]—though, like "real toads" in "imaginary gardens," each retains its own integrity as well. At the same time, both positions—in this case the modernist and the reactionary—are endowed with Moore's own neutrality and are thereby removed from the "category" of poetry.

By 1919, Moore has come to judge herself very much as critics like Louis Untermeyer and Harriet Monroe would judge her two years later.[59] She does not consider herself to be writing as a poet. She sees herself rather as an "interested" observer, one who is separated from poetry as by the "locked doors" of "Sojourn in the Whale" and looking through a partially opaque lens at her own work and that of her contemporaries—and what she sees does not strike her as meriting her title. For she sees a group of "autocrats"—herself among them—busily passing judgment and prescribing aesthetic criteria like Oliver Wendell Holmes at the Breakfast-Table, a disunited collection of "Critics and Connoisseurs" who have so far proved incapable of rising "above / insolence and triviality" to deliver "the genuine" article called "Poetry."[60]

We may say, then, that the isolation Moore enjoys in "Poetry" and from which she derives her authority is very different from the isolation she had feared so much in "So far as the future is concerned." She begins by claiming to "dislike" poetry—a strange admission from one who seems to be presenting herself as a poet. But even as this confession isolates her from us, it draws us by rhetorical means into a stance very much like hers. "I too, dislike it," she confides: evidently there is a community of people who share Moore's distaste for poetry, and evidently Moore considers that we, "too," are among its citizens. That community, moreover, is larger than we might think.

In an essay called "Impressionism," published in *Poetry* in September 1913, Ford Madox Hueffer writes that his own youthful "attempt to read Tennyson, Swinburne and Browning and Pope" had given rise to "a settled dislike for poetry" from which he had never fully recovered.[61] He justifies that "dislike" on the grounds that his reading had left him with the distinct impression that "all poets must of necessity write affectedly, at great length, with many superfluous words"—defects Hueffer spent the rest of his career trying to eliminate not only from his own work but also, crucially, from Pound's.[62] The "perfect contempt" with which Hueffer rejects "Tennyson, Swinburne and Browning and Pope" in a single breath seems consciously hyperbolic, just as Moore's does; but it is necessary. For if we dismiss his comments as absurd or unfair, we will be confounded by the words of the young George Santayana, explaining (in an essay republished just two years earlier) that "When Ossian, mentioning the sun, says it is round as the shield of his father, the expression is poetical. Why? Because he has added to the word sun, in itself sufficient and unequivocal, other words, unnecessary to practical clearness. . . ."[63]

The philosopher may be right about Ossian; but Hueffer and Pound and Moore would say that he is exactly wrong in his account of what makes an expression "poetical." It is easy to imagine Hueffer responding to this pronouncement as he responded to Pound's *Canzoni* in 1911—by throwing himself on the floor and rolling with laughter;[64] but we do not have to guess at Pound's answer, or Moore's. Pound's response, learned the hard way from Hueffer, is the second rule of Imagisme: the injunction "To use absolutely no word that does not contribute to the presentation." Moore's is in "To a Snail": "'compression is the first grace of style.'"[65]

Moore responds in a more complex way in "Poetry." Having implied her allegiance to Hueffer and Pound, Moore separates herself from them by insisting that "there are things that are important beyond all this fiddle" and suggesting a means by which those "things" may be discovered: "Reading it, however, with a perfect contempt for it, one discovers that there is in / it after all, a place for the genuine." That "perfect contempt" is the necessary antidote to the poet's incessant "fiddle" with unnecessary words, and to the reader's fiddling as well.

We must not assume, however, that the phrase "perfect contempt" simply designates the feeling one has while reading poetry, or even what one ought to feel. It is not really a feeling, and it is not so much a by-product of reading as it is a way of reading—a means by which the reader may "stand outside and laugh," as "New York" suggests one must, in order to avoid getting "lost." A few other poems will help us to define the *virtú* of "perfect contempt" more clearly.

It is what Moore calls in "In This Age of Hard Trying Nonchalance Is Good And—" a "polished wedge" to drive between oneself and the poem one is reading, a "weapon" like that "self-protectiveness" which, as Moore writes in the same poem, is most clearly revealed by a "feigned inconsequence of manner." It is also one of "Those Various Scalpels" used in the laboratory to "dissect" specimens and in the operating theater to remove dead or diseased tissue and restore the body to health.[66] William Carlos Williams, writing in *The Dial* in 1925, offers a useful description of its practical value (though he is not talking specifically about "perfect contempt") when he writes:

> Miss Moore gets great pleasure from wiping soiled words or cutting them clean out, removing the aureoles that have been pasted about them or taking them

> bodily from greasy contexts. . . . With Miss Moore a word is a word most when it is separated out by science, treated with acid to remove the smudges, washed, dried and placed right side up on a clean surface. Now one may say that this is a word. Now it may be used. . . .[67]

Like her writing, Moore's reading is guided by a certain edginess, an urge to penetrate quickly and get out fast, for protracted involvement is risky: "to go in is to be lost." But "perfect contempt" affords her exactly the narrow standpoint she needs—a position from which she may "discover" in what she reads "a place for the genuine" without having to "go in" herself.

Responsibility for determining the precise nature of "the genuine" belongs to the poet, and to "Poetry." Proceeding from her contemptuous dismissal of "all this fiddle" to the "important" "things" "beyond" it, the poet suddenly discovers "a place for the genuine," and no sooner has she done so than she proceeds to fill that "place" by apposing a list of "things." These give provisional definition to "the genuine," even as they are in turn defined by it:

> Hands that can grasp, eyes
> that can dilate, hair that can rise
> if it must, these things are important not because a
>
> high sounding interpretation can be put upon them
> but because they are
> useful;

One senses initially that the words have been strung together as if by hyphens, as though each phrase were an ideogram: "Hands-that-can-grasp" are "useful" and therefore "important," but a hand without its prehensile ability is trivial, insignificant, false. Moore's economy is such that the poem has already acquired considerable momentum without wasting any motion: "Hands that *can* grasp, eyes / that *can* dilate, hair that *can* rise / *if it must,* these things" are potential energy: nothing moves until it has to.

It is worth pausing for a moment over the word "useful," which is evidently an important element of "the genuine." Placed with a "feigned inconsequence of manner" at the beginning of a line, it has the same kind of shock value as "expediency," and similarly it aims a blow at the genteel school of thought which exposes poetry to Hueffer's charge of superfluity. The word stands at the head of a line—but it feels as though it comes at the end of an extremely long and difficult one that bristles with sharp sounds, and in a sense it does. After almost two full lines and twenty-nine syllables that stretch the sentence across the stanza-break without a pause, we strain for "useful" with the last of our breath; and then a semicolon pins us to it. "Hands that can grasp" are "important not because a / high sounding interpretation can be put upon them but because they are / useful; . . . " What makes them "useful" is that they can be put into a poem (this poem) and used, disembodied as they are, to flesh out the abstract concept of "the genuine" and hold its "place." Taken singly, "these things" are perhaps not very "important," not very "useful"; taken together, they serve a real function. For "these things" are not emotions, but together they can indicate emotion—fear, perhaps; but they have no necessary, no fixed relation to any one emotional condition, and they might just as easily be used to indicate surprise or joy. What makes them "important," then, is their capacity to signal the presence of that "Ecstasy" which "affords / The occasion" for poetry—of some state of being beside oneself. They do not give that state its conventional name, however, and here again Moore implicitly aligns herself with Pound, and specifically with the first technical rule of Imagisme: "Direct treatment of the 'thing' whether subjective or objective." Imagiste theory sought to join what genteel aesthetics had put asunder: thought and feeling. (It is precisely that fusion that Eliot singles out for praise in his first review of Moore in 1918.[68]) Among other things, Pound's redefinition of the "'image'" as "that which presents an emotional and intellectual complex in an instant of time" means that "Direct treatment of the 'thing'" makes possible the indirect treatment of emotion. Such indirect treatment deprives those critics for whom "ecstasy would be everything"[69] of the signs by which they are accustomed to recognize the presence of feeling in poetry, and nowhere is that outraged sense of deprivation more clearly evident than in the response to Moore. "If there can be a poetry without passion," writes Louis Untermeyer, "—and one could as easily imagine a music without sound—Miss Moore's achieves a special distinction."[70]

For Moore, however, the problem is that the very importance and utility of the "things" by which the poet indicates emotion may deprive them of their force and their provisional status as constituents of "the genuine." They can be used too often, so that "external action" becomes "effete"; and

> . . . when they become so derivative as to become unintelligible, the
> same thing may be said for all of us—that we
> do not admire what
> we cannot understand. The bat,
> holding on upside down or in quest of something to

eat, elephants pushing, a wild horse taking a roll, a tireless wolf under
a tree, the immovable critic twinkling his skin like a horse that feels a flea, the
base-
ball fan, the statistician—case after case
could be cited did
one wish it . . .

The members of this new list are neither disembodied limbs nor other unattached parts, but whole beings in intense motion—or so it seems at first glance. On looking more closely, however, we see that only the first four are actually moving, and all four are animals; the sense of their activity is so powerful that it seems to carry over to the three human figures, who do not move. It is characteristic of Moore's acid wit that the critic should be made to serve as the transitional figure: half man, half horse, he is not immobile but "immovable." Part of him—his skin—is in motion, however; and since this is what makes him "like a horse that feels a flea," it is as if motion were only an animal and not a human capacity. For what characterizes baseball fan and statistician alike—and Moore was both—is that their activity at its most intense takes the form of a rapt stillness. If we neither "understand" nor "admire" these figures, then we have failed to apprehend something crucial about what they are and what they do. As R.P. Blackmur has said,

> They are as they succeed the springboards of ecstasy. . . . [W]e come to be aware, whether consciously or not, that these animals and these men are themselves, in their special activities, obsessed, freed, and beside themselves. There is an exciting quality which the pushing elephant and the baseball fan have in common; and our excitement comes in feeling that quality . . . as it were beside and for itself, not in the elephant and the fan, but in terms of the apposition in the poem.[71]

But "the immovable critic" is "beside himself" in a different way than the others, helplessly "twinkling his skin like a horse that feels a flea" because whatever he is reading (this poem, perhaps) has gotten under his skin and he feels it beneath his dignity to scratch; after 1921, he "twitch[es]," a much better word because it renders him even more ludicrously helpless.

In reading "Poetry," we must bear in mind that it is we who have "hands that can grasp," and if we are not to make ourselves ridiculous "Critics and Connoisseurs," we must be prepared to use our "hands" to "detain and appraise such bits / Of food as the stream" of Moore's verse bears "counter" to our expectations. Not to make that effort is to display the "ambition without / Understanding" that Moore condemns in "Critics and Connoisseurs"; to take up what she offers us, however, is to begin to understand that what makes "all these phenomena"—even the critic—so "useful" and "important" is not only their capacity to act as what Moore calls in "England" an "emotional / shorthand," but also their ability to clarify the nature of "the genuine." What they are beginning to show us is that "the genuine" is not so stable as we might like to think.

We take it for granted that "the genuine" is worthy of our admiration, but we read without really expecting to find it: an early draft of "Picking and Choosing" begins with the weary declaration that "The half of what is written is not like a play / for enjoyment nor is it rich in material that one can use after- / ward and it is permissible to / say so. . . ."[72] The ultimate goal of reading, then, is the discovery of "material that one can use" in one's work; but the discovery guarantees nothing. Use becomes overuse very quickly, and what had been "genuine" and "useful" will soon "become so derivative as to become unintelligible." Like the disembodied "Hands that can grasp, eyes / that can dilate, hair that can rise / if it must," the idea of "the genuine" is "useful" because, by itself, it can be made to mean and to accommodate almost anything. It is not a quality intrinsic to objects or to words, which have no meaning until they are used, and which cease to have meaning when they are used up.

Radically unstable, "the genuine" is as susceptible to the corruption or decay of the terms used to define it as those terms are susceptible to overuse. We thus discover, in the fickleness and instability of "the genuine" itself, the grounds for reading poetry "with a perfect contempt for it": "perfect contempt" makes words useful again by "taking them bodily," in Williams's phrase, from the "greasy contexts" in which it finds them, and then reusing them in such a way as to make them "genuine." Genuineness depends, therefore, on the poet's treatment of the material she has found. And that treatment poses a real problem, for she must use "material" which has already been handled by someone else and is therefore especially prone to deterioration. If she is to avoid becoming "so derivative as to become unintelligible," therefore, Moore must first of all escape the rigid limitations imposed by genteel criticism upon the poet's choice of subject-matter. "Prose is *is,*" said one typical critic in 1912, "the ever-present fact, today . . . . [It] deals with things as they are—school, marriage, wills, dress, laws, civilisation, order and degree."[73] Poetry, on the other hand, is "the voice of the infinite in man." It has to "sing of things that know no place or time," so it must not be "limited by the use of local phrases and allusions."[74]

Above all, it must not deal with "things as they are." For "Poetry is not description."[75]

Moore must have the widest possible range of "material" at her disposal, however, and she cannot afford to overlook anything. This is why the bat, the critic, and the other members of that set are left hanging, "holding on upside down," until the penultimate clause of the long sentence that brings them one by one into the poem; then the logical operator, "nor," reaches back to gather them into a new class of "phenomena" whose importance has not been sufficiently taken into account:

> . . . The bat,
> holding on upside down or in quest of something to
>
> eat, elephants pushing, a wild horse taking a roll, a tireless wolf under
> a tree, the immovable critic twinkling his skin like a horse that feels a flea, the
> base-
> ball fan, the statistician—case after case
> could be cited did
> one wish it; nor [is it] valid
> to discriminate against "business documents and
>
> school-books"; all these phenomena are important.

The items Moore catalogues here are precisely the sort of "phenomena" which the genteel tradition considers to be beneath the poet's dignity. It consigns them to prose and then, fearing contamination, takes "refuge" on "a little isle," in a "remoter world."[76]

Just when "Poetry" claims for itself the subject-matter conventionally assigned to prose, moreover, the "Hands that can grasp" do grasp—and, with "perfect contempt" for "the old aesthetic canons" of the genteel tradition's careful demarcations between poetry and prose,[77] Moore seizes upon an entry from Tolstoy's diary. It is, of course, a prose entry in which, fruitlessly attempting to locate the essential difference between poetry and prose, Tolstoy finally throws up his hands, choosing an arbitrary point and drawing a line through it: "Where the boundary between prose and poetry lies, I shall never be able to understand. The question is raised in manuals of style, yet the answer to it lies beyond me. Poetry is verse: prose is not verse. Or else poetry is everything with the exception of business documents and school-books."[78] Declaring that it is not "valid to discriminate against 'business documents and / school-books'" either, Moore goes beyond Tolstoy's position and seems to imply that poetry is indeed "everything," schoolbooks and business documents not excepted.

If we recall that "So far as the future is concerned" defines the analogy between Moore's situation and Pound's by using a quotation from Turgenev in conjunction with Habakkuk's name, we may see that "Poetry" uses Tolstoy in a similar way, as an indirect means of suggesting an affinity between Moore and another contemporary figure whose poetry and criticism she is coming to esteem even more highly than Pound's. For Tolstoy's inability to decide just "where the boundary between prose and poetry lies" rhymes very closely with Eliot's inability to locate what he calls "The Borderline of Prose." Writing in *The New Statesman* in May 1917, Eliot says:

> It is noticeable that poetry which looks like prose, and prose which sounds like poetry, are assured of a certain degree of odium and success. Why should this be so? I know that the difference between poetry and prose is a topic for the school debating societies, but I am not aware that the debating societies have arrived at a solution. Do the present signs show that poetry and prose form a medium of infinite gradations, or is it that we are searching for new ways of expression? There are doubtless many empirical generalisations which one may draw from a study of existing poetry and prose, but after much reflection I conclude that the only absolute distinction to be drawn is that poetry is written in verse, and prose is written in prose; or, in other words, that there is prose rhythm and verse rhythm. Any other essential difference is still to seek.[79]

Moore's earliest response to these questions had been a gesture of annoyance. "Why that Question?" she asks in an unfinished poem written about 1917—

> "What is the difference between prose and poetry"—
>   If it is one? Why that wart
> On so much pleasantness? If the world is right about the
>
> Thing it is entitled to a place on some feature
>   Of enquiry and there may
> Be a difference, only no one says so who is sure:
>
> Because it is the people who know, who say nothing—
>   Against whose principles it
> Is, to be ~~interested~~ in what is ~~uninteresting~~.[80]
>   irritated   unirritating.

"Poetry" presents a far more interesting and powerful response to the problem of definition. Instead of merely restating Tolstoy's position, as she does in "Why that Question?" Moore now uses his words as a means, first, of establishing his priority and, second, of establishing her own covert relation to Eliot. She thus brings Eliot actively onto her own ground and engages him in her own effort to define the essential features of poetry. But by establishing an equivalence between Eliot's position and her own, she effectively removes his work, too, from the "category" of poetry.

For in fact Moore does not imply that "poetry" is "everything," as I said she seems to do; and neither her redrawing of the Tolstoyan "boundary" nor the interest in "conserving everything" which she expresses in "Radical" four months earlier should be taken to mean that "everything" may automatically be regarded as "poetry."[81] That Moore erases Tolstoy's arbitrary line of demarcation does mean, however, that "everything" may be considered available to poetry—that "everything" is now potential "material." But the problem of treatment, of how to turn that material into poetry, still remains.

It is to this problem that Moore now turns her attention, and here the poem takes a crucial turn. The poet has just made an enormous claim on poetry's behalf, but her assurance seems to wobble a bit as she adds, anticlimactically, that "One must make a distinction / however: when dragged into prominence by half poets, the result is not poetry. . . ." The ironic disclaimer has the advantage of shifting the argument to new ground. No longer faced with the impossible task of defining the "essential difference" between poetry and prose, Moore is now free to set "poetry" on one side against its mirror-image, "not poetry," on the other. That shift also allows her to draw a final, crucial distinction before bringing "Poetry" to an uneasy close. If it is not "valid / to discriminate *against* 'business documents and / school-books,'" it is both valid and necessary to discriminate *between* "the raw material of poetry in / all its rawness and / that which is on the other hand, / genuine. . . ." This makes it absolutely clear that genuineness does not inhere in the material of poetry—and forces us to consider the nature of that material more closely than we have yet done. For it is not enough to say that "everything" is potential material.

The phrase "raw material" comes from a review published in *The Spectator* (London) in May 1913. Discussing a book called *Ancient Gems in Modern Settings* by G.B. Grundy, the reviewer—who signs him- or herself "C"—explains at one point that *The Greek Anthology* continues to interest readers for

> reasons [which] are not far to seek. In the first place, no productions of the Greek genius conform more wholly to the Aristotelian canon that poetry should be an imitation of the universal. Few of the poems in the Anthology depict any

> ephemeral phase or fashion of opinion, like the Euphuism of the sixteenth century. All appeal to emotions which endure for all time, and which, it has been aptly stated, are the true raw material of poetry.[82]

The "raw material of poetry" is emotion, then—but as Moore's handling of this phrase suggests, emotion "in / all its rawness" is utterly useless to the poet. However "genuine" that emotion may be, emotion is not the "material that one can use" because it cannot be put directly into a poem. Its "place" can only be held for it, as by "Hands that can grasp, eyes / that can dilate, hair that can rise / if it must"—and these are not emotions, as I have said, nor are they fleshly parts of bodies; they are only words. Words are not "raw material": they have already been treated, used, like the phrase "raw material" itself. But they are all the poet has at her disposal.

According to one view of poetry, the poet works within a lexical and formal range that has been established and validated by usage and tradition, so that to employ a particular vocabulary or a particular form in dealing with a similarly prescribed issue or problem is in effect to guarantee that in writing a poem one has played by the rules. "It is supposed," says Wordsworth in the preface to *Lyrical Ballads*, "that by the act of writing in verse an Author makes a formal engagement that he will satisfy certain known habits of association; that he not only thus apprises the Reader that certain classes of ideas and expressions will be found in his book, but that others will be carefully excluded."[83] From the standpoint Wordsworth describes, one might almost say that insofar as one values the "formal engagement" between author and reader, it will be necessary to be "derivative" in order to satisfy the terms of the contract. This is the standpoint of genteel criticism more than a century after Wordsworth; but the relationship between a given poem and the conventions and traditions of poetry need not be affirmative, and from another standpoint it may almost have to be antagonistic. For as soon as "the genuine" ceases to be regarded as either a stable entity or an essential characteristic of certain words or objects—as soon, that is, as one begins to discover that there is no such thing as an inexhaustible storehouse of certifiably and permanently poetic language and subject-matter—then originality becomes a major issue and begins to be taken as a defining feature of poetry itself. But when the demand for originality is coupled—as it is in Moore's case—with the discovery that virtually all one's "material" has already been used, the very possibility of poetry is put in doubt.

Like the "elephant-skin" the poet "inhabit[s]" in "Black Earth" (1918), all the "material" she discovers must be tested for durability.[84] That testing is conducted by removing that "material" from the context in which it has been discovered and inserting it into a new context, a totally alien structure by which it may be "goaded" into revealing its full usefulness and perhaps its "poetry." Like the phrase "raw material," the quotation from Tolstoy is one instance of this procedure, and there are many others. They include the crucial phrase "perfect contempt," which occurs in a bit of conversation between the poet and her mother in the spring of 1919, and we may take Moore's treatment of this phrase as exemplary:

> Alphabet.   You took no
> interest in it   no more than you took
>   in the Baedekers in Eng[land]—in fact
> had a perfect contempt for it. Reading
> somehow it came about. . . .[85]

This seems to be an anecdote about the poet as a child (though it embraces another, briefer one, about her visit to England in 1911), when her "perfect contempt" apparently operated at a very fundamental level indeed; yet, Mrs. Moore seems to be saying, despite the fact that her daughter "took no interest" in the alphabet—"in fact had a perfect contempt for it"—"somehow it came about" that she learned to read.

The poem seizes upon a thoroughly commonplace expression and bends the line containing it into a completely different shape—one that is, nevertheless, oddly like the line in its "raw" form. As if the poem were a mirror distorting the image of the notebook, *had a perfect contempt for it. Reading* becomes *Reading it, however, with a perfect contempt for it*; only the headings—"Alphabet," "Poetry"—tell us in each case what "it" stands for.

As a description of the young Moore's lack of interest in the alphabet, the phrase is of no great value; but "Poetry" makes of "perfect contempt" what Moore calls in "Radical" a "wedge-shaped engine with the / secret of expansion," and when driven home, that "engine" uproots a word or a phrase and places it within a system where its significance is expanded to the fullest possible degree—a system by which words are treated with an apparently complete disregard not only for their origins but also for their mere physical integrity. If a line-ending happens to coincide with the middle of a word, for instance, the word is simply broken over the end of the line as a stick is broken over the knee—and even if the breakage creates a new "expansion" of the word's force, as when the splitting of the phrase "base- / ball fan" makes "the immovable critic" seem "base," the poem goes on without seeming to notice. This is the kind of treatment which allows "perfect contempt" to convert the poet's mere "dislike" for poetry into the active force driving her search for "the genuine": the change of context as the phrase is transferred from notebook to poem is so complete that the poem can proceed as if the words had never meant anything but a way of reading poetry. Just as the ocean at the end of "A Grave[yard]" "advances as usual, looking as if it were not that ocean in which dropped things are bound to sink,"[86] so Moore "advances" as if she had no idea where her words had come from.

But she cannot do so in every case. It may be possible for "perfect contempt" to cover its own tracks, but a poet trying to establish the importance of "all these phenomena" cannot avoid dragging some of them into a dangerous "prominence." When that happens, moreover,

> the result is not poetry,
> nor till the autocrats among us can be
> "literalists of
> the imagination"—above
> insolence and trivality and can present
>
> for inspection, imaginary gardens with real toads in them, shall we have
> it. In the meantime, if you demand on one hand, in defiance of their opinion,
> the raw material of poetry in
> all its rawness and
> that which is on the other hand,
> genuine then you are interested in poetry.

And so the poem comes at last to what seems to be a definition of poetry, only to take it away from us again. For we do not "have / it" yet, nor "shall we have / it" until certain conditions have been met—and those conditions are as difficult to meet as they are to define. They amount neither to a demand for convincing fictions nor to an insistence that poets be faithful to the literal truth of their imaginings, though they may include both of these things. The problem is that Moore's first stipulation—that "the autocrats among us" must become "'literalists of / the imagination'"—sorts oddly with the second, which requires that after their transformation the erstwhile "autocrats . . . present / for inspection, imaginary gardens with real toads in them. . . ." I may seem either willful or obtuse in refusing to admit the obvious implication that "literalists of the imagination" are those who see real toads in imaginary gardens, but this sort of tautological argument tells us little about what it means to see real toads in imaginary gardens. If, moreover, we try to say directly what that would mean, we shall first of all have to abandon literalism—and even that "of the imagination" is literalism of a sort—and we shall also have to resort to the kind of "high sounding interpretation" which, in favoring the "useful," the poet has explicitly rejected as a criterion of importance.

Yet the poem has just presented us with a definition of poetry, if only to tell us that we shall have to settle for something less "In the meantime." If we do not try to learn what that definition means and what it is that we have to accept in place of "poetry," we will have been wasting our time. I propose, therefore, to "detain and appraise" the phrase which has been "dragged into prominence" by quotation marks, in order not only to determine what that phrase may be "useful" for, but also to find out why "the result is not poetry. . . ."

Let me begin by recalling that Moore has already "dragged" a phrase of Tolstoy's "into prominence" by the same means. That phrase, we have seen, comes from a journal entry asserting the impossibility of defining the difference between poetry and prose; and we may note, too, that Moore ventures to correct Tolstoy by erasing the line he had drawn to separate the two media. But she does not establish a new boundary; instead, she leaves it undefined, with the result that the phrase she quotes can no longer be assigned with any certainty to either category. But it is very "useful": not only does it bring Tolstoy's uncertainty about the division between prose and poetry actively into "Poetry"—whose own status is now very much in doubt—but it also points to a contemporary figure: Eliot, who has recently arrived at a conclusion very similar to Tolstoy's. It therefore suggests that confusion over the nature of poetry is by no means uncommon; and it is precisely because that confusion is so widespread that we do not and cannot "have" poetry for the time being. It remains, however, for the nature of this lack of clarity to be defined more precisely; for we do not yet know what it is that we do not "have."

According to Moore's notes, the phrase "literalists of the imagination" was suggested by an essay by W.B. Yeats, who speaks disapprovingly of Blake as a "too literal realist of the imagination, as others are of nature; and because he believed that the figures seen by the mind's eye . . . were 'eternal existences,' symbols of divine essences, he hated every grace of style that might obscure their lineaments."[87] Yeats's quarrel with Blake seems to be that Blake insists on clarity at the expense of "grace"—and Moore corrects him as she has already corrected Tolstoy, though in this case she does so by altering Yeats's words to fit her own purposes. She has no quarrel with Yeats's description of Blake's priorities; she only disagrees with Yeats for disagreeing with Blake.

Like Habakkuk, Blake is among those whom Moore described to Pound as "direct influences bearing on [her] work."[88] We may learn something about what she values in Blake by looking briefly at an early poem called, very simply, "Blake," which appeared in *Others* in December 1915, alongside "So far as the future is concerned."

> I wonder if you feel as you look at us,
> As if you were seeing yourself in a mirror at the end
>   Of a long corridor—walking frail-ly.
> I am sure that we feel as we look at you,
> As if we were ambiguous and all but improbable
>   Reflections of the sun—shining pale-ly.[89]

Moore can only "wonder" whether Blake would recognize in her work, and in that of her contemporaries, an image of his own; but in the second half of the poem, which mirrors the first, she uses an image strongly reminiscent of genteel poetry and criticism, an image which makes of her work not only a distorting "mirror" but also a satellite revolving at great distance and in a vacuum. She declares herself unhappily "sure" that in the work of the moderns (and especially in her own) she finds no more than "ambiguous and all but improbable / Reflections" of Blake's "sun." In subsequent chapters we shall be looking at the means she takes to improve this uncomfortable situation; what we are looking at in "Poetry" is the result of that effort.

For just as Moore's rhymes set her apart from Habakkuk in "So far as the future is concerned," so in "Poetry" she separates herself from Blake in the very act of "revert[ing]" to him. She does not address him directly, as she does in the earlier "Blake"; she can no longer afford to do so. In demanding that poets become "literalists of the imagination," she is quoting Yeats, or rather deliberately misquoting him in order to correct him—but she is also obliquely measuring herself and her autocratic contemporaries against the standard of Blake's "shining" clarity, and the obliqueness of her procedure is itself a measure of the degree to which she and Yeats, along with more immediate contemporaries like Eliot, have departed from that standard. Indeed, it is precisely because Moore does find herself (and herself in particular) so sadly lacking that she must drag her modification of Yeats's phrase "into prominence." In doing so, however, she places herself among the "half poets" whose work ends in something that "is not poetry"—and she takes her contemporaries down with her. To measure herself directly against Blake (or perhaps against any poet), or to allow us to take such a measurement, would be to hold herself up like a candle to the sun and, overwhelmed by the far more powerful light, become altogether invisible. Thus, Moore can continue to do her own work, and to admire the work of her contemporaries, only by concealing the intensity of her admiration for and her sense of affinity with Blake and the other prophetic writers she so admires. She must, therefore, "obscure [the] lineaments" of her ideal—which is precisely what Yeats complains that Blake will not do—with what she disapprovingly calls in "Picking and Choosing" an "opaque allusion," hiding Blake's light not only with Yeats's disapproval, but also with her own disapproving correction of Yeats's judgment. To do so, of course, only widens the gulf that separates her from Blake; thus, in deliberate self-contempt, she drives herself farther away from the prophetic clarity which she implicitly identifies with poetry itself—a clarity she tries again and again to achieve, not only in subsequent poems but also in her disastrous revisions of "Poetry" itself.

For she is uncomfortably aware that "poetry" becomes more impossible to attain the harder she tries to define it, and that awareness motivates the drastic revisions of "Poetry" which have baffled Moore's readers for so long. The second edition of *Observations* (1925) contains a substantially revised version of "Poetry" (quoted here in full):

> I too, dislike it:
> there are things that are important beyond all this fiddle.
> The bat, upside down, the elephant pushing,
> a tireless wolf under a tree,
> the base-ball fan, the statistician—
> "business documents and school books"—
> all these phenomena are pleasing,
> but when they have been fashioned
> into that which is unknowable,
> we are not entertained.
> It may be said of all of us
> that we do not admire that which we cannot understand;
> enigmas are not poetry.[90]

R.P. Blackmur and Guy Davenport have mistaken the text just quoted for a kind of *Ur*-"Poetry."[91] Blackmur looks back at it from the vantage-point afforded ten years later by Moore's *Selected Poems,* which contains a version much closer to the one we have been considering, and he sees "the difference between the poem and no poem at all, since the later version delivers—where the earlier only announces—the letter of imagination. But," he goes on, "we may present the differences more concretely, by remarking that in the earlier poem half the ornament and all the point are lacking. . . . [T]he earlier version . . . did not, indeed, become a poem at all."[92]

It is certainly true that a great deal is "lacking" in the version of "Poetry" I have just quoted. But the missing element is not mere "ornament," as Blackmur calls it; it is precisely "the point," which emerges only through Moore's careful elaboration and arrangement of detail. And that detail is lacking not because Moore has yet to discover it, but because she has made a deliberate decision to excise it from the text. The revised version fails, but not because Moore has yet to figure out what she means by calling something "Poetry." It fails because she has already arrived at a very firm conception, and she is now trying to live up to it. Blackmur is right in trying to read the two versions against each other; but when he reverses the chronological sequence, he necessarily misconstrues their relationship entirely. To read the new version in relation to its predecessor, however, is to see it clearly as a gesture of disgust, an angry and embarrassed confession on Moore's part that, as she was to say many years later, "when I am as complete as I like to be, I seem unable to get an effect plain enough."[93] In eliminating so many of the poem's crucial details, along with the elaborate formal pattern that holds them in constantly shifting relation to one another, Moore is trying to bring "Poetry" more closely into conformity with the Blakean clarity she holds up to herself in the earlier "Poetry" as the implicit (and somewhat startling) ideal that version fails to achieve. For that failure has become intolerable to her, and when she says "I too, dislike it" this time, Moore is both joining ranks with the critics who have been enraged by her work and emerging as her own harshest critic: "there are things that are important beyond all this fiddle."

Lines 3–6 parody the long catalogues of the earlier poem, rushing through an enervated, partial list of things that had once been considered vitally "important." That earlier judgment is now repudiated, and "these phenomena" are condescendingly allowed to be merely "pleasing." As though accusing herself of having been excessively preoccupied in the earlier "Poetry" with the dictum that "the result is not poetry" when things have been "dragged into prominence," the poet now does an about-face, angrily indicating that the charm of even these "pleasing" "phenomena" has been spoiled because "they have been fashioned into that which is unknowable"—have been turned into an enigma, and "enigmas are not poetry."

It is in this regard that the glaring absence of the stipulations concerning "literalists of the imagination" and "imaginary gardens with real toads in them" is most significant. In the earlier version, various "phenomena" are subjected to the desperate expedients of a poem which has had to present itself as an irreducible enigma because the clarity it seeks is unattainable by Moore or her contemporaries—but the new version allows itself no riddles, and so it cannot internalize the standard against which it is to be judged. To do so—and especially to do so obliquely—would be to admit that reading the poem poses real problems, and that is what Moore is no longer willing to admit in this case. "Poetry" can no longer afford to demand very much, therefore. In order to preserve its transparency, it must refrain from prescribing to other poets—so "literalists," "gardens," and "toads" all have to go. It must refrain, too, from prescribing to its readers: the "perfect contempt" which has served us (and Moore) so well must therefore be eliminated, along with the formerly "immovable critic"—whose part has been played with such vigor by the poet herself that the critic can no longer find anything to "dislike." But without that "perfect contempt," the poem cannot hope to find "a place for the genuine," and indeed there is no "place for the genuine" in this version. The "result is not poetry," either.

These revisions present an extreme instance of the concern for clarity which impels Moore's work in the early 1920s. But "Poetry" cannot be dismissed so easily. This is why Moore restored something closer to the original version when she prepared *Selected Poems* for publication in 1935, and for the same reason, thirty years later, she felt compelled to print that text (miscalled "Original Version") in the notes to the *Complete Poems* of 1967. The three-line version in the *Complete Poems* is Moore's final attempt to speak directly about poetry without obscuring its lineaments; but again the result is self-parody and an even greater obscurity:

> I, too, dislike it.
> Reading it, however, with a perfect contempt for it, one discovers in
> it, after all, a place for the genuine.[94]

This is only a remark waiting to be tested, made "genuine" by a poem; but that poem has been relegated to the Notes.

The self-contempt that informs these revisions is wasted: Moore got "Poetry" right the first time. And she got it right precisely because she had been willing to acknowledge that she had reached an impasse in her increasingly desperate struggle to define the obscurity surrounding the essential clarity of poetry.

2

The Forms of Resistance

I

The elaborate patterns into which Moore cast her poems have attracted the notice of her readers since the beginning of her career, but have rarely received more than cursory attention; few critics have asked what function those patterns might serve.[1] If we seek to account for this neglect, we need not go far: we have only to observe, for instance, that the concluding lines of "So far as the future is concerned" not only blur the conventional distinctions between poetry and prose, but seem also to contravene the widely accepted organic analogy by which Emerson, among American writers, had most powerfully asserted the priority of thought to form. "For it is not metres," Emerson wrote, "but a metre-making argument that makes a poem—a thought so passionate and alive that like the spirit of a plant or an animal it has an architecture of its own, and adorns nature with a new thing."[2]

Thus the problems raised by Moore's suggestion that poetry differs from prose only in possessing something vaguely defined "as a sort of heightened consciousness" are further compounded by her coupling of a reference to the "ecstasy" that prompts a poem with the apparent contention that it is not that ecstasy but rather an unspecified "'expediency'" which "'determines the form.'" This seems to imply so radical a disjunction between form and content that the meaning which the critic seeks to elicit seems unlikely to emerge in the querying of form; it is hardly surprising, therefore, that many of Moore's early readers, regarding the form of her verse as perversely arbitrary, should virtually have dismissed her work out of hand.

Nor is it especially surprising that more recent critics, confronted—and often confounded—by the products of Moore's incessant revision, should conclude that she ascribes to form no particular significance. There are, she writes in "Poetry," "things that are important beyond all this fiddle," and when apparently at whim she alters or departs from the stanzaic pattern of a given poem—altering or omitting rhymes, adding and subtracting syllables, deleting or restoring stanzas, or portions thereof; even, on occasion, eliminating the pattern altogether—the critic might well be tempted to say that "mystery of construction diverts one from what was originally one's / object—substance at the core. . . ."[3] But the only way "beyond" is through: Moore "fiddles" with form not out of any disregard for it but because it matters in the extreme.

By "form" I designate first Moore's use of rhyming syllabic verse in conjunction with a diction more usually associated with prose, and the shape that usage gives to her basic unit of composition—the stanza.[4] But in the larger sense—which matters most—I mean it to designate her conception of form as "the outward equivalent of a determining inner conviction." Neither this statement nor the accompanying remark that "the rhythm is the person" (both included in a brief "Note on Poetry" written in 1938[5]) represents the adoption of a new position; rather, they restate long-standing convictions. For when Moore writes in "Roses Only" (1917) that "spirit creates form," she makes explicit an assumption which implicitly governs her use of form, in "So far as the future is concerned," to define her isolation as a poet, thus casting doubt on any reading of the latter which takes it for granted that "ecstasy" and "expediency" stand to one another simply as polar opposites.

It is in "Black Earth" (1918)—a poem whose speaker repeatedly but unsuccessfully seeks to deny any connection between its "skin" and its "soul"—that the intimate bonding of meaning and form, poet and poem, is most fully articulated. For in drawing out the implications of her Emersonian conviction that "spirit creates form" (and "Roses Only" is heavily indebted to Emerson), Moore discovers a crucial corollary: that "form" thereby becomes the only available means of defining "spirit"—the only available means, that is to say, of giving definition to the self. Form thus assumes a signal importance as a means, also, of limiting the self, inhibiting its aggressive tendencies while at the same time protecting it against those "phases of life" which are most difficult to control and therefore most dangerous to confront.

Moore does not speak lightly when, in "Picking and Choosing" (1920), she proposes to herself neither to be "afraid" of "Literature" nor to approach it "familiarly." For, as she writes in the opening line, "Literature is a phase of life," perhaps the most potent type of that "experience" to which, she has "heard men say," she will ultimately "be forced to give / In"—and for all the rage such condescension provokes, she *has* been afraid, as we shall see, not just of "literature" but of "experience" more generally. Controlling that fear even while giving expression to it, following Emerson in her "liking for everything / self-dependent," Moore makes strictness of form the principal instrument in her desperate resistance to the compulsions of what "Black Earth" calls "unpreventable experience," seeming—as in "The Fish" (1918)—most self-contained when she is most in danger of losing her self-possession. To immerse herself in "the life of things," to "give / In" to "experience," would be "to disappear like an obedient chameleon" into her surroundings, to risk the dissolution of the self in a protean ecstasy of helpless imitation.[6]

II

"Roses Only" begins by overturning the convention by which the rose, prized for its delicate, unthinking beauty, is held out to women as an invitation by analogy to enter into sexual relations.

You do not seem to realise that beauty is a liability rather than
An assest—that in view of the fact that spirit creates form—we are justified in supposing
That you must have brains. For you, a symbol of the unit, stiff and sharp,
Conscious of surpassing—by dint of native superiority and liking for everything
Self-dependent—anything an

Ambitious civilisation might produce: for you, unaided to attempt through sheer
Reserve, to confute presumptions resulting from observation, is idle. You cannot make us
Think you a delightful happen-so. But rose, if you are brilliant, it
Is not because your petals are the without-which-nothing of pre-eminence. You would look—minus
Thorns—like a what-is-this, a mere

Peculiarity. They are not proof against a worm, the elements, or mildew
But what about the predatory hand? What is brilliance without coordination? Guarding the
Infinitesimal pieces of your mind, compelling audience to
The remark that it is better to be forgotten than to be remembered too violently,
Your thorns are the best part of you.[7]

In complaining of the rose's failure "to realise that beauty is a liability rather than / an asset" (a phrase which belongs to the "'business documents and / school-books'" that "Poetry" claims for its own rather than to the subgenre of poems dealing with women and roses),[8] Moore does not adduce the argument one might have expected—that beauty makes its possessor an object of male desire, and therefore susceptible to the sort of expert flattery that Waller offers in "Goe, lovely rose," and that Moore is determined to avoid. Instead, she takes the rose's beauty as warrant for a series of unanswerable "presumptions resulting from observation"—that, for one, it "must have brains"; for "in view of the fact that spirit creates form we are justified in supposing" that the beauty of the rose is not imposed from without but is the external manifestation of the "spirit" within. Since the rose has "brains," it must also be capable of understanding the second presumption, that it is "conscious of surpassing—by dint of native superiority and liking for everything / Self-dependent—anything an / Ambitious civilisation might produce. . . ."

Convention would lead us to presume that the rose owes its "native superiority" to its status as a natural object—and so the rose would like us to think. But the poem has already made it clear that beauty is a product of intelligence, and the rose's presumptive effort to "confute" the poet's presumptions "through sheer / Reserve" (for apparently the rose, like Peter the cat, "can talk, but insolently says nothing") is *so* "sheer" that we see right through it: "You cannot," says the poet, "make us / Think you a delightful happen-so." Indeed, that the rose should even "attempt" to do so makes it liable to the contrary, though seemingly arbitrary, presumption that it is not "natural" at all, but rather a work of art, self-conscious and self-created.

The ground is tricky, but firmer than it appears—for in her presumption that the rose is "conscious of surpassing—by dint of native superiority and liking for everything / Self-dependent—anything an / Ambitious civilisation might produce," Moore invokes Emerson's distinction, in "The Transcendentalist" (1842), between "material facts," such as the products of an "ambitious civilisation," and "spiritual facts," and she does so in Emerson's words: like the Transcendentalist, she "affirm[s] facts not affected by the illusions of sense, facts which are of the same nature as the faculty which reports them, and not liable to doubt; facts which in their first appearance to us assume a *native superiority* to material facts, degrading these into a language by which the first are to be spoken; facts which it only needs a retirement from the senses to discern."[9]

Although the personification is so opaque throughout the first half of the poem that the rose is scarcely visible, Moore "does not deny the sensuous fact" of its "beauty": rather, by personifying the rose she effects an Emersonian "retirement from the senses" which enables her to "discern" in the "sensuous fact" of its "beauty" what the Transcendentalist would recognize, in Emerson's words, "as the reverse side of the tapestry, as the *other end*, . . . a sequel or completion of a spiritual fact which nearly concerns [her]."[10] The strategy is crucial in removing the rose from nature, for according to Emerson, "This manner of looking at things transfers every object in nature from an independent and anomalous position without there, into the consciousness."[11] But there is a further twist, for we have seen that Moore is acutely aware that she herself occupies what might be called "an independent and anomalous position," and we shall see later that in bringing the rose into her own "consciousness" she will rather accentuate than alleviate that sense of detachment.

Having very nearly refined the rose out of existence by "degrading" the "material fact" of its beauty "into a language" by which the pertinent "spiritual facts" may be "spoken," Moore now brings it more fully "into the consciousness" by "speaking" the rose itself, naming it for the first and only time in the body of the poem. In doing so, she reaffirms the priority of "spiritual fact," of thought to form, for it is only when the rose has been named that its hitherto-suppressed formal features become visible: "But rose," she writes, "if you are brilliant, it / Is not because your petals are the without-which-nothing of pre-eminence."

Despite the rhetorical "if" and her evident mockery, the poet's characterization of the rose as "brilliant" carries a positive force not evident in her initial insistence that its "beauty is a liability rather than / An asset," suggesting that she is now prepared to admire the rose for possessing qualities which could not appear so long as it retained its "independent and anomalous position without there. . . ." Having used the word "beauty," which normally applies to "form," in establishing the existence of the rose's "spirit," she is now in position to refer simultaneously, with the word "brilliant," to operations of the intellect and to certain qualities of the surface. Thus she carries the earlier emphasis on intelligence into a study of the rose's formal vocabulary that inverts the conventional hierarchy of values.

In a "Bridal Song" attributed to John Fletcher, the future happiness of the couple whose marriage the poem celebrates is emblematized by flowers strewn along the path to the bridal house.[12] At the head of the list are, not surprisingly, some roses; but they have been specially treated, for in order to avoid any small mishap that might bring bad luck to the new marriage, their thorns have been removed. "Their sharp spines being gone," the flowers are rendered harmless, and may be enjoyed solely for their delicate fragrance and the "royal" "hues" of their petals. For the author of the "Bridal Song," then, the roses' beauty inheres in their petals, and beauty, to use Moore's terminology, is their chief "asset"; the "spines," on the other hand, are a distinct "liability." For Moore, however, "beauty" and "brilliance" are not necessarily identical, though they may coexist; and the most obviously beautiful parts of the rose are conspicuously *not* what "Roses Only" calls "the without-which-nothing of pre-eminence." The clumsy, Latinate "pre-eminence" on which the sentence closes collides heavily with the ludicrous and patently unnecessary translation of the Latin tag-phrase that precedes it, upsetting the balance so that as the poet considers the prospect of a rose "minus / Thorns," the entire structure collapses of its own weight into "a what-is-this, a mere / Peculiarity." But it is just here that the conventional image of the rose is most powerful, for in attempting to deflate the value conventionally ascribed to the rose's petals by overwhelming them with language as ponderous in its "peculiarity" as they are light and delicate, Moore reveals the degree of effort required to "resist," as Emerson says the Transcendentalist does, "all attempts to palm other rules and measures on the spirit than its own."[13]

The effort is necessary, however, for the "self-dependent" rose, like a great many of the creatures in Moore's poems, is in almost constant danger. Thus its thorns are more than the readily disposable nuisance that "the Bridal Song" makes them out to be—and more, too, than compositional elements whose function is simply to save the rose from "peculiarity." The threats come from a variety of sources—some natural, some human—and the thorns serve the rose in a protective, though severely limited capacity. "They are not proof against a worm, the elements, or mildew / But what about the predatory hand?" Although the thorns can do nothing against the natural enemies of the rose, they do offer a limited measure of protection against human depredations, and for that reason they constitute "the best part" of the rose's claim to "pre-eminence." "What is brilliance without co-ordination?" the poet asks, and we begin to see that the rose's "brilliance" consists in its "co-ordination" of the defensive role played by the thorns with the attractive force of the petals' beauty.

As the arguments which have been withheld from the outset are at length brought into play, we find that what makes "beauty a liability rather than / An asset" is indeed its power to attract those whose admiration almost inevitably takes form as a desire to pluck the rose, to appropriate it to themselves. This is, of course, to kill the rose in order to enjoy it for a short while; but it is not only that: within the context of the poem, to pluck the rose is to attack its independence, to violate the integrity of its "spirit." The thorns are there to stand guard over the "infinitesimal pieces" of the rose's "mind," a mind whose only hope of survival lies in its "brilliance," in its creating the possibility that its "beauty" may hold the admirer's attention until "the predatory hand" has reached out, only to be pricked and hastily withdrawn, its owner preferring—like the rose—rather "to be forgotten than to be remembered too violently."

From the rose's standpoint, "to be remembered too violently" is to be destroyed. The "Bridal Song," for instance, has to mutilate the rose in order to make it fit its celebratory role properly: no sharp thorns are wanted to suggest that either member of the wedding party will one day become a thorn in the other's flesh, and so the roses' "spines" are trimmed off before the flowers are placed in the couple's path. Waller, to take a more famous example, makes the rose an emissary to his lady in an attempt to win her favor by comparing her beauty to the perfection of the flower. Perhaps anticipating that flattery will get him nowhere, however, his final instructions are that the rose should "die—that she / The common fate of all things rare may read in thee." In dying, the rose becomes a text wherein the lady "may read" a thinly veiled threat that she will die "uncommended" and unwed unless she accepts the poet's admiration and thereby resumes her place in the natural order of things. This is Herrick's burden also, as he reminds his audience of "young Virgins" that "Old Time is still a-flying"; therefore, he admonishes them, "Gather ye rosebuds while ye may."[14] These examples suggest that the graceful (or flowery?) language of these poems conceals or blinds us to the violence with which both the flower and the woman are actually treated: each poet finds it necessary to destroy the flower, and each finds it more natural that the woman should submit her will to that of a male admirer than that she should continue in "an independent" and (therefore) "anomalous position."

By contrast, Moore has set herself the problem of finding a way to admire and "remember" the rose without doing it a violent injury, without laying on it the "predatory" "Hands that can grasp." She thus transforms it into a work of art in an effort not only to remove it from the depredations to which it is subject at the hands of poets who treat it as what William Carlos Williams scornfully calls "a symbol of nature,"[15] but also to demonstrate her own ability to resist the temptation to treat it similarly. For Moore is a "lover and worshipper of Beauty," like the Transcendentalist;[16] and the Emersonian translation of the acknowledged "beauty" of the rose "into a language" also "transfers . . . into the consciousness" of the poem an analogue for the language of poems whose beauty is conventionally regarded as being closely analogous to that of the rose. She must, therefore, either deny the worth of that beauty or succumb to the temptation to incorporate it into her own poem; expending "all [her] criminal ingenuity" in an effort "to avoid" what she calls in "Marriage" "the strange experience of beauty" —which "tears one to pieces"—she resorts to a diction which is, by conventional standards, extravagantly unpoetic and defiantly her own.

For Moore to incorporate the language of these *English* poems would be to adulterate with delicacies imported from a foreign and "ambitious civilisation" the "native" stock of Americanisms out of which, as T.S. Eliot noted,[17] "Roses Only" has been so painstakingly constructed. But that in turn would be to retreat from her "liking for everything / Self-dependent," thereby denying what Emerson calls the "height, the deity of man," which consists in being "self-contained," in "need[ing] no gift, no foreign force" to supplement one's own powers—and that Moore cannot afford to do, for "Everything real is self-existent."[18] I suggested in chapter 1 that "Sojourn in the Whale" registers Moore's fury at being "locked" out of the literary world by "men" who "say" that her work is weak because it is "Circumscribed by a heritage of native / Incompetence"; "Roses Only," which was first published together with "Sojourn in the Whale," counters with an equally angry refusal to "give / In" to the suppositions of the men who advance such charges. That refusal is accomplished, moreover, by so thoroughgoing an *acceptance* of what those critics would describe as circumscription that Moore herself appears to acknowledge no limits at all; rather, as the reviewer for the *Times Literary Supplement* remarked upon reading "Roses Only" in 1921, she seems "entirely ignorant" of all previous writing.[19] Opposing to the imputation of her "native incompetence" a "native superiority to material facts," Moore transforms limitation into "that weapon, self-protectiveness"—and she wields that weapon so effectively that she seems not only to "repel influences," as the Transcendentalist does,[20] but also to repel the *reader*, and so to stand entirely apart— inviolate, "self-dependent," and therefore "real."

For when, in order to make the rose "proof against . . . the predatory hand," Moore elevates its thorns to an unaccustomed "pre-eminence," she translates the "material fact" of the thorns into a "spiritual fact," which in turn "creates [the] form" of the poem itself. Knowing as she does that "beauty is a liability rather than an asset"—for beautiful language constitutes an almost irresistible temptation to those who would, in remembering the poem, inevitably *dismember* it by plucking out its words—she makes the poem appear as "stiff and sharp" as the rose, as if the only way to ensure its survival were to render it inaccessible and perhaps a bit dangerous.

"My Apish Cousins" (which also appeared with "Sojourn in the Whale" and "Roses Only") exults—a little prematurely—in the success of this effort, which has left her critics

"... trembling about
In inarticulate frenzy, saying
It is not for all of us to understand art, finding it
All so difficult, examining the thing

As if it were something inconceivably arcanic, as
Symmetrically frigid as something carved out of chrysoprase
Or marble—strict with tension, malignant
In its power over us and deeper
Than the sea when it proffers flattery in exchange for hemp,
Rye, flax, horses, platinum, timber and fur."[21]

In exchange "for hemp, / Rye, flax, horses, platinum, timber and fur," the sea allows us the illusion of mastery; but like "the land" which, in Emerson's "Hamatreya," renders to the farmers' "toil / Hay, corn, roots, hemp, flax, apples, wool and wood," the sea will not be owned—least of all by those who say, "'Tis mine, my children's and my name's."[22] So, too, Moore's poems would refuse themselves to any who laid claim to their secrets. But, like the American literature Emerson described, this is written "in the optative mood,"[23] for "My Apish Cousins" is much less elusive than it claims to be, as Moore's revisions of 1924 acknowledge.

Here we find the same critics, "trembling about" in the same "inarticulate frenzy," and

"... saying
it is not for us to understand art; finding it
all so difficult, examining the thing

as if it were inconceivably arcanic, as symmetrically frigid as if it had been carved out of
chrysoprase or marble—strict with tension, malignant
in its power over us and deeper
than the sea when it proffers flattery in exchange for hemp,
rye, flax, horses, platinum, timber and fur."[24]

The differences are almost invisible: two syllables are lost when "it is not for all of us to understand art" becomes "it is not for us to understand art," and the rhyme-scheme is unbalanced by the loss of the rhyme on *as / chrysoprase* in the opening lines of the final stanza. The latter change occurs, however, just at the point when the poem's careful symmetry is under direct attack, and it calls attention to the fact that Moore has quietly introduced asymmetries into each of the poem's controlling patterns where none had been tolerated previously. Those whose "half fledged protestations" the poem reports with such scorn are thus made to look exceedingly foolish, for their "inarticulate frenzy" has made them inattentive critics; their insistence that "it is not for us to understand art" comes to rest squarely on their own shoulders.

The earlier version is aimed squarely at the critics who resist it, who will not allow themselves to be moved by what "they" evidently regard as the "malignant" power of a poem which appears to be "as / Symmetrically frigid as something carved out of chrysoprase / Or marble"; but in the later version Moore pokes fun at herself as well, turning away from the critics to comment ironically on the earlier version of the poem. Acknowledging that version's insistence on symmetry while destroying symmetry, the revision sharpens Moore's attack on her critics by granting their point and taking it away from them in the same motion.

Balking the efforts of those "scarecrows / Of aesthetic procedure" who would—like the "trembling" critics of "My Apish Cousins" and the condescending "men" of "Sojourn in the Whale"—"palm other rules and measures on the spirit than its own," the "thorns" of "Roses Only" afford a measure of protection against the "predatory hand" of the reader who does not share Moore's assumptions. "They are not proof against a worm," however, nor does the poet wish them otherwise. For Moore, as for Emerson's Transcendentalist, "it is really a wish to be met,—the wish to find society for [her] hope and religion,—which prompts [her] to shun what is called society."[25] And so the poem closes itself to a certain class of readers in order that Moore's "secret love" for Blake may be "met" on her own ground, in order that she may offer a place to the "invisible worm" of "The Sick Rose" without giving herself away.[26] Having insinuated itself into the "life" of "Roses Only," however, the now-visible worm threatens by its very visibility to "destroy" the poem, and lest the "dark secret" of her susceptibility to a male and "foreign force" be exposed, Moore must naturalize the "worm" by linking it to the hazards of exposure to "the elements, or mildew," thereby containing its destructive "tension" within the "strict" measures of the patterned symmetry by which she affirms that it is indeed (in Emerson's words) "simpler to be self-dependent."[27]

III

We turn our attention now to "The Fish" (1918), an elegant and widely anthologized poem which seems almost hermetically self-contained in the austerity of its form, though it is more often cited as illustrating Moore's approach to nature than as representing her formal procedures. Indeed, the typographical modification by which in 1935 Moore transformed a poem arranged in six-line stanzas into stanzas of only five lines (the form in which it is most often reprinted) seems to hint at the futility of the formalist approach and seems also to warn against any categorical assertion that form, in Moore's verse, always involves more than the imposition of merely arbitrary patterns. This transformation, which entails neither a change in wording nor a rhetorically strategic sacrifice of symmetry (as does the revision of "My Apish Cousins" discussed above), is quite evidently *not* an effort to lessen the enigmatic character of the poem, which retains its collection of incongruous and unnatural objects: ash-heaps, a fan, spun glass, an iron wedge, a cornice, rice-grains, and so on.

Still, as Hugh Kenner has pointed out, the exchange of one symmetrical structure for another, equally symmetrical one,

> is not a trivial change, since it affects the system by which pattern intersects utterance, alters the points at which the intersections occur, provides a new grid of impediments to the over-anxious voice, and modifies, moreover, the intrusiveness of the system itself. . . . We can nearly say that we have a *new* poem, arrived at in public and without changing a word, by applying a system of transformations to an existing poem.[28]

The changes Kenner describes are not the product of a mere restless urge to tinker, as they may seem to be; but they will remain incomprehensible unless we realize that the six-line stanza from which Moore derived the new pattern is itself a revision. When "The First" first appeared in the August 1918 issue of *The Egoist*,[29] it moved in rather breathless four-line stanzas, thus:

The Fish

Wade through black jade.
Of the crow blue mussel-shells, one
Keeps adjusting the ash-heaps;
Opening and shutting itself like

An injured fan.
The barnacles undermine the
Side of the wave—trained to hide
There—but the submerged shafts of the

Sun, split like spun
Glass, move themselves with spotlight swift-
Ness into the crevices—
In and out, illuminating

The turquoise sea
Of bodies . . .

Several early drafts of the poem assure us that this was neither editorial fiat nor a printer's error; they indicate, also, that the lines about the barnacles on "the / Side of the wave" had given Moore considerable difficulty.[30]

"The Fish" was recast into eight six-line stanzas for publication in Alfred Kreymborg's *Others for 1919: An Anthology of the New Verse*.[31]

The Fish

wade
through black jade.
    Of the crow blue mussel shells, one
        keeps
        adjusting the ash-heaps;
    opening and shutting itself like

an
injured fan.
    The barnacles which encrust the
        side
        of the wave, cannot hide
    there; for the submerged shafts of the

sun,
split like spun
    glass, move themselves with spotlight swift-
        ness
        into the crevices—
    in and out, illuminating

the
turquoise sea
    of bodies . . .

It last appeared in this form in *Observations*, where Moore set beside it another poem which had preceded it in *The Egoist* by one month. This other poem, which was dropped from collections of Moore's work after 1925, appears here exactly as it did in *Observations*.

Reinforcements

The vestibule to experience is not to
    be exalted into epic grandeur. These men are going to
their work with this idea, advancing like a school of fish through

still water—waiting to change the course or dismiss
    the idea of movement, till forced to. The words of the Greeks
ring in our ears, but they are vain in comparison with a sight like this.

The pulse of intention does not move so that one
    can see it, and moral machinery is not labelled, but
the future of time is determined by the power of volition.[32]

"Reinforcements" opens with an injunction against exalting "into epic grandeur" the activity of replacement troops on their way to a war already four years old, and it carries out that injunction in a simile designed rather to diminish than to enlarge—as epic simile customarily enlarges—the stature of the men it describes. These are not godlike figures hurling themselves heroically into the fray: they are only "men" on their way to "work," "advancing like a school of fish through / still water." For a faintly ridiculous, but strangely beautiful, "sight like this," the epic mode is entirely inappropriate: "The words of the Greeks / . . . are vain" not only because they use "exalted" language to inflate the value of the work these men are "going to," but because in attempting thus to glorify the occasion, they miss—or rather deny—its awful significance. The significance here consists precisely in the *insignificance* and anonymity of the men themselves, and in the sense of routine with which they move off together. These men are not so much moving as *being moved*—impelled, "like a school of fish," by a "pulse of intention" which belongs to the group rather than to any single individual, and thus can be seen neither by the men themselves nor by the poet, who sees only men going matter-of-factly "to their work" as if, so she writes in "A Graveyard," "there were no such thing as death."[33]

Moore wrote in 1940 that "the power of the visible / is the invisible"[34]

—and "The Fish" achieves its "power" by keeping so much of what most concerns it "invisible" that the reader is forced to take up the necessarily speculative work of supplying the "connectives" which, Williams wrote in 1925, Moore had told him she "despised."[35] We may begin by noting that the title is in fact a quotation, unmarked because in this instance Moore preys upon her own work. What had been a simile, used in "Reinforcements" with self-conscious didacticism to illustrate and enforce the poet's argument that war poetry works most appropriately by understatement, is in "The Fish" cut off from its referent and made to serve as the new poem's starting point. Brilliantly pushing understatement to the brink of silence, "The Fish" is a war poem, as the date suggests. Most likely prompted by the assignment of Moore's brother, a Navy chaplain, to sea duty in the North Atlantic late in 1917, it is all the more chilling for having suppressed all overt reference to the men who are seen in "Reinforcements" "advancing like a school of fish through / still water." The fish are abruptly launched into the poem through the title (which thus becomes the "vestibule to experience," divested now of any association with "epic grandeur"), but their advance is blocked immediately by the wall of "black jade" which they encounter at the end of the opening sentence.

The most significant "revision" of "The Fish" in 1935 does not really touch the poem directly: rather, it is the combination of Moore's decision not to reprint "Reinforcements," and T.S. Eliot's skillful manipulation of the contents of her *Selected Poems.* Removed from the chronological sequence of composition which Moore had followed ten years earlier in *Observations*, and placed by Eliot in an entirely different configuration, "The Fish" assumes a significantly different character. The poem is no less enigmatic, but it now follows the most recent poem in the collection ("Nine Nectarines and Other Porcelain" [1934]), a celebration of artistry in the imaginative apprehension of "'the spirit of the wilderness'" which directs the reader's attention to *Moore's* artistry in representing the otherness of the sea.[36] And when we turn the page, "In This Age of Hard Trying Nonchalance Is Good And—" (1916) leads us to recognize a certain "self-protectiveness" in "The Fish" as well. But there is nothing to tell us what is being protected against, and by comparison with the earlier version quoted above, the sharp edges of that "self-protectiveness" have been blunted.

Changing the shape of the stanzas themselves does not effect a radical difference in meaning so much as it alters the force of the presentation: what Kenner is so nearly willing to call "a *new* poem" seems less spare, less stark, less "defiant" (to borrow from the poem itself) than it once had been, for in eliminating the monosyllabic fourth line of the previous version Moore has softened the poem considerably. That softening is appropriate, moreover, because the relative fluidity of the new version is in accord with the generally more relaxed movement of Moore's poems of the 1930s; it is also appropriate because, without "Reinforcements" to help account for its severity, the formal pattern Moore devised for "The Fish" in 1919 seems excessive, even arbitrary, as Kenner suggests when he writes that the "new version relents a little its self-sufficient arbitrariness." In context, however, it is neither excessive nor arbitrary.

In the first version (1918), both the fish and the reader are impelled too quickly through the entire poem, as through the first sentence:

The Fish

Wade through black jade.

Here the primary emphasis falls on "jade," which concludes both the line and the sentence; the strong closure, enforced by punctuation and a heavy internal rhyme, creates a swift-paced line that belies the sluggishness of the movement in which we are being asked to believe. But when the same fish are made to

wade
through black jade

the new pattern slows their advance dramatically by isolating the verb, and so accentuates the great effort of their motion. With the verb singled out for attention, moreover, we become conscious of its oddity, for only creatures equipped with feet can wade: these "fish" are at least half-human — like the creatures of whom Moore was to write in "The Plumet Basilisk" (1933), they are "interchangeably man and fish."[37] The verb thus retains, and augments by extreme compression, the force of the simile by which the replacement troops had been discerned in "Reinforcements," "advancing like a school of fish through / still water." In "Reinforcements," "still water" is also *clear* water, as transparent as the simile itself; "black jade," however, is as opaque as the "black glass through which no light / Can filter" that forms the thick skin of the elephant in "Black Earth"—published only a few months before "The Fish." Having forced their way "through black jade," the all-too-human fish are lost from sight.

The reader, too, must now "wade / through black jade," stumbling over line-breaks as surprising in their placement as "still water" gone suddenly black and solid. Following the fish into the poem's stone sea, we find ourselves in a strange, ominously silent landscape filled with ruins. Amid scores of "crow blue mussel-shells" one moves, "adjusting the ash-heaps" to reveal that these are not living creatures but piles of empty, burned husks; and the lone survivor is weak, feebly "opening and shutting itself like / an / injured fan." Again the pattern does its work: by forcing the new stanza to begin on an insignificant word, it shifts emphasis to the second line, where because the fan is "injured" rather than *torn* or *damaged*, the line nags us once more with the faint, disturbing sense of a human presence, of a frail, crumpled body.

Although all seems quiet, the scene is still fraught with danger: barnacles looking for a place to hide "encrust the side" of a (solid) wave, but find no security. (The original version, which tells us that these "barnacles" are "*trained* to hide / There," hints that they, too, are human.) The sun's rays, refracted and "split like spun / glass" as they pass through the hard surface of the water, are themselves solidified: they become "submerged shafts," stabbing into the sea "with spotlight swift- / ness," probing (as the lineation suggests their quick, unpleasantly arhythmic motion) "into the crevices." No place is safe, and neither are we: when the searching light transmutes the sea from "black jade" to another stone, "turquoise," the syllabic pattern holds the image for a split second—just long enough for us to become conscious of a gentler, more soothing beauty—before allowing the light-change to reveal, with terrible deliberateness, that we are moving in a "sea / of bodies."[38]

The poem now arrives, quite literally, at its crisis: pressing relentlessly forward in the present tense, it turns *back*, chronologically, to discover the violence which has brought these bodies here. The "submerged shafts of the / sun," moving like spotlights, have found a target; and with sudden explosive force, "The water drives a / wedge / of iron through the iron edge / of the cliff."[39] (Wedges in Moore's poems are always weapons, and like the one that "might have split the firmament," they always possess tremendous explosive force.[40]) Just so, a submarine's spotlight finds its target, and a torpedo is driven through the iron hull of a ship, which looms clifflike above the surface. The concussion throws the undersea world into chaos:

. . . the stars,

pink
rice grains, ink

bespattered jelly-fish, crabs like
green
lilies and submarine
toadstools, slide each on the other.

Seemingly oblivious to such massive destruction, the stanzaic pattern isolates two splotches of bright color, pink and green, highlighted against the at-first-black and now turquoise sea, while the blasted troop-ship, scarred with "All / external / marks of abuse . . . all the physical features" of an "ac- / cident" which is no accident but an act of war, settles to the bottom. There it rests, a "defiant edifice" with a gaping "chasm" in its "dead" "side."

The "submarine" world into which the poem has taken us, then, is what Moore calls in "A Graveyard" "a well excavated grave," and "The Fish" is a bitterly elegiac poem mourning a loss which it is as helpless to restore as it has been helpless to prevent. But it *can* register the poet's guilt and horror at her troubled discovery of what a note in the margin of an early draft called "beauty intertwined with tragedy,"[41] and it *can* register the loss. "Dead" though it is, "the chasm side" lives "on what cannot revive / its youth"—on a poem which records and perpetually re-enacts its destruction, and which in doing so takes responsibility for it, although it can "revive" neither the "youth" of the ship nor the "youth" who went down with it. The poem can only note, with something like despair, that the sea filling the ship's hold "grows old in it."

The four-line stanzas in which "The Fish" was first published rush the poem so quickly to conclusion that much of its force is dissipated in the rapidity of its movement, as if Moore had been concerned to finish the poem before she could be betrayed into greater explicitness, and thus overwhelmed by the very intensity of her emotion. The risk of succumbing to what she would describe many years later as "A Burning Desire To Be Explicit"[42] may best be measured by setting "The Fish" against one of Moore's most popular works. Confronted by another war, she offers in "In Distrust of Merits" (1943) "testimony—to the fact that war is intolerable, and unjust."[43]

Strengthened to live, strengthened to die for
medals and positioned victories?
They're fighting, fighting, fighting the blind
man who thinks he sees—
who cannot see that the enslaver is
enslaved; the hater, harmed. O shining O

firm star, O tumultuous
    ocean lashed till small things go
as they will, the mountainous
    wave makes us who look, know

depth. Lost at sea before they fought! . . .[44]

In writing this poem Moore was, she said later, "overpowered" by emotion; and as a result, "In Distrust of Merits" is a mere "protest—disjointed, exclamatory."[45] The poet signifies her anguish by insistent, heavily rhetorical repetitions which seem, at times, almost a helpless stammering: *O . . . O . . . O. . . .* But the exclamation point, a form of punctuation extremely rare in Moore's *oeuvre*, tells the story best, for it confesses the flaccidity of the sentence, which must rely upon punctuation to provide an emotive force it would otherwise lack.

By contrast, "The Fish" derives much of its considerable force from the tension created by its effort to abstain from any overt reference either to the war or to the men who are, like those in the later poem, "lost at sea" before they reach the battlefront. The six-line stanza into which Moore recast "The Fish" in 1919 heightens that tension, and thus supplies the poem with additional power, by releasing the poem's energy in gradual increments, cutting it sharply back, and releasing it again slowly, only to curtail it once more with the opening of a new stanza. The new form exerts itself against the over-hasty movement toward closure that so evidently weakens the first published version.[46] Indeed, the syllabic pattern drags so strongly against what Moore once called "the pull of the sentence"[47] that the poem is forced to continue in spite of being nearly choked off, twice in each stanza, by a formal structure that allows only a single syllable to articulate itself. The poem thus seems to complete itself in defiance of the iron control imposed upon it.

All
external
    marks of abuse are present on
        this
        defiant edifice—
    all the physical features of

ac-
cident— lack
    of cornice, dynamite grooves, burns,
        and
        hatchet strokes, these things stand
    out on it. . . .

The poem, then, appears as a defiant linguistic edifice marked by the "burns, / and / hatchet strokes" of a formal pattern which blasts its way through the sentences. What at first sight appears to be opposition, however, is in fact cooperation, for the sentences and the pattern into which they fall are made of the same substance, and cannot be separated. Each is what it is by virtue of the shaping power of the other: language articulates a pattern which in turn articulates language, and which, in doing so, controls and coerces meaning. Just as "The water drives a / wedge / of iron through the iron edge / of the cliff," so the sentences drive through the pattern. And although "the chasm side is / dead,"

> Repeated
> evidence has proved that it can
> live
> on what cannot revive
> its youth. The sea grows old in it.

As the iron cliff gives way before, but contains, the force of the iron wedge, so the pattern yields to, but controls, the poem that thrusts itself against and through it. Visibly, violently shaping the sentences, it is in turn shaped and sustained—"repeated"—by their terrible, explosive knowledge of "dynamite grooves, burns, / and / hatchet strokes." The pattern "lives on" sentences which "cannot revive its youth," and the poem "grows old" in the knowledge with which it has scored the pattern, which in turn impresses that knowledge back upon the poem. In defiant opposition to the insane violence of the First World War, they keep each other alive.

IV

First published in *The Egoist* in April 1918, "Black Earth" (later retitled "Melancthon") is an anomaly in Moore's *oeuvre*,[48] for of all her poems only this one purports to be spoken in its entirety by a voice other than the poet's. Indeed, that voice seems as far removed from Moore's as possible, since ostensibly it is not human at all: the speaker is an elephant, fretful, self-aggrandizing, and so vastly proud of the figure it cuts that although it wants desperately to save its "soul," it can think only of saving its "skin." But the poet's playfully "feigned inconsequence of manner" gives place to a far more intimate and consequential drama, for in choosing a nonhuman speaker Moore necessarily injects *herself* into the play of speech and pattern, only to find that the integrity of her own "soul" depends entirely upon her ability to defend her chosen form.

Moore's choice of a speaker is at once playful and extremely significant. In the earlier "Diligence Is to Magic as Progress Is to Flight" (1915), the "tough-grained" elephant is clearly a figure for the sort of poetry Moore believes herself to be writing. The elephant, like the poetry, is prized chiefly for its "ability to endure blows" from those critics who would frighten it, if they could, by holding up "scarecrows / Of aesthetic procedure"—critical standards by which her poems are judged to be "ephemera," mere closely worked "curios" not worth preserving. "Diligence" represents the poet as having deliberately chosen "to travel laboriously": she has "clambered up" onto the elephant, which serves as her vehicle. Like "The Fish" then—and, in a slightly different way, like "Roses Only" as well—"Black Earth" animates a rhetorical figure, for here the *elephant* speaks, suggesting both that the poem now speaks for itself (whereas in "Diligence" the poet speaks for it) and that the poet has, as it were, "clambered" into her vehicle: she now "inhabit[s]" the tough "elephant skin," and her voice issues from within the elephant. The elephant is, in the truest sense, a persona, a mask which conceals the features while amplifying the voice of the actor.

In "Black Earth" the poet takes advantage of the protection afforded by the elephant's thick hide to proclaim not only the poem's impenetrability to criticism (and to other predatory poets) but her own imperviousness as well. "My soul," the speaker boasts, "shall never / Be cut into by a wooden spear. . . ." The elephant is not completely invulnerable, however, for its "back / Is full of the history of power" and its skin, thick and hard as it is, has been "cut / Into checkers by rut / Upon rut of unpreventable experience" whose very unpreventability demonstrates the need for protection. "New York" (1921), with its uneasy celebration of a new-found "accessibility to experience," resonates all the more powerfully for the knowledge that, three years earlier, "experience" had been something to shut out, to ward off: in "Black Earth," the poet takes undisguised pride in the fact that although a certain amount of experience has proved to be "unpreventable," her "soul" remains inviolate and inaccessible. The elephant's thick skin, like the rose's thorns, is there to guard the consciousness within against "the predatory hand."

We learn in "Roses Only" that "spirit creates form"; and just as thorns and petals together comprise the form of the rose, so the elephant's skin is its form, the external manifestation of the "soul" within. We are, therefore, altogether "justified in supposing" (the phrase is from "Roses Only") that this elephant is every bit as self-conscious as the rose—the more so as the elephant, unlike the rose, is not silent. Indeed, we know the creature only as its speech reveals it to us.

The I of each is to

The I of each,
A kind of fretful speech
Which sets a limit on itself. . . .

Form by its very existence manifests "spirit," and the elephant's form—its skin—*is* the poem that is its speech. Thus speech itself is the mask, the persona which conceals the poet who not only speaks through it but who also, and more importantly, *speaks* it. Because speech is perceived to be coeval with form, however, we are justified in inferring the presence of the "soul" within the speech. The mask of speech thus reveals as it conceals, conceals as it reveals: "Now I breathe," says the speaker, "and now I am sub- / Merged." Both conditions obtain simultaneously.

Speech, however, answers a double obligation: generated by internal pressure, by the outward thrust of the "spirit" or "soul" working within, it yet "sets a limit on itself"—and is therefore formed—in response to its "experience" of the speech of *another*, speech which has likewise taken form by imposing limits on itself. Forming itself by delimiting itself against other speech, the poem defends itself against the speech of the other and, at the same time, guards the integrity of the other's speech. As the elephant's skin is "cut / Into checkers by rut / Upon rut of unpreventable experience," so the speech comprising the poem is everywhere conscious of and responsible to the self-imposed limits of rhyme (*aabc*) and syllable count (4, 6, 13, 13); these "cut" the poem into carefully symmetrical four-line stanzas in response to the "unpreventable" (that is, both unforeseeable and unstoppable) "experience" of T.S. Eliot's "The Hippopotamus," which appeared in *The Little Review* in June 1917.

The broad-backed hippopotamus
Rests on his belly in the mud;
Although he seems so firm to us
He is only flesh and blood.[49]

So begins Eliot's poem; ten months later, *The Egoist* (with Eliot as assistant editor) printed "Black Earth," which begins disingenuously:

Openly, yes,
    With the naturalness
    Of the hippopotamus or the alligator
    When it climbs out on the bank to experience the

Sun, I do these
Things which I do, which please
    No one but myself. . . .

The firm, deliberate rhythms of the initial lines betray the studied "naturalness" with which the speaker "openly" drops the hippopotamus' name into the interior of a line which does not stop short, as the first two lines do (*hippopotamus* is only one syllable shorter than the entire second line, and it is a syllable longer than the first), but instead goes on quickly to name another, more recognizably dangerous animal, only to pass into the next line and then to the next stanza before pausing for breath. By the time the sentence ends, midway through the third line of the second stanza, the hippopotamus' cameo appearance is all but forgotten. "Openly, yes," and with a great deal of deliberateness (in one early draft Moore wavered, uncertain whether she ought not to announce her "deliberateness" rather than her "naturalness"),[50] "Black Earth" naturalizes, and thus neutralizes, "The Hippopotamus."

As "The Fish" disappear into the "black jade" of the sea, so "the hippopotamus" (which in Eliot's poem emerges—on wings—"from the damp savannas," whence it ascends to Heaven) sinks back into the "black earth" as suddenly as it had first appeared, and with far less fanfare. Eliot's satiric hymn is thus "sub- / Merged" in "Black Earth" in much the same way that "Reinforcements" is "submerged" in "The Fish," but it makes its mark nonetheless, for "The Hippopotamus" is written indelibly upon "Black Earth"; it is very much a part of what Henry James called "the impress that constitutes an identity."[51] Deriving its identity from its form, "Black Earth" carries the impress of Eliot's quatrains in its own four-line stanzas: adhering to careful symmetries, the elephant "sets a limit on itself" in order to avoid taking on the form of "The Hippopotamus." It is only in risking that possibility, however, that the poet's speech may take form at all: "The I of each" so closely resembles "The I of each" in being constituted as speech that each *must* "set a limit on itself," must take on form, in order to avoid taking (or mistaking) the other for itself.

As Eliot's quatrains impress themselves upon the four-line stanzas of "Black Earth," so the language of James's *The Portrait of a Lady* (the preface is quoted above) informs the poem's speech in ways equally significant.

For Moore's argument about the self and its limits brings together the apparently irreconcilable positions advanced by Isabel Archer and her antagonist, the worldly, corrupt Madame Merle. In a crucial encounter, Merle tells her young protégée:

> ". . . When you've lived as long as I you'll see that every human being has his shell and that you must take the shell into account. By the shell I mean the whole envelope of circumstances. There's no such thing as an isolated man or woman; we're each of us made up of some cluster of appurtenances. What shall we call our 'self'? Where does it begin? Where does it end? It overflows into everything that belongs to us—and then it flows back again. I know a large part of myself is in the clothes I choose to wear. I've a great respect for *things*! One's self—for other people—is one's expression of one's self; and one's house, one's furniture, one's garments, the books one reads, the company one keeps—these things are all expressive."

But Isabel cannot and will not assent. "I think just the other way," she retorts; ". . . I don't know whether I succeed in expressing myself, but I know that nothing else expresses me. Nothing that belongs to me is any measure of me; everything's on the contrary a limit, a barrier, and a perfectly arbitrary one."[52]

Moore knows—or discovers as "Black Earth" proceeds—that far from being mutually exclusive, the two positions shade constantly into one another, overflowing and then flowing back again. Thus her initial declaration of independence—"I do these / Things which I do, which please / No one but myself"—echoes Isabel's defense of her choice in husbands: "Whatever I do," says Isabel to her aunt Lydia, "I do with reason."[53] But from Isabel, Moore moves straight to Madame Merle, for she inhabits an "elephant skin / . . . fibred over like the *shell* of / The coco-nut . . ." (emphasis added); later in the poem, though, she will seem to dismiss that "shell," scorning the "tree trunk without / Roots" which is "accustomed to shout / Its own thoughts to itself like a shell. . . ."

It is easy enough to see that either position taken by itself becomes a trap; what "Black Earth" seems to imply, however, is that the trap remains even when the two are allowed to come together. The circularity of the poem's linguistic definition of the self—according to which "The I of each" mirrors and is mirrored in "The I of each," upon which each in turn depends for recognition and for the limit that is its form, its identity, and its protection—suggests that form draws a circle about the self, enclosing, containing, and at the same time expressing it: "through- / Out childhood to the present time," says the remarkable elephant, "the unity of / Life and death has been expressed by the circumference / Described by my / Trunk. . . ." It is, we note, the *form*—the "circumference" itself—that is expressive: "The I of each" is contained in and expressed by the circle of its form, as "the I" of the poet is expressed by and held securely within the form of her speech. Conferring distinction, form simultaneously affords the poet a protective "skin."

Wholeness, "unity," the completeness and integrity of the self, are concepts aptly "expressed" by the circle: for the circle, a single line returning continuously upon itself without beginning or end, is the most perfect of forms. It is, therefore, also the most dangerous. Moore warns in the truncated final stanza of "In the Days of Prismatic Colour" that "Truth is no Apollo / Belvedere, no formal thing,"[54] and the self that concentrates exclusively upon achieving the circularity of perfect form may in the process *de*-form "truth." To concentrate upon form is to be intent upon externals and so to risk mistaking what may be dangerously superficial perfections for true "feats of strength." But, the elephant says,

> I
> Perceive feats of strength to be inexplicable after
> All; and I am on my guard; external poise, it
>
> Has its centre
> Well nurtured—we know
> Where—in pride, but spiritual poise, it has its centre where?

Turning inward from the circumference that proudly maintains the integrity of self and poem, "Black Earth" stumbles over the sudden recognition that the "feats of strength" by which it turns aside the "wooden spear" of the hunter, who is both critic and poet, are "inexplicable": the line has one syllable too many, and the following line has one too few. Although the stanza maintains a total syllable count equal to that of the eight preceding stanzas, this cannot disguise the fact that just past midpoint (we are at line 35 of a 68-line poem), "Black Earth" has lost its "external poise": each of the next three stanzas is also unbalanced.

This loss, however, is only a prelude to and a prefiguration of the more severe disturbance that follows: just as pride goeth before a fall, so the slippage of "external poise" goes before the loss of "spiritual poise." The second line of the tenth stanza sacrifices not only a syllable but its rhyme as well (this is the only stanza without the *aa* rhyme): *where* should have rhymed (imperfectly, of course) with *centre*, but it has been dropped down into the third line. That line, which acquires *another* extra syllable from line four, now stretches its awkward syntax uncomfortably between the certainty of a *where* that signifies a center which has been too easily located and a far more disturbing uncertainty: the unbalanced line closes on a hexameter hemistich that puts metrical as well as rhetorical stress on the final *where*?

The question goes unanswered as the elephant turns, with apparent inconsequence, to contemplate its own ears. Gradually, however, it becomes clear that the elephant is searching for the elusive center of spiritual poise by taking stock of itself.

> My ears are sensitized to more than the sound of
>
> The wind. I see
> And I hear, unlike the
> Wandlike body of which one hears so much, which was made
> To see and not to see; to hear and not to hear;
>
> That tree trunk without
> Roots, accustomed to shout
> Its own thoughts to itself like a shell, maintained intact
> By who knows what strange pressure of the atmosphere . . .

The last line of stanza eleven lacks a syllable which cannot be accounted for in previous lines (thus leaving the stanza as a whole unequal to the others); but the balance is restored by an extra syllable in the first line of the succeeding stanza (which therefore has a total of 37, against a norm of 36). As if to underscore the difficulty—and the importance—of making up the balance in this way, the eleventh is the only stanza in the poem that concludes with an end-stopped line.

The fact that such an interstanzaic balancing act has replaced the former method of accounting, by which differences were made up internally, suggests that other developments may be taking place as well. Indeed, as it moves toward conclusion, the poem enters an important new phase in which regularity or perfection of form seems to *signal* "truth" rather than threaten to deform it, while the *absence* of "external poise" appears to imply that the statement being made may be less than fully honest. Thus, the apparent poise with which the elephant scornfully dissociates itself from the tendency of the "wandlike" human to "shout / Its own thoughts to itself like a shell" is betrayed by the syllabic imbalance of the stanza in which the denunciation occurs, and shown to be at best self-delusive, at worst the last defense of a stubborn pride. (But it is not the last, as we shall see.)

We have known from the outset that the speaker "inhabit[s]" an "elephant skin / . . . fibred over like the *shell* of / The coco-nut" (italics added) —a skin made of "black glass through which no light / Can filter." She thus *resists* illumination, as the human—"that / Spiritual / Brother to the coral / Plant, absorbed into which, the equable sapphire light / Becomes a nebulous green"—does not (the Transcendentalist, said Emerson, "believes . . . in the perpetual openness of the human mind to new influx of light and power").[55] The "openly" proud declaration with which the poem begins—"I do these / Things which I do, which please / No one but myself" —now seems as hollow as the human shell she disdains, as hollow as the circle "Described" by the elephant's trunk. It does not seem so to the speaker, however—or if it does, she will not say; for she has been trying all along—is still trying—to suppress the knowledge that she is only talking to herself.

As she moves, in the thirteenth stanza, toward an apparent acknowledgment of her resemblance to the human "shell," the poem returns to the syllabic norm which had been established in the earlier stanzas. Stanza thirteen ends with the beginning of the crucial definition of the self:

> The I of each is to
>
> The I of each,
> A kind of fretful speech
>   Which sets a limit on itself. . . .

With it comes the knowledge that to "The I of each" the elephant is only a husk, "a cortex merely," as at first "the wandlike body" is to the elephant merely a "tree trunk without / Roots, accustomed to shout / Its own thoughts to itself like a shell. . . ." Each, trapped within the closed circle of form, looks at each, and sees only a distorted image of itself, a shell of a slightly different size and shape. But the elephant has seen that the human "shell" is capable of admitting light, even as it is "maintained intact / By who knows what strange pressure of the atmosphere," and here she seems to find the solution to the troublesome opacity of her own form. Thus the poem concludes with a question which seems to invite the reader to look deeply into the interior of the circle:

>   Will
> Depth to depth, thick skin be thick, to one who can see no
> Beautiful element of unreason under it?

In the beginning, "Black Earth" flaunts as its chief virtue—and its own chief delight—the thickness of the elephant's skin, the impenetrable opacity of its form; but, having perceived that only a dangerous pride takes credit for having performed "feats of strength" now understood to be "inexplicable after / All," the poem undertakes a major internal revision, reevaluating the question of form. As a result, it seems to give up a measure of its opacity in order to preserve its impenetrability. For if in its opacity the poem should be perceived as "the circumference / Described" by the elephant's trunk has been perceived—as pure form surrounding a hollow center, as "a cortex merely"—it would then have neither thickness nor depth, but only the one-dimensionality of line pursuing itself to no end. There would then be, from the reader's standpoint, no reason *not* to penetrate the circle of form, no reason not to burst the bubble—as when, in Hawthorne's "The Artist of the Beautiful," the "child of strength" maliciously crushes the delicate mechanical butterfly that Owen Warland has labored so many years to perfect.[56]

Only by convincing us that its principles of form are not those of Hawthorne's watchmaker can "Black Earth" hope to save itself from destruction; and so it seems to allow us, in its abrupt departure from symmetricality, a brief glimpse of the "Beautiful element of unreason" that plays beneath the surface, generating form with its "fretful speech." But if we are invited to peer through a shell that has finally purported to become rather translucent than fully opaque, we are not, even now, to consider this an invitation to probe the interior. The reader who might be tempted to try the shell of form with a "wooden spear" is called upon to acknowledge that this elephant is no mechanical butterly but, like Eliot's hippopotamus, "only flesh and blood"—and hence even more fragile, more delicate than anything either the watchmaker or the maker of Prince Rupert's Drops might contrive.[57] It is the *reader*, then, who grants to depth that it is deep, to thickness that it is thick, by taking care to form and limit his own speech in response to that of the poem in such a way that his speech and the poem's remain separate and distinct, leaving the elephant's skin intact, the painstakingly regenerated circle of form unbroken.

The poem's solution to the problems posed by its own opacity is thus a purely rhetorical one, and this is perhaps the reason for Moore's eventual decision to exclude it from the *Complete Poems*. Having announced that "external poise" "Has its centre / . . . in pride," and having offered no arguments to the contrary, the poem nevertheless works desperately to recover that "poise" and, with it, its pride. It has only asked the reader's assent to the opacity it must vainly preserve.

V

Quotation, which we may now define as speech which oversteps the limit that it "sets . . . on itself," clearly presents a serious problem for a concept of poetic form in which the self is implicated in speech, and which in effect defines form as a limit that confers identity by establishing difference. If "The I of each is to / The I of each, / A kind of fretful speech," then to incorporate another's speech into one's own is necessarily also to incorporate "The I of each" into "The I of each," and so to break down—or at least to threaten seriously—the difference on which identity depends.

Such transgressions may occur from either of two directions. The poet may think of herself as violating the limits of her own speech when seizing a word or phrase written by someone else and therefore may define quotation as a predatory act; or she may think of the other's speech as having crossed both its limits and her own, forcing its way into the poem by dint of the sheer "creative power" which, in "The Labours of Hercules," "flies along in a straight line like electricity / and devastates those areas that boast of their remoteness." In the latter case, the poem is prey to other texts—unless it adopts what Moore calls in "Critics and Connoisseurs" an "attitude of self-defense" to guard against both the "wooden spear" aimed by the "predatory hand" of the reader, who would violate the integrity of the poem by dismembering it, and against the "electricity" discharged by other texts. That "attitude" is clearly manifest in "Black Earth," which, together with "Roses Only," "The Fish," "Critics and Connoisseurs," and a number of other poems written between 1916 and 1918, contains no marked quotations.

The poem finds that protection in its form. To the eyes of the reader, the elephant of "Black Earth" is

a cortex merely—
That on which darts cannot strike decisively the
first

Time, a substance
Needful as an instance
Of the indestructibility of matter; it
Has looked at the electricity and at the earth-

Quake and is still
Here. . . .

What the reader may not see at first glance (and is not at first *permitted* to see) is that the "cortex" surrounds living material, the "Beautiful element of unreason" by which it has been produced and which it now defends against that "creative power" which "flies along like electricity" and, like the "earth- / Quake," "devastates" remote areas, opening yawning chasms in the (black) earth's crust.

The reader may not see, either, that the strength of form lies precisely in the "element of unreason under it." No discernible logic *within* Moore's patterns governs the initial decision that a given line shall have so many syllables and the next line so many syllables more or less than the first, just as no discernible logic within the pattern determines a particular rhyme scheme. Yet once the form of the original stanza has been repeated—once form has become pattern—pattern *becomes* a logic and derives its power not only from the fact that it is pattern, but also from its very unreasonableness, its arbitrariness: it is "inexplicable after / All."

That unreasoned and unreasoning adherence to a set of self-imposed limits (in "Critics and Connoisseurs" Moore calls it "unconscious / Fastidiousness") which gives to each poem in Moore's *oeuvre* a distinctive form of its own, also enables—and to a certain extent requires—the poem to withstand the "creative power" of other texts, and particularly of other poems. As in "Black Earth" the elephant's tough skin is "That on which darts cannot strike decisively the first / Time," so in the patterned poems generally the sense of form as limit, which enables Moore to differentiate her poems from those written by others, also allows her to fend off phrases which might otherwise, like words that stick in the memory, embed themselves in her texts. Paradoxically, however, the visible and audible differences between, say, "Black Earth" and "The Hippopotamus" are predicated upon and stipulated by Moore's perception of their fundamental *likeness*. The relation between the two poems might be represented by a pair of magnets with like poles held toward each other, and so repelled by the contact of their similarly charged electrical fields. Neither magnet can draw the other toward itself, and neither poem can "attract" the other; nor can one poem bond itself to the other. The poems are held apart by virtue of their likeness, for Moore so forms her own speech as tacitly to acknowledge the power of Eliot's language by setting strict limits upon *it* as well—by confining it within its own formal boundaries. She thus protects the identity of both poems, and in doing so makes it clear that the formal differences between her poem and Eliot's are also substantive differences: "The Hippopotamus" sarcastically uses the form of the conventional hymn to expose the form of the Visible Church, shrouded in mist; "Black Earth," with a similar mixture of playfulness and gravity, uses its unconventional form to manifest a deep concern with the state of the individual soul as revealed —and concealed—by the visible form of its speech.

Moore's procedure in the patterned poems very nearly disallows the possibility of quoting from conventional poetry. The conventional poem is obligated to a set pattern as Moore's syllabic poems are, and to this extent they may still be said to resemble each other. But the patterns of Moore's verse are so different in kind that to integrate one into the other is almost necessarily to *deform* one of them. The perfect balance of the hexameter hemistich in the tenth stanza of "Black Earth" becomes, in that context, an *imbalance* which throws the entire stanza out of kilter, because the relative predictability of the *syllabic* patterns of conventional verse forms depends upon an *accentual* regularity which is completely alien to the carefully controlled irregularities of Moore's pattern. Moore can use a clause like "beauty is a liability rather than / An asset" only because she does not worry as poets usually do about where the stresses will fall. For the purposes of her patterns, though not for the purposes of the voice, all syllables have the same formal value: there is no fixed ratio of stressed to unstressed syllables within the line, and the line itself is rarely more than a purely syllabic —that is, typographic and therefore inaudible—unit, rather than a rhythmic one. Sentences most often begin and end within the line, a practice which overrides Moore's stated preference for the end-stopped line and makes enjambment her characteristic procedure.[58] In fact, many of her sentences not only run over from one line into the next, but often carry through several enjambed lines, even crossing stanza breaks. ("Black Earth," as I have pointed out, has only one end-stopped stanza—and even then, the sentence is still not complete; "The Fish" has two end-stopped stanzas, "My Apish Cousins" one, and there are none in "Roses Only" or in "Poetry.") All of this makes it even more difficult for Moore's patterns to accommodate the formal structures of more conventional verse, where the line is very frequently not only an auditory unit but a syntactic and semantic one as well, and where, more often than not, the stanza is coterminous with the sentence. When, in a patterned poem, a sentence which begins in one stanza ends in the middle of the next, the pattern exerts its force, demanding another sentence to meet its formal requirements. This is not to say, however, that Moore's patterns bar quotation altogether; even a cursory glance will indicate that many of her patterned poems do incorporate clearly marked quotations. Nevertheless, the patterns do control the nature and even the length of those quotations, as well as the poet's attitude toward the act of quotation itself.

Quotation, for Moore, relies on both similarity and difference. The most fundamental similarity inheres in the fact that the poem, which is made of language, necessarily quotes language; the difference is in the fact that in Moore's case poetry almost invariably quotes *prose*. Although prose, like poetry, "sets a limit on itself," that "limit" is less immediately evident —one might even say that it is less *physical*—than it is in poetry, and particularly in poems which follow a clearly defined pattern. Prose may well employ such conventionally "poetic" devices as rhyme, assonance, and alliteration; it may even become metrical on occasion (although when it does so, we often think of it as an unconscious lapse into meter). In the course of our reading, however, we do not generally regard such devices as serving an organizational function in prose, as we do when reading poetry. Unless they recur with such regularity as to assume a definite and obtrusive pattern, we usually pass them over, preferring to address ourselves to the larger structures of grammar and syntax, logic and narrative, to which they are evidently subordinate.

Moore's syllabic verse may be said to resemble prose, not only to the extent that it uses diction more usually associated with prose (as discussed earlier), but also to the extent that its auditory features appear to be irrelevant to the structure of the sentences in which they occur. In conventional verse forms, rhyme and meter often aid in determining syntactic and semantic relationships; in Moore's verse, however, there is no identifiable metric base, and because stress is unregulated we tend to pay less attention to her structures of sound. Her rhymes (to take only the most obvious example) are singularly unobtrusive, not only because they are usually arhythmic and depend upon such odd collocations as *Ming / something, Spiritual / coral,* and *as / chrysoprase* (to name only a few),[59] but because they are usually buried deep within a syntactic structure which does not and cannot pause for them, and so neither displays them nor is itself displayed by them.

Yet, unobtrusive as Moore's formal patterns may be, they serve a very real controlling function in her verse. Let us consider, for a moment, a few representative sentences from her review of *The Sacred Wood*:

> The connection between criticism and creation is close; criticism naturally deals with creation but it is equally true that criticism inspires creation. A genuine

> achievement in criticism is an achievement in creation; as Mr Eliot says, "It is to be expected that the critic and the creative artist should frequently be the same person." Much light is thrown on the problems of art in Mr Eliot's citing of Aristotle as an example of the perfect critic—perfect by reason of his having the scientific mind. Too much cannot be said for the necessity in the artist, of exact science.[60]

Now let us try to arrange them in a syllabic pattern:

> The connection between criticism and
> creation is close; criticism nat-
> urally deals with creation but it is
> equally true that
> criticism inspires creation.
> A genuine
>
> achievement in criticism is an
> achievement in creation; as Mr
> Eliot says, "It is to be expected
> that the critic and
> the creative artist should fre-
> quently be the
>
> same person." Much light is thrown on the problems
> of art in Mr Eliot's citing
> of Aristotle as an example of
> the perfect critic—
> perfect by reason of his hav-
> ing the scien-
>
> tific mind. . . .

It seems easy enough to coax six lines into a weak semblance of a Moore stanza; but to make the *next* six lines conform both to the syllabic pattern and to the rhyme scheme established by the initial "stanza" is impossible without making drastic changes in the sentences themselves. Moore's sentences work, and work very well, as prose. The passage contrives to blur the distinction between "criticism" and "creation" (we will see later on how important a move this is for Moore) by setting up an increasingly rapid oscillation between the terms themselves, until finally all sense of difference between them is worn away and they become virtually interchangeable. This is what allows Moore's leap from "Mr. Eliot's citing of Aristotle as an example of the perfect *critic*—perfect by reason of his having the scientific mind," to her own comments on the "necessity in the *artist*, of exact science" (the emphases are mine), to appear perfectly logical. Set in a syllabic pattern, however, the same sentences strike the reader very differently. In her verse, Moore's sentences move simultaneously within and against the pattern, at once shaping it and being shaped by it, drawing energy from the tension between the outward thrust of the sentence and the limiting force of the pattern; but the passage under consideration actually loses most if not all of its energy in being subjected to a pattern that Moore in no way tried to predict as she wrote. These sentences merely collapse under the pressure of the formal conditions imposed upon them, as those of Moore's verse never do.

This small experiment demonstrates that the language of Moore's poems is controlled and limited by aural and visual patterns in a way that has no real analogue in most prose, even her own.[61] It suggests, too, that for Moore the prose writer's comparative freedom from such limits differentiates prose sufficiently from verse to make quotation possible. If one wishes one's readers to recognize a quotation's source as poetic, it is necessary to quote a passage of sufficient length to allow the formal features which mark it as poetry to become evident (this is one reason why William Carlos Williams found it difficult to quote Moore's work "convincingly");[62] for Moore to do so, however, would entail a massive, probably irreparable disruption of her own formal structure. On the other hand, to quote only as much as her pattern would bear would require her to ignore the formal signature of the poem being quoted, and thus to deny its identity as poetry. But prose can be assimilated to her patterns as conventional verse cannot, because it does not rely upon the same kind of formal limits for control or identity, and so cannot rely upon their "protection" either.

Although it is not bound by the formal strictures of conventional poetry, and does not fall automatically into the patterns characteristic of Moore's work, prose cannot be called "formless." On the contrary, my failed effort to impose a Moore-like syllabic pattern on a segment of her own prose demonstrates that prose does indeed assume a distinctive form once it has reached a certain length. Small bits and pieces, therefore, are all that the patterned poem can use: Moore's syllabic patterns are no more capable of taking in long pieces of prose than they are of assimilating other poetry. A lengthy prose quotation, like a recognizably poetic borrowing, would break the pattern completely.

Not only does the pattern control the length of the passages that a given poem may incorporate, but it imposes other conditions as well. In order to overcome the difference between poetry and prose that Moore's patterns enforce, to bridge the distance between texts that the patterns are designed to maintain, she must violate the limits imposed upon her by her own formal decisions. She is, therefore, constrained to take the sort of predatory action which is forcibly restrained in "Roses Only" but permitted—and justified—in "Poetry" and "Picking and Choosing." In "Poetry" it is just at the moment when the poem claims for itself the subject matter conventionally associated with prose that Moore, with "perfect contempt" for the conventional distinctions, reaches beyond the limits of her own speech to seize upon Tolstoy's diary, quoting a fragment from a prose entry in which Tolstoy is explicitly concerned with his own inability to define the boundary between prose and verse.

The poem acts upon such bits and pieces of prose like a magnet on iron filings, arranging them along its own lines of force, pulling them into the pattern; but since the poem necessarily violates its own limits in appropriating to itself the language of another text, it must set additional, compensatory limits on itself in response to these alien words. Thus, Moore uses quotation marks as *internal* limits which both mark the boundaries of the borrowed phrase and redefine the boundaries of the poem itself.

By marking the phrase as borrowed, Moore simultaneously defines it as an interruption and gains a measure of control over it, in effect withholding it from the pattern even while leaving it in place. At once *in* the poem without being fully *of* the poem, the quoted phrase has a curious double identity. The inverted commas distinguish it from the poem, thus allowing it to retain its identity as prose; at the same time, however, because the quotation marks define the boundaries of the phrase just as the pattern defines the boundaries of the poem, setting limits upon speech which has hitherto been regarded as unlimited, they make it resemble the poem as well. The quotation has the effect, therefore, of internalizing (and complicating) the debate over the distinction between poetry and prose.

If Moore's use of prose quotations is made possible by her sense of a significant difference between her poetry and the prose it incorporates, then it must bother her very much that the only internal means of differentiating one from the other is an arbitrary convention by which borrowed phrases are set off in inverted commas. For it suggests that the only boundary between prose and verse—or, at least, Moore's verse—is a purely typographical one, a matter of punctuation alone. It thus becomes easier to understand Moore's continuing reluctance to classify her "product" as poetry: her writing bears considerable resemblance to what has conventionally been defined as poetry in its strict adherence to formal patterns, but its capacity for assimilating bits of prose suggests an even closer and more dangerous affinity with prose. Just as the phrases she borrows are, once they have been set into the pattern, at once prose and not prose, poetry and not poetry, the texts in which she uses them can be adequately defined neither as prose nor as poetry: "What I write," she said to Donald Hall, "could only be called poetry because there is no other category in which to put it."[63]

It is precisely the indeterminate status of her texts which makes it imperative that she identify at least some of her borrowings. The marked quotation calls attention in several ways to the problematic status of the poem, but by its stubborn resistance to complete assimilation, it also provides the poem with an internal measure by which to redefine itself once it has breached its own limits—for in reaching past those limits, the poem has come very close to lapsing into the unlimited and unprotected condition of the prose upon which its own "predatory hand" is bent. As when in "Critics and Connoisseurs" the swan's "hardihood" is finally "not proof against its / Inclination to detain and appraise such bits / Of food as the stream / [Bears] counter to it," so the hardihood of Moore's patterns is not fully proof against the poet's own predatory tendencies. Indeed, the very effectiveness with which the pattern separates her poems from other texts forces Moore into the disingenuous attitude of "perfect contempt" which enables her to pick and choose among other people's words at will; at the same time, by denying her admiration for them, she evades full consciousness of the extent to which she has put herself in their debt. Quotation threatens the poem's independent existence; quotation *marks* allow it to sustain, with only slight damage, the illusion of "self-dependence" and absolute difference.

The effort to sustain that illusion puts the poet in an extremely uncomfortable position, for the need to preserve the integrity of the poem against her own trespasses does not so much limit the number of possible borrowings as prevent her from acknowledging all of them—for like "Roses Only" and "Black Earth," a great many of the poems contain words or phrases taken from other sources but not marked as quotations in the text. To mark all of them would be openly to confess not only that the pattern has failed to act as an absolute limit by which the poem defines itself against and separates itself from all other texts, whether prose or verse, but also that the poet herself has been either unwilling or unable to treat her self-imposed limits with the respect and tact she has asked of her readers.

VI

In the work published in the late 1910s, however, a new emphasis on honesty and truth increasingly puts Moore's concept of form under great strain. A subtle but significant disturbance in the pattern of four internal stanzas of "Black Earth" is precipitated by a sudden anxious awareness on Moore's part that her desire to achieve and maintain an inviolable perfection of form may be grounded in false pride—in the wish not only to believe in but also to secure widespread recognition of her own superiority by rendering her poems so opaque to the understanding that they become impressive by the sheer scale of their incomprehensibility. Until this point, Moore has worked actively to prevent discovery of the "Beautiful element of unreason" that informs and motivates her work; in consequence of the spiritual crisis I have described, however, she seems in the final stanzas of "Black Earth" to invite precisely the sort of scrutiny to which she has been so hostile. Even now, however, we are not so much allowed to *see* that "Beautiful element of unreason" as we are asked to take its existence on faith, for although the poem registers its moments of self-doubt in the formal "blemishes" that "stand up and shout when the object / In view was a / Renaissance," the proleptic "was" announces well in advance (these lines occur very near the beginning of the poem, long before the "blemishes" are in evidence) that the "object" will not be attained, that the "Renaissance" that would permit "light" to "filter" through the skin of "black glass" will not occur. In the thirteenth stanza, the poem recovers its "external poise," which "Has its centre / Well nurtured . . . in pride": returning to the syllabic pattern established in the first eight stanzas, it leaves us peering at a "cortex" for whose thickness it would make *us* responsible: "will / Depth be depth, thick skin be thick, to one who can see no / Beautiful element of unreason under it?"

Moore is aware, however, that if such a question is to have real force, if the "Renaissance" is to succeed, she must undertake to lighten her own obscurities, and she confronts the problem more directly in "In the Days of Prismatic Colour," first published in the Bryn Mawr *Lantern* in 1919, and revised late in 1920.[64] (The revised version forms the basis of my discussion here.) Complexity, she says there, "is not a crime," for it is inevitable in a fallen world that is by definition cut off from the clarity and "originality" of the pre-Lapsarian period; but some have gone to culpable extremes, not simply tolerating complexity as inescapable but actively embracing it for its own sake. This is to "carry / it to the point of murkiness"—to the point where complexity becomes obscurity, "and nothing is plain." At that point, too, complexity begins to take on a life of its own; filled with self-importance and "committed to darkness," it would make itself the ruling principle of the universe. In the effort to establish dominion it

> moves all a-
> bout as if to bewilder us with the dismal
> fallacy that insistence
> is the measure of achievement and that all
> truth must be dark. . . .

But in the murky "darkness" to which complexity has "committed" itself, it is hidden most of all from itself. Bewildered by its own "dismal / fallacy," it cannot or will not see itself for the "pestilence that it is," and it fails or refuses to understand that it "is as it al- / ways has been—at the antipodes from the init- / ial great truths," whose original clarity is unaffected even when temporarily obscured by the "wave" of complexity.

Excessive complexity, then, is a monster, so huge and so unwieldy that it can move only in segments: "'Part of it was crawling, part of it / was about to crawl, the rest / was torpid in its lair.'" As we hear the "gurgling" and note "all the minutiae" of this creature's appearance, we discover that in its "short legged, fit- / ful advance" the monster Complexity is becoming isomorphic with the poem's form. The quotation that brings the monster to light is taken from the Loeb Library's *Greek Anthology*: thus, like the monster, both the quotation that reveals it and the poem that discovers the quotation have the English equivalent of "the classic / multitude of feet."

However, such complexity of form must collapse under the burden of the knowledge that "Truth is no Apollo / Belvedere, no formal thing" (an argument which, by implication, stunningly turns a classic—and classically formal—representation of the Greek god of the sun and of poetry into a monstrosity). As at the close of *Billy Budd* Melville destroys what he has come to regard as a factitious symmetry that would, if allowed to stand, expose his "inside narrative" as a tale more interested in external questions of form than in telling the truth,[65] so in the final stanza of "In the Days of Prismatic Colour" Moore breaks the formal pattern of the poem. She must do so, for to sustain the pattern in the face of the claim just advanced about the nature of "Truth" would be to sacrifice Truth to form—to countenance, not an inevitable complexity, but the lie of willful symmetricality. (The *Lantern* version suggests a closer resemblance between "Truth" and excessive complexity, or "sophistication," than does the later text. It is fitting, therefore, that in the earlier version it should also be far more difficult to detect Moore's break with the formal pattern: she retains the five-line stanza she has used throughout, thus making it necessary to count the syllables, while the later text cuts the final stanza to four lines, so that the abandonment of the pattern is immediately apparent.) Nor can she restore the pattern, as we have seen her do in "Black Earth," for to do *that* would be to engulf Truth once more in the folds of obscurity, to bury it beneath the wavelike movements of a monstrously complex form. The wave of form breaks now, not merely for the poet to gesture toward Truth, but to make Truth *visible* by the only means available to the poem—by letting it speak. Thus Truth has the last word: "'I shall be there,'" it says, "'when the wave has gone by.'"

Locating "the days of prismatic colour"—that lost moment of original clarity—"not in the days of Adam and Eve but when Adam / was alone," Moore implies that woman is to blame for introducing complexity in the world.[66] Although in the later "Marriage" (1923) she contemptuously describes the temptation of Eve as "that invaluable accident exonerating Adam," it seems clear that in "In the Days of Prismatic Colour" Moore does not mean to exempt herself from the general condemnation: only the previous year she had taken as a persona an elephant whose skin, "fibred over like the shell of the / coco-nut," is an opaque "piece of black glass through which no light / Can filter," and in "The Fish," published only a few months after "Black Earth," she had led her readers into a sea of "black jade." "In the Days of Prismatic Colour" is an intensely, almost savagely self-critical poem, and even as she moves toward the light, Moore is painfully aware that *hers* is "a complexity / . . . which has been committed to darkness."

One must be doubly cautious in examining that complexity, moreover, for Moore's commitment "to darkness" takes a variety of guises, and may even appear as a commitment to "brilliance" (the word is from "Roses Only"). In "Blake" (1915) she ruefully compares her own work to a mirror, "pale-ly" and ambiguously reflecting, as though from a great distance, the strong clear "sun" of Blake's art;[67] but the mirrorlike surface of "An Egyptian Pulled Glass Bottle in the Shape of a Fish" serves a very different purpose:

> Here we have thirst
> And patience from the first,
>   And art, as in a wave held up for us to see
>   In its essential perpendicularity;

Not brittle but
Intense—the spectrum, that
    Spectacular and nimble animal the fish,
    Whose scales turn aside the sun's sword with their polish.[68]

Like so many cunningly angled mirrors, the polished "scales" of "the fish" break up the white light of "the sun" so that what we notice is not "the sun" but "the spectrum," which seems to belong to, or rather to *be*, the fish itself; and, like the scales of the fish, the formal elements of the poem[69] reflect, and in reflecting *deflect*—"turn aside"—the light that would pierce the poem like a "sword." The poem, then, works with the effect of a prism; but it is all done with mirrors. Now, however, the light that the mirrors give back is not pale or "ambiguous" (as in "Blake"), "but / Intense"—even dazzling; thus, Moore implies that if her art shines by the reflected light of some antecedent's "sun," its own special brilliance is in showing *itself* to advantage by using form simultaneously to catch and to deny that light.

Whereas "An Egyptian Pulled Glass Bottle in the Shape of a Fish" breaks up the light by turning it aside, "The Fish" splinters the light as it passes through a surface of "black jade." The light, moreover, is not only "split like spun / glass" by the difficulty of its passage into the stony sea; it is also trapped in such a way that it is "submerged" beneath the waves while the water appears opaque to anyone standing outside or above it. We can learn what happens to the fish only by following them into the poem; and once we have waded after them "through black jade," we find ourselves in a medium which, if not exactly transparent, is at least clear enough to allow certain things to appear with terrible distinctness. For all its apparent opacity, "The Fish" is shot through with "submerged shafts" of light which not only transform the sea from "black jade" to "turquoise," but also galvanize the water—and the poem itself—into devastating action. As the poem's language is held in check, and its power increased, by the stringencies of the syllabic pattern against which it reverberates, so the power of the light trapped below the surface is intensified by its reverberation against the darkness that contains it.

In a sense, "The Fish" has discovered what "Black Earth" had been looking for: a way to admit the light—to "experience the / Sun"—without being overwhelmed by it, and a way of putting that light to use without fully acknowledging the extent to which it has done so. By splintering the sunlight, the poem asserts its own power over the light, rather than the sun's power to affect the poem. By contrast, the elephant in "Black Earth," prompted by its recognition of the photosynthetic process at work in the coral plant ("absorbed into which, the equable sapphire light / Becomes a nebulous green," signifying that the plant has converted sunlight into energy it can use for its own purposes), tries to convince us that its skin is "translucent like the atmosphere." But if the elephant has allowed light to "filter" through its skin, we have not been allowed to see it: we are left staring at a wall of "black glass" because, although the elephant knows that it ought to follow the coral plant's example, it would clearly prefer not to: it is afraid of losing its shape, of becoming "nebulous." In token of its earnestness, however, "Black Earth" leaves its "blemishes" to "stand up and shout" because "the object / In view was a / Renaissance," and although the "object" has not been achieved, it is crucial to record the fact that an attempt of such historical magnitude has been made.

3

Getting Closer to the Truth: Free Verse and the Acknowledgment of Debt

I

In 1967, Moore took three poems—"Picking and Choosing," "England," and "Peter"—and converted the syllabic patterns in which they had originally been cast into free verse.[1] Although all three poems were more than forty years old by then, Moore, as usual, did not explain her reasons for making such a change; indeed, there is nothing in the text of the *Complete Poems* to say that there has been any change at all. Yet it is an important gesture. It pays a debt of gratitude; it marks the limits of a period of central importance in Moore's career, a period of significant experimentation; and it demonstrates the particular form of that experiment. For, six months after the appearance of the revised version of "In the Days of Prismatic Colour," with its abrupt and conclusive abandonment of the syllabic pattern in the final stanza, Moore began publishing poems in free verse, and continued to do so for the next three and a half years. Given the intimate connection between formal definition and self-definition set out in the previous chapter, this is clearly an important development. My aim in this chapter and the two that follow is to account for the shift to free verse and to explore its ramifications as fully as possible.[2]

The first of the free-verse poems, "When I Buy Pictures" and "A Graveyard," were printed together in *The Dial* in July 1921, and the last one, "The Monkey-Puzzler," appeared in the same magazine in January 1925. As it turned out, "The Monkey-Puzzler" was Moore's last poem for seven and a half years: a few months after it appeared she was named editor of *The Dial* and, though the magazine closed its doors in 1929, she produced no new work until June 1932, when "Part of a Novel, Part of a Poem, Part of a Play" came out in *Poetry*. The resumption of her poetic career also marked her return to syllabic verse, from which she never again departed—that is, until 1967.

Two of the poems she then converted to free verse—"England" and "Picking and Choosing"—had been the first of her poems to appear in *The Dial*, where they were published in April 1920; the third one, "Peter," was not published until 1924 (in *Observations*), but we may infer both from the fact of the revision itself and from the poem's placement in *Observations* that it was composed at roughly the same time as the other two.[3] By changing these three poems, then, Moore set all the work produced during the years of her association with *The Dial* apart from the rest, giving it a distinctive formal identity of its own.[4]

In so doing, she both indicates the central importance of that work—this is the only period of Moore's career to be fully represented in every major collection of her verse from 1924 on—and pays a debt of gratitude to the magazine itself. In its heyday the best-financed, best-produced, most wide-ranging, and most widely distributed periodical with a modernist bias in America, *The Dial* in early 1920 became Moore's chief outlet for publication. She was both a regular contributor and a staff member; the magazine carried her articles and reviews as well as the vast majority of the poems she produced during this period, and the editor, Scofield Thayer, called attention to her with his enthusiastic editorial commentaries.[5] The announcement that the two thousand dollar *Dial* Award for 1925 had gone to *Observations* gave further impetus to Moore's career by ensuring that the volume received prominent, and generally favorable (if somewhat baffled), coverage in the book-review sections of major newspapers like the *New York Times* and the *Herald-Tribune*, as well as other important periodicals.[6] And although promotion to the editorial chair in 1925 seriously disrupted Moore's poetic activity, it also substantially enhanced her position in the literary world, making it clear that she was no longer an outsider "Trying to open locked doors with a sword."

This not only explains why Moore still felt obligated to *The Dial*, even as late as 1967, but it also (and more importantly) helps to account for the major reorientation of her work between 1921 and 1925. The increasingly active sense of engagement manifest from poem to poem is both responsible for and responsive to Moore's increasingly prominent position within *The Dial* organization; and that position serves her as a base from which to thrust herself still more deeply into the literary community.

The decision to switch to free verse is of crucial importance here, and Moore's association with *The Dial* is directly implicated in that decision. When Donald Hall asked her in 1960 how she had come to be associated with the magazine, Moore replied:

> "Let me see. I think I took the initiative. I sent the editors a couple of things and they sent them back. And Lola Ridge had a party—she had a large apartment on a ground floor somewhere—and John Reed and Marsden Hartley, who was very confident with the brush, and Scofield Thayer, editor of the *Dial*, were there. And much to my disgust, we were induced to read something we had written. And Scofield Thayer said of my piece, 'Would you send that to us at *The Dial*?'
>
> "'I did send it,' I said.
>
> "And he said, 'Well, send it again.' That's how it began, I think. Then he said, one time, 'I'd like you to meet my partner, Sibley Watson.' . . . And they asked me to join the staff at *The Dial*."[7]

This anecdote is nicely revealing. It was "England" that Moore was "induced to read" that night,[8] and she must have been struck by the difference between Thayer's rejection of the poem he had *seen*, and his far more sympathetic response to the same poem when he heard it read aloud. It is not difficult to understand why he reacted so differently. In the syllabic poems, the visual pattern of the verse often works against the flow of the sentence, as in "The Fish." But when she read aloud, Moore read her syllabic poems as if they were free verse; and the free-verse poems under consideration here suit themselves to the needs of the voice by removing the impediments placed in the way of the eye by the syllabic patterns. The free-verse poems thus *look* less forbidding, and their movement seems easier to follow—but this does not make them easy by any stretch of the imagination.

Of course, Moore did not rush straight home from Lola Ridge's party to convert "Picking and Choosing" and "England" to free verse, but the change that began the following year with "When I Buy Pictures" and "A Graveyard"—the next pair of her poems to appear in *The Dial*—set the pattern for that final gesture. Both "When I Buy Pictures" and "A Graveyard" exist in syllabic versions that clearly predate the published free-verse texts, as do a number of other poems, including the free-verse "Poetry."[9] Evidently syllabic verse remained the form with which Moore was most comfortable, the one that came most naturally to her.

We are left with the curious fact that she wrote in syllabics but published in free verse. This illustrates vividly the tension between what Moore later called her "natural reticence"[10] and her equally "Burning Need To Be Explicit." Like the syllabic poems we have been looking at in previous chapters, the syllabic drafts from which the free-verse poems of the early 1920s emerge are essentially *private*, written in much the same spirit that prompts the elephantine speaker of "Black Earth" to declare, "I do these / things which I do, which please / no one but myself. . . ." The syllabic poems set their own terms, demanding to be engaged on their own ground or not at all; but the free-verse poems give public expression to what Moore calls in "The Labours of Hercules" (1921) "the principle of accommodation."

Collectively, they reveal Moore's effort to open up her work, both to her readers and to those manifestations of "creative power" (to quote "The Labours of Hercules" again) that were appearing all around her, and to which her association with *The Dial* in particular demanded that she pay heed. To indicate the force of these manifestations, it is only necessary to point out that Moore's *Observations* is contemporaneous with some of the seminal works of Anglo-Irish and American modernism: the late poems of Yeats and Hardy; Williams's *Spring and All* and Stevens's *Harmonium*; Pound's early *Cantos*; and, pre-eminently for Moore, the poetry and criticism of T.S. Eliot. (Eliot's influence on Moore's work will be discussed at length in the next chapter.) The extent to which the writers I have just named share common ground is, of course, still open to debate; Moore seems to have heard them as isolated and competing voices, to which she could accommodate herself only in the process of reconciling them as far as possible to one another.

The shift to free verse is crucial to that process, that search for community, for it makes the poems more readily accessible—as Moore puts it in "New York"—to an "experience" which the syllabic poems had worked to "turn aside," even while they acknowledged that it was "unpreventable": the experience of "creative power." Free verse accommodates quotation to a much greater degree than the syllabic patterns do—and in Moore's verse quotation serves as both the direct and the indirect manifestation of the creative power wielded by other writers. That is, quotation is the form of "experience." Thus we may take at least a partial measure of Moore's sense of her place within the community by examining her use of quotations within the larger context of the poems.

She uses them sparingly in the beginning, as befits one taking the first exploratory steps of a new venture. Their first purpose is to acknowledge poetic debt and to clarify the thrust of the poems. What they reveal most clearly, however, as we see in "When I Buy Pictures" and "New York," is Moore's continuing reluctance to let go of the protective devices which have served her thus far. Her reluctance to abandon them is outweighed only by her fear of the consequences should she refuse or fail.

II

At the end of "In the Days of Prismatic Colour," Moore is still in the untenable position she had occupied earlier in the poem—despite the climactic breaking of the syllabic pattern, she is still "at the antipodes from the init- / ial great truths." For it is not enough simply to assert, as she does in the closing lines, that truth "will be there when it says, / 'I shall be there when the wave has gone by.'" Getting "closer to the truth," as Moore seeks to do in "When I Buy Pictures" and the poems under consideration here, requires a commitment to *action*, a thoroughgoing revision of her art.

She has already declared her right to exercise her predilections, arguing in "Picking and Choosing" that "If he must give an opinion, it is permissible that the / critic should know what he likes." The "critic" in this case is also the poet, who devotes much of the poem to saying explicitly what she likes (and dislikes) in the work of James, Shaw, Hardy, Gordon Craig, and Edmund Burke. But there is a considerable difference between saying *what* one likes and saying *why* one likes it; and that, in a sense, is the difference between "Picking and Choosing" and "When I Buy Pictures."

It is not the whole difference, though, nor is it the most important one: "When I Buy Pictures" also redefines, in a complex and elliptical way, the poet's relation to the material selected by her critical intelligence, allowing her to take hold of what she likes more openly than she has yet done. "Picking and Choosing" implicitly restrains the poet's ability to "use" what she finds,[11] for it ends by enjoining us to "remember" what Xenophon said about hunting-dogs: that it is their function "to put us on the scent," not to bring down the quarry. By contrast, in the closing line of "When I Buy Pictures," the poet takes her prize "in hand," and thereby concludes her purchase: this is not a hunt, but an economic transaction.

But in fact Moore is not buying pictures at all. The title merely offers a first approximation of what she is doing, and the words are no sooner out than she corrects them:

When I Buy Pictures

or what is closer to the truth,
when I look at that of which I may regard myself as the imaginary possessor,
I fix upon what would give me pleasure in my average moments: . . .

The full import of the shift from prospective buyer to "imaginary possessor" will not become clear until the end of the poem. The first effect of that shift, however, together with the poet's declaration of interest in "what would give [her] pleasure in [her] average moments," is to prevent any special and perhaps temporary need from influencing her judgments about value: instead of having to select a particular object to answer a particular purpose, she is free to indulge the eclecticism of her tastes.

It may seem, then, that Moore is simply unwilling to commit herself financially, unwilling to pay the price that buying pictures requires. But in fact she is willing to go much farther: for if she has freed herself of the need to make a specifically financial commitment, she has put herself at risk in even more fundamental ways: to "look at" these things at all is necessarily to "regard [her]self" at the same time. She will therefore discover herself in what she sees, and I mean that in a double sense: not only will she see herself in a certain way, perhaps for the first time, but in offering us a representative sampling of what would please her, she will reveal herself to *us* as well. It might be

the satire upon curiosity, in which no more is discernible than the intensity of the mood;
or quite the opposite—the old thing, the mediaeval decorated hat-box,
in which there are hounds with waists diminishing like the waist of the hour-glass
and deer and birds and seated people;
it may be no more than a square of parquetry; the literal biography perhaps—
in letters standing well apart upon a parchment-like expanse;
an artichoke in six varieties of blue; the snipe-legged hieroglyphic in three parts;
the silver fence protecting Adam's grave or Michael taking Adam by the wrist.

Like "that which is better without words, which means"—according to the earlier syllabic version—"just as much or just as little as it is understood / to mean by the observer,"[12] this catalogue of objects is a "satire upon curiosity." It is a self-contained (and silver-fenced) exhibit in which little more than a certain "intensity of . . . mood" is at first "discernible," an intensity which inheres both in the formal precision of the objects themselves and in the poet's passionate interest in them.

We can hardly expect that Moore will explain her preferences in any explicit way, since even the subject of that "literal biography" is unnamed; and, indeed, she writes in the following line that "Too stern an intellectual emphasis upon this quality or that, detracts from one's enjoyment." But she does not leave us completely in the dark. Just as Michael takes "Adam by the wrist" and shows him God's grand design, so Moore leads us past the enclosing finality of "Adam's grave" and gives us a glimpse of her own design:

> Too stern an intellectual emphasis upon this quality or that, detracts from one's enjoyment;
> it must not wish to disarm anything; nor may the approved triumph easily be honoured—
> that which is great because something else is small.

These lines suggest that we have been looking at a collection of what Moore would later call "uninsistent masterpieces"[13]—works that do not claim greatness for themselves by striving for what art historians call "monumentality." The poet's attention is drawn to them, in fact, by their very refusal to draw attention to themselves. Their success does not depend upon their ability "to disarm" the beholder by making concessions, whether formal or otherwise, to conventional expectations; rather, success depends upon the beholder's discernment, upon the understanding of "the observer." Thus, in disavowing "the approved triumph[,] . . . that which is great because something else is small," the poet makes it clear that she is not belittling the objects the poem has catalogued: the poem does not mean to call itself "great" by measuring itself against "small" and insignificant objects. On the contrary, these are objects whose qualities the poem seeks to emulate. In laying down the standards by which they are to be judged, Moore is also establishing a set of criteria for her own work.

Nor are those criteria merely proscriptive. These admirable objects have also satisfied certain positive requirements:

> It comes to this: of whatever sort it is,
> it must acknowledge the forces which have made it;
> it must be "lit with piercing glances into the life of things;"
> then I "take it in hand as a savage would take a looking-glass."

Here, in the closing lines, "the satire upon curiosity" is turned back upon the poet herself, reflecting ironically upon her status as "the imaginary possessor" of the things she has seen. And—without quite telling us how the objects in the catalogue have gone about acknowledging "the forces which have made" them, or in what ways they may be "'lit with piercing glances into the life of things'"—these lines reveal the ways in which the poem has met its own requirements.

The differences between this poem and its syllabic predecessor amount to much more than a difference in lineation, and a brief examination of the earlier version will help considerably in clarifying the extent to which Moore has redefined her principles as well as her practice. (I should point out that by the time the syllabic version appeared in print, Moore no longer intended to publish it: the copy H.D. included in her edition of Moore's *Poems* had been obtained without Moore's knowledge, presumably from Scofield Thayer, and it was only by a strange coincidence that both versions were printed in July 1921.[14]) Ironically, in abandoning the syllabic pattern, Moore brings to the poem as a whole a much greater clarity of design.

The catalogue of objects in the syllabic version is arranged somewhat haphazardly, in keeping with its primary function there, which is to demonstrate the catholicity of the poet's taste. This makes it perfectly appropriate to end the catalogue as she does (in the syllabic version), with "a bed of beans / or artichokes in six varieties of blue," but it also involves the poem in a logical contradiction from which it cannot recover.

For the poem does not—and in its syllabic form cannot—meet the conditions it lays down. The list of things proscribed is essentially the same in both versions—the only difference is that the syllabic version specifies irony as one of the banned types of "intellectual emphasis." What is at issue, therefore, is not simply the qualities present in the works themselves, but also, as we have seen, the observer's ability to discern them.

The prescriptive requirements, however, are very different indeed, and again the poem is involved in an impossible contradiction. The final stanza leaves virtually nothing to the discernment of the beholder, and in a certain sense the beholder scarcely exists. The audience, it now appears, is only *incidentally* human: the real exchange takes place between the artist and "the spiritual forces which have made" his or her work, and the work itself is only the medium of that exchange. Consequently, the stanza outlines a *rhetorical* strategy, a mode of presentation or display whose aim is precisely to "make known" to those "forces" that they are being addressed, and by whom—that is, "to disarm" their indifference so as to win for the artist approval and even gratitude:

> It comes to this: of whatever sort it is, it
> must make known the fact that it has been displayed

> to acknowledge the spiritual forces which have made it;
> and it must admit that it is the work of X, if X produced it; of Y, if made
> by Y. It must be a voluntary gift with the name written on it.[15]

This stanza has less in common with the free-verse text of "When I Buy Pictures" than with the closing lines of an early poem called "Feed Me, Also, River God" (1916). There, the poet's prayer for sustenance is cut short by her unwillingness to "dress" her words in any but a fashion of her own choosing, an almost Miltonic refusal to use the prescribed forms of address:

> . . . if you may fulfill
> None but prayers dressed
> As gifts in return for your gift—disregard the request.[16]

The defiance so clearly evident here has softened considerably in the five years that separate these lines from "When I Buy Pictures." The final stanza of the later poem implies that Moore is now willing to offer "prayers dressed / As gifts in return" for gifts granted her earlier—but if the will is there, the capacity is not. There is really no significant diference between Moore's refusal, in 1916, to "dress" her "prayers"—her poems—except as she saw fit, and her present insistence that the work "admit that it is the work of X, if X produced it; of Y, if made / by Y." It is a question of *form* in both cases: we have seen that syllabic verse *is* Moore's signature, the writing that establishes and guarantees her identity—and that it serves that function by thwarting any overt display of indebtedness or relationship.

This is precisely the sort of display that "When I Buy Pictures" calls for—but it is also precisely the sort that is precluded, both by the syllabic pattern and by the way Moore has defined the objects of her attention. By requiring that each one be presented as "a voluntary gift with the name written on it," she effectively writes herself out of the poem, and makes it impossible that she should use those objects as part of her own effort to "acknowledge the spiritual forces" to which she herself is indebted. Since each object has been specifically addressed by a particular artist to "the spiritual forces which have made it," for the poet to take those objects into her possession in any way would be tantamount to stealing thank-offerings from the altar.

This is the impasse through which Moore has to break in revising "When I Buy Pictures" for *The Dial*. Her first move is to alter the arrangement of the "pictures" themselves, so that the revised catalogue and the poem itself partake, in effect, of the shape of "the hour-glass"—a double image, in which each half mirrors the other and which, like the Vortex or Yeats's gyres, allows for both concentration and expansion. Beginning as in the earlier version with the broadly defined "satire upon curiosity, in which no more is discernible than the intensity of the mood," and proceeding immediately to "quite the opposite," the poet gradually narrows her gaze until what she sees is "no more than a square of parquetry"; then the scope widens again, so that the culminating image (which does not appear at all in the syllabic text) implies the whole course of providential history revealed to Adam by Michael. In the context of the poem as a whole, however, the image of "Michael taking Adam by the wrist" is a point of concentration, "the waist of the hour-glass." What Michael is pointing to is what cannot be quite conceived in "In the Days of Prismatic Colour": a way to proceed after the Fall. He is not indicating a way of reaching "truth," which is impossible in the poet's postlapsarian state, for it requires "such power as Adam had and we are still devoid of"—as Moore would write in "An Octopus" three yeas later. Rather, Michael indicates a way of *approximating* truth, a way of getting "closer" to it than has been possible so far.

Everything depends upon the closing lines, then, and it is here that Moore makes her most drastic revisions. These changes serve to complete the analogy between the poem and the objects it catalogues—to make it approximate them as closely as possible—so that, like them and unlike the syllabic version, it may "acknowledge the forces which have made it." But if analogy is a way of moving "closer to the truth," it is also, and simultaneously, a way of defining distance—a device signifying the poet's awareness that the gap separating her from "the truth" has not been bridged in any *real* sense: she is only "the imaginary possessor."

The syllabic version requires the object to "admit that it is the work of X," or "Y," or whoever may have "produced it." But the objects themselves are remarkable for their anonymity, among other things, and neither version of the poem has anything at all to say about the artists—artisans, rather—who made those objects. It is fitting, therefore, that in revision Moore should drop this requirement. True, her name is printed above the title, so that the poem *is* signed; but unlike the title (which is also the first, subordinate clause of the opening sentence), the name does not play an active part in the composition. As I have said, the poet's real signature is the syllabic pattern; but that too has been dropped, as if to say that it had been little more than an elaborate way of disguising the extent to which Moore's materials are taken from the work of others—an illicit claim on someone else's property.

But Moore has not renounced the use of such materials. On the contrary, in giving up the syllabic pattern—thereby relinquishing her formal claim to possession of the materials that compose the poem—she virtually commits herself to using them, and to presenting them in their true character. Thus, the last two lines of the poem consist almost entirely of quoted phrases. After insisting that the object "must acknowledge the forces which have made it," Moore introduces a new requirement, then ends by stipulating her own response:

> it must be "lit with piercing glances into the life of things;"
> then I "take it in hand as a savage would take a looking-glass."

Neither of these lines appears in the syllabic text, nor could it have contained them; it is no accident that there are no quotations at all in the earlier version. "When I Buy Pictures" has its starting point, I think, in the opening paragraphs of "Where I Lived and What I Lived For"—the second chapter of *Walden*, where Thoreau begins his account of how he came to "settle" the American wilderness with a comic, punning sketch of himself walking roughshod over the neighboring farmers' "premises" about property and ownership, taking imaginative possession of "all the farms in succession" without the farmers being the richer or the wiser for it:

> At a certain season of our life we are accustomed to consider every spot as the possible site of a house. I have thus surveyed the country on every side within a dozen miles of where I live. In imagination I have bought all the farms in succession, for all were to be bought, and I knew their price. I walked over each farmer's premises, tasted his wild apples, discoursed on husbandry with him, took his farm at his price, at any price, mortgaging it to him in my mind; even put a higher price on it—took everything but a deed of it,—took his word for his deed, for I dearly love to talk,—cultivated it, and him too to some extent I trust, and withdrew when I had enjoyed it long enough, leaving him to carry it on. . . .
>
> My imagination carried me so far that I even had the refusal of several farms,—the refusal was all I wanted,—but I never got my fingers burned by actual possession. . . .[17]

Thoreau presents this little narrative for our instruction, but the playful imitation of economic activity which it recounts profits no one but Thoreau himself—which is precisely the point. *Walden*'s premise is that the "mass of men" are enslaved to the conventional standards of the communities in which they live, and Thoreau argues in his opening chapter on "Economy" that the instrument of that enslavement is precisely economic—that is to say, financial—commitment: what we own ends by owning us. It is, then, only by refusing to buy into the community that we may purchase the freedom to pursue, and even more crucially to define, our own ends. In *Walden* as in "When I Buy Pictures," the *imitation* of the act of buying is a means of self-contemplation.

Like Thoreau, Moore wants to "buy pictures" only "in imagination," without getting her "fingers burned by actual possession." Whereas "the refusal was all [Thoreau] wanted," however, Moore wants to go beyond refusal—wants, indeed, to make of mere refusal a form of acknowledgment, of acceptance. The practical means of doing so must elude her, however, so long as she concerns herself exclusively with *pictures* (and this is why, in the syllabic version, the poet is finally so passive before the objects of her interest): "actual possession" is a moot point where pictures are concerned, for visual material cannot be incorporated directly into the poem. The problem of possession arises only when possession and refusal are genuinely possible—that is (since only verbal material can be assimilated by the text), only if some verbal analogue to the pictorial matter presents itself.

Quotation must still have seemed, in the syllabic version, like getting your "fingers burned by actual possession"—for Moore's quotations are presented in the free-verse text precisely as verbal analogues to the pictures catalogued earlier. The pictures Moore catalogues belong to what are usually regarded as minor artistic genres; so, too, her quotations are drawn from sources not usually considered "poetic." These phrases, then, have been carefully chosen in accordance with the poem's criteria and in accordance with its purposes. Not only do they allow the poem to "acknowledge the forces which have made it," but, like the pictures, they present the poet with "'a looking-glass'" which shows her to herself—and to us—by means of an analogy. For when she takes the phrase "'in hand,'" she appears as she does in her "average moments," as something very like "'a savage.'"

The first of these quotations (I have been unable to locate a source for the second) is taken from A.R. Gordon's *Poets of the Old Testament.* The quotation fulfills the stipulation that art "acknowledge the forces which have made it" by affirming the seriousness of Moore's religious and poetic interest in the Bible, while acknowledging the considerable extent to which both her understanding of biblical poetry and her conception of poetic language in general are indebted to Gordon's study of the prophets. Less obvious, perhaps, is the message that such acknowledgments *must* take the form of quotation: in order for the work properly to confess its indebtedness, "it must be 'lit with piercing glances into the life of things.'" As in earlier poems like "Black Earth," light is seen here as a penetrating agent; now, though, rather than attempt to ward off the light by using form as a shield to turn it aside, Moore pays homage to Gordon for the light he has cast on poetry by allowing a shaft of that light to pierce her own poem.

The last line (which has been deleted, unfortunately, from all subsequent editions) reinstates the poet as an active force in the poem, and so allows us to define more clearly what it is to be "the imaginary possessor." When an object has met her standards, the poet says, "then I 'take it in hand as a savage would take a looking-glass.'" The *light* that penetrates the poem comes to be recognized as a *mirror* in the process: turning Gordon's language back to reflect praise on his work—piercing it, as it were, with its own light—Moore discovers that she has simultaneously offered us a "'piercing glance into the life'" of her own work, a reflection of the admiration for and continuing sense of affinity with the prophets of the Old Testament, which finds its fullest expression two years later in the closing lines of "Novices."

At the same time, however, she has revealed herself in a more disturbing light, as a "savage." "My Apish Cousins" heaps scorn on critics who "tremble" before the work of art as if it were "malignant / in its power over us and deeper / than the sea when it proffers flattery in exchange for hemp, / rye, flax, horses, platinum, timber and fur." Moore turns this radical distrust of art inward in "When I Buy Pictures," fearful that she may be exchanging "flattery" for more valuable commodities. By turning the poem into a mirror, she offers to Gordon what is intended as a pleasing reflection on his work; but a compliment may seem scant compensation for the knowledge she has taken from him, and it must seem even less substantial when she considers that the reflection is created by a phrase of which she is only "the imaginary possessor"—a phrase she has used *as if* it were her own in trying to thank the man who composed it. It is as though the attempt straightforwardly to "acknowledge the forces" to which her work is indebted were inevitably to cheapen the acknowledgment, to cheat those forces by returning less than value received.

The final quotation also reflects Moore's fear that she may be the victim as well as the perpetrator of fraud. The phrases she appropriates are initially of interest to her as the looking-glass is of interest to the savage who doesn't know what it is—as a bright thing that throws light on *something else*. The savage has to learn to recognize her own face in the glass, and so, too, the poet comes belatedly to discover herself reflected in the phrase she has taken for a bit of light and confidently thought to keep well "in hand."

The savage may be frightened at first by the seemingly magical appearance of a face in the glass, but she is nonetheless absorbed by what she sees, and so risks the fate of Narcissus. Nor does the mirror lose its fascination once she has learned to recognize herself there: now she seems to possess herself as never before. She therefore takes the looking-glass as an object of considerable value, a prize to be displayed, much as the poet displays the bright bits of language she has taken from other texts by putting them in quotation marks.

But to the white man who offers the looking-glass, it is only a cheap trinket, an almost worthless piece of glass which, like the sea, "proffers flattery in exchange for" things of incomparable value not only to the white man and his "ambitious civilisation" (the phrase is from "Roses Only"), but to the savage as well: food, for instance, or horses, or huge tracts of land which the savage regards as her hunting grounds, but from which she will soon be hunted, barred forever. By taking the looking-glass in hand, then, the savage makes herself "the imaginary possessor" of all she surveys: her worldly goods are now hers in imagination only; they are henceforth the white man's real estate.

Even her relation to herself is altered irrevocably. In her absorption with the looking-glass, she becomes increasingly concerned with an insubstantial image of her outward appearance, with her *form*—a preoccupation which may lead, as it does in "Black Earth," to a devastating loss of self-possession. The looking-glass gives her the illusion of self-possession, but it robs her of the "spiritual poise" that might have helped her see through the fraud—for it teaches her to see herself as the white man sees her. The Indians, after all, did not call themselves "savages."

Thus form remains a major (though now a veiled) concern, and the final quotation vividly reflects Moore's ambivalence toward the process she has initiated. Recognizing that she must abandon the syllabic pattern in order properly to acknowledge the "forces" to which she is indebted, she fears nevertheless that she may be robbing those forces of what she actually owes them. She fears also that in giving up her characteristic form so that her poems may be "lit with piercing glances into the life of things" she may also be giving up her own real estate—her uniqueness, her self-dependency—in exchange for what may prove to be cheap bits of language which have, by an unrecognized appeal to the very pride she is trying to subdue, led her to betray herself as an ignorant "savage," wild and out of place amid the artifacts of civilization, endangered and dangerous.

III

It would seem, then, that "imaginary possession" is at best a possibility to be explored and discarded; but "A Graveyard," which served as companion-piece to "When I Buy Pictures" in *The Dial* for July 1921, shows us what happens when "imaginary" possession becomes "actual."[18] "A Graveyard" is the only one of Moore's free-verse poems without a single marked quotation, the only one that makes no gesture of acknowledgment. It represents the sea as a graveyard whose deadly acquisitiveness is matched only by its inscrutability; it implies that "actual possession" is more potent than "imaginary possession." And it demonstrates its potency as well: "A Graveyard" is undoubtedly a more poweful poem than "When I Buy Pictures" —but it is also confessedly a poem that kills and corrodes, one which is truly "malignant / in its power over us. . . ."

The syllabic draft of "A Graveyard" that I mentioned earlier was composed toward the end of 1917, not long after Moore's brother had sailed for the North Atlantic; and like "The Fish," which it predates by several months, the poem is prompted by the poet's sense of the horror of the war and her terror lest her brother should be killed at sea.[19] But the syllabic pattern is so obtrusive, so extravagant (the opening line of each stanza comprises thirty-two syllables) that it takes up the whole "view" and fixes the reader's attention entirely upon the poet. I shall argue later on that this is just where our attention ought to be, but for very different reasons; what we are most aware of in the unpublished syllabic version is the poet's distance from the scene, her evident reluctance to enter fully into it. In "The Fish," by contrast, the poet takes us through the opaque surface and into a world of submarine ruins, imagining the tragedy of a torpedoed troop-ship with a gaping "chasm" in its "dead" side; the strangled articulation of the syllabic pattern shows us how close Moore is to coming undone, manifests the intensity of her struggle to keep from becoming one of the "bodies" she has found floating in "the / turquoise sea" of her imagination, and to preserve some line of demarcation between her sense of self and the terrifyingly "beautiful element of unreason" into which she has waded.

The limit between self and sea is completely eradicated in the published version of "A Graveyard," and it is *we* who are deprived of the protection afforded by the visible signs of the poet's presence. For "the sea is a collector," too, but it is far less discriminating than the art-collecting poet of "When I Buy Pictures" and, unlike her, it takes "actual," not "imaginary," possession of all that comes near it; it makes its acquisitions secretly, too, never putting its treasures on display. Indeed, it forestalls any attempt to determine the extent of its holdings by presenting to the eye a surface not so much opaque as blandly transparent; yet it is both fiercely protective and mirrorlike in its quickness "to return a rapacious look" even as it conceals its own rapacity.

The stony surface of the sea in "The Fish" is so opaque that we must be led through it if we are to see anything at all; but here the only obstruction is a "Man, looking into the sea, / taking the view from those who have as much right to it as" he has, and the poet reproves him so harshly that we automatically take the part of those who have been so rudely deprived and press forward for a closer look. Before we can realize that to "have as much right" to "the view" as this man has is to have no "right to it" at all—that we go too far merely by looking—we are in over our heads, afloat in something we "cannot stand in the middle of. . . ." The sea is dangerous precisely because it presents no obstacle to our "looking into" it, gives us no warning that even the desire to look is a form of rapacity that will be repaid in kind.

We are in fact two-thirds of the way through the poem before we see the surface at all. We look past the man to the silent, funereal "procession" of fir trees, "each with an emerald turkey-foot at the top," and past them in turn to the "others . . . who have worn" that "rapacious look"—only to find that there is nothing left of them to see, "for their bones have not lasted." We then look to the fishermen who "lower nets, unconscious of the fact that they are desecrating a grave, / and row quickly away . . . as if there were no such thing as death"—men too ignorant to realize that the sea collects, among other things, those who come to plunder it. Only then do we learn that the waves, deceptively "beautiful under networks of foam," form a skin of "wrinkles" which in turn comprise "a phalanx"—a conquering force advancing behind a barrier of interlocking shields, capable of destroying those in its path and moving on as before, its ranks unbroken. Even this faintly visible skin dissolves in the next instant: the "wrinkles . . . fade breathlessly while the sea rustles in and out of the seaweed," leaving the water transparent once more: the ocean "advances as usual, looking as if it were not that ocean in which dropped things are bound to sink— / in which if they turn and twist, it is neither with volition nor consciousness."

This near-transparency is a highly effective means of concealment. Released from its obligation to a formal pattern, the language of "A Graveyard" seems to relax, also, from the intense, "fretful" self-consciousness of the syllabic poems; turning outward, it seems to become descriptive, referential rather than self-reflexive. The opening lines seem straightforwardly addressed to a figure standing at a remove from both the poet and the reader, so that our attention converges with hers on a third point; similarly, the poem as a whole directs attention away from its own performance to the prospect on which it seems to open, so that we look through it without the heightened awareness of the medium that the syllabic pattern engenders—and without pausing to consider that the poem *is* what we see.

The speaking voice, seemingly disembodied without the pattern to give it definition, is difficult to locate, the speaker herself invisible. At first it seems that the words must come from someone standing on the shore, asserting her own "right" to the obstructed "view," but once the hapless man has been gotten out of the way—or rather, once we *believe* he is out of the way—the poet does not come forward to make herself the dominant figure in the scene, to lay claim to the composition. ("Picking and Choosing" celebrates Gordon Craig for his "'this is I' and 'this is mine'"; but such acts of identification and appropriation have customarily been performed, in Moore's verse, by the formal patterns and by quotation, and there is none of that here.) Far from seeming proprietary or exclusive, in fact, the poet acts as a kind of tour guide, discreetly holding herself back out of sight while she points out the more interesting features of "the view." Instead of looking *at* her, therefore—or even looking *for* her—we seem to be looking at and "into" the sea.

Only the brief, delayed glimpse of the surface betrays the depth of the poet's interest in the sea. For as the "wrinkles" resolve themselves into "a phalanx" (one of the digital bones of the hand or foot), skin dissolves and gives way to bone, leaving only a single skeletal finger as a gruesome, mocking index of the poet's presence. It is, if we know how to read it, a signature—a name "writ," like Keats's, "in water"; "beautiful under networks of foam," it beckons us closer, but it points a warning as well, and, again, if we know how to read it, we know, too, that it is too late for us to save ourselves. The "phalanx" vanishes; the "wrinkles . . . fade breathlessly"; and the poet's dissolution is complete. She is not just *in* the sea; she *is* the sea, and it is as the sea that she has spoken. As we look into the sea we invade the poet with our stare, not realizing that we have done so, not recognizing ourselves in what the poem has shown us: I am that "Man, looking into the sea"; this is direct address.

Tempting our gaze by the transparency with which it hides itself and the poet, the poem, like the sea, captures and reflects the rapacity of our interest: like the men who "lower nets . . . and row quickly away as if there were no such thing as death," we are on a fishing expedition, trying "to get something out of the poem" without paying for it. But the "sea has nothing to give but a well excavated grave," and just as the poet has paid for transparency with the skin and "bones" whose final dissolution we have just witnessed, so we must pay with our lives for our "right" to this "view." What we get out of the poem is only what we've put into it: the "rapacious look" with which we have tried to make it our own, and with which the poem, repaying our interest by taking it far more seriously than we had bargained for, devours us. We have looked into the water only to fall for our own image, having learned too late that the grave we have been desecrating is our own.

This is indeed "that ocean in which dropped things are bound to sink," but the reader has no way of knowing, until it is too late, that he is "looking into" something which has concealed what may be its most crucial elements by assimilating "the forces which have made it" so thoroughly that —as "When I Buy Pictures" has it—"no more is discernible than the intensity of the mood." Indeed, the poem has effectively concealed the fact that it *has been made*—not only by refusing to acknowledge its debts, but also by dissolving the formal pattern which has served in the past to indicate the controlling presence of the poet. Poet and poem alike appear to have been subordinated to their presentation of the sea, thereby veiling the urgency of Moore's desire to be taken seriously as an artist. What she conceals most of all, then, is her awareness that her "life" as a poet depends upon our discernment—upon the reader's ability to recognize *after the fact* the very things of which the poem has worked to keep him ignorant; for our necessarily belated acknowledgment of Moore's artistry coincides with our recognition that we have long since been consigned to a watery and "well excavated grave."

IV

Moore must take hold of the looking-glass, then, in order not only to "acknowledge the forces" to which her work is responsible, but also to allow her *readers* a clear "view" of her design—and to achieve a clearer look at herself as well. She must do so, moreover, in the full knowledge that to accept the looking-glass is to give up what she calls in "New York" (December 1921) "the savage's romance": the "illusion," in Henry James's words, of

> experience liberated, so to speak; experience disengaged, disencumbered, exempt from the conditions that we usually know to attach to it and, if we wish so to put the matter, drag on it, and operating in a medium which relieves it of the inconvenience of a *related*, a measurable state, a state subject to all our vulgar communities. The greatest intensity may so be arrived at evidently—when the sacrifice of community, of the "related" sides of a situation, has not been too rash. It must to this end not flagrantly betray itself; we must even be kept if possible, for our illusion, from suspecting any sacrifice at all.[20]

Only substitute the word *poetry* for James's *experience*, and we have in his description of "projected romance" a strikingly apt description of Moore's syllabic poems. The syllabic pattern serves precisely to "relieve" the poem "of the inconvenience of a *related*, a measurable state, a state subject to all our vulgar communities"; for by requiring that its integrity *as pattern* be preserved, it fosters the illusion that the poem is a unique and completely "self-dependent" entity, not "subject" to "the conditions we usually know to attach" to poetry and therefore not "measurable" by the usual standards, an entity which does not seem to have "sacrifice[d] . . . community" because, like the savage, it appears (to the white man, that is) never to have belonged to a community in the first place.

The syllabic pattern, then, is "the savage's romance" which isolates the poet-savage from the pressures of "our vulgar communities." By preventing the poem from acknowledging "the forces which have made it," the pattern blocks the poem's full participation in the rituals of exchange which constitute the community—prevents it, that is, from giving anything in return for the predatory raids on the community's stores by which the poem covertly nourishes itself. But when the savage succumbs to the lure of the looking-glass, the illusion of self-sufficiency must give way before the pressure for payment of debts incurred, for what she sees in that glass is not only her *own* likeness, but the resemblance between herself and the writer she quotes—and so by taking the looking-glass she acknowledges a community of interest between them, acknowledges, that is to say, "the 'related' sides" of her "situation." Like the vanished buildings of New York for which Henry James mourns in *The American Scene*,[21] "the savage's romance" has "accreted where we need the space for commerce," and so the pattern, like the buildings, must be torn down to make way for newer, leaner structures in which that commerce may be carried on, and by which its triumph may be proclaimed.

Moore's newfound willingness to say "Let there be commerce between us"—as Ezra Pound had put it in an address to Whitman some years earlier[22]—is largely the result of a twofold change in her situation. That change was initiated in 1918, when, fulfilling a desire which had been growing steadily since her first visit to New York in 1915, Moore moved from Chatham, New Jersey, to Greenwich Village—"a far cry" indeed, as "New York" clearly implies, from the small Pennsylvania town near "the conjunction of the Monongahela and the Allegheny" where Moore had grown up. Living in Manhattan, at the center of the nation's literary, artistic, and commercial activity, Moore was for the first time within easy reach of libraries and museums, and galleries like the one that provides her with a setting for "When I Buy Pictures"; and just as it exposed her to material she could not have seen elsewhere, so too it gave her access to people she could not otherwise have met, and made possible such encounters as the decisive meeting with Scofield Thayer.

That encounter came at a crucial moment, for the magazines which had become Moore's principal outlets for publication—Alfred Kreymborg's *Others* and the London-based *Egoist*—had either just ceased publication or were just about to do so.[23] *Others* had been conceived from the outset as providing space for writers whose work, like Moore's, was too radical to gain ready acceptance elsewhere—a magazine, that is, for outsiders. Thayer's initial rejection of the poems Moore sent to *The Dial*, coming as it did when she had virtually no other place to take her work, must have confirmed her already strong sense of herself as just such an outsider. As a result of meeting Thayer, however, Moore not only secured the publication of "England" and "Picking and Choosing"; she also became one of *The Dial*'s regular contributors, and by 1921 she had become a paid member of the staff as well.

Thus, prompted by a newspaper item reporting that "In 1921 the centre of the wholesale fur trade shifted from St. Louis to New York,"[24] Moore celebrates in "New York" the completion of a parallel movement in her own career. The effect of that movement is to dissolve the need—and the justification—for her posture of resistance to "the scholastic philosophy of the wilderness, / to combat which one must stand outside and laugh / since to go in is to be lost." For she has moved from "the wilderness," where "plunder" is the order of the day, to find herself at the commercial "centre of the wholesale fur trade, / starred with tepees of ermine and peopled with foxes"; and what counts here—as the closing lines of "New York" acknowledge—"is not the plunder, / it is the 'accessibility to experience.'" As a member of *The Dial*'s editorial staff, involved like the white man who proffers the looking-glass and the savage who takes it in the buying and selling of literary works, Moore is now an active participant in that "wholesale" trade—so active, indeed, that she is at once the white man, the savage, and the animal. In order to engage fully in "commerce," Moore has had to sell off such appurtenances of form as the "elephant-skin" she had worn in "Black Earth" to protect her "soul" from the "wooden spear" of the hunter, the sharp pencil of the critic. That skin had also provided an effective shield against the ravages of "unpreventable experience," allowing the poet who had "looked at the electricity" to affirm, however shakily, that she was indeed "still here." But, as Moore writes in "The Labours of Hercules" (which appeared in *The Dial* as a companion-piece to "New York"), it is time now for "the bard" to learn "that one detects creative power by its capacity to eliminate detachment"—time to admit that her own detachment has been eliminated by that "creative power" which "flies along in a straight line like electricity / and devastates those areas that boast of their remoteness." The "ground" of "New York" is "dotted with deer-skins, white with white spots— / 'as satin needle-work in a single colour may carry a varied pattern'"—and the looking-glass for which Moore has traded her skins to Henry James shows her, in the closing line, a new vulnerability, a novel "'accessibility to experience.'"

4

The Principle of Accommodation: Moore, Eliot, and the Search for Community

I

Much of the impetus for Moore's interest in literary "commerce" comes from her reading of T.S. Eliot's work, and especially of his criticism. Eliot is clearly the major force behind Moore's exploration of what in "The Labours of Hercules" she calls "the principle of accommodation," that is, a way of adjusting herself to the related sides of her situation as a poet. Thus Eliot is also the guiding spirit in what I have called Moore's search for community. Equally clearly, however, he is also the figure to whom she finds it most difficult to accommodate herself.

Moore's ambivalence toward Eliot becomes evident as early as April 1918, with the appearance of "Black Earth" (in which, I have shown, she tries to neutralize Eliot by setting strict limits on both his "speech" and her own) and of her first review—of *Prufrock and Other Observations.*[1] The simultaneous publication of these two pieces strongly suggests that Moore had been working concurrently on both. When we take the two together, we find that the review evinces a respect for Eliot which the poem cannot afford to acknowledge "Openly," but which nonetheless underlies Moore's effort to circumscribe his power. Even in this brief review she is unable to speak of Eliot's verse without adopting some sort of protective cover. Just as she hardens herself against him in "Black Earth" by taking for her persona the elephant whose thick skin protects her "soul," so the manner in which she expresses her admiration for *Prufrock* betrays a kindred anxiety. Here she adopts a male persona who describes himself—with utter lack of conviction—as "this hardened reviewer."

No such embarrassment, though, is evident in her next recorded response to Eliot. Reviewing *The Sacred Wood* (1920) for *The Dial* in March 1921, she unhesitatingly declares the book to be "especially rich" "in what it reveals as a definition of criticism," and goes on confidently to address that definition:

> The connection between criticism and creation is close; criticism naturally deals with creation but it is equally true that criticism inspires creation. A genuine achievement in criticism is an achievement in creation; as Mr Eliot says, "It is to be expected that the critic and the creative artist should frequently be the same person." Much light is thrown on the problems of art in Mr Eliot's citing of Aristotle as an example of the perfect critic—perfect by reason of his having the scientific mind. Too much cannot be said for the necessity in the artist, of exact science.[2]

In writing that "criticism inspires creation," Moore quietly acknowledges that her own work has already been inspired by Eliot's criticism. But this does not say that she is completely uncritical of *The Sacred Wood.* Objecting to the treatment Swinburne receives at Eliot's hands, Moore invokes Swinburne's name and accomplishment at every turn, and at length justifies her insistence by hanging her final assessment of *The Sacred Wood* on a direct comparison of the two writers. Eliot wins the competition easily, but Swinburne gets the last word:

> Although Swinburne was not as Mr Eliot says he was not, "tormented by the restless desire to penetrate to the heart and marrow of a poet," it is evident that Mr Eliot is. In his poetry, he moves troutlike through a multiplicity of foreign objects and in his instinctiveness and care as a critic he appears as a complement to the sheen on his verse. In his opening a door upon the past and indicating what is there, he recalls the comment made by Swinburne upon Hugo:
>
> "Art knows nothing of death; . . . all that ever had life in it, has life in it forever; those themes only are dead which never were other than dead. No form is obsolete, no subject out of date, if the right man be there to rehandle it."[3]

Here as in the passage quoted earlier, Moore emphasizes the complementarity which makes the "connection between criticism and creation" so "close" that "'the critic and the creative artist [are] . . . frequently the same person.'" In this respect, her review of *The Sacred Wood* elaborates upon and extends the argument of "Picking and Choosing," which had been published eleven months earlier.

The poem's subject is criticism; it sets up two models of criticism and tries—not altogether successfully—to move from one to the other. The opening stanzas define criticism as little more than the expression of opinion about works of literature; criticism is something that happens after the fact. By the end of the poem, however, as the result of an encounter with Eliot, criticism has been reconceived as an act of selection, an informed picking and choosing which is an integral part of the creative process itself. But Moore is unwilling to abandon the cruder model with which she began, nor is she able to assimilate it into the more sophisticated model she develops at the end.

The poem ends by enjoining the critic to

remember Xenophon;
only the most rudimentary sort of behavior is necessary
to put us on the scent; a "right good
salvo of barks," a few "strong wrinkles" puckering the
skin between the ears, are all we ask.

These lines define the critic's role in terms very closely analagous to those in which we have seen Moore praising Eliot for "opening a door upon the past and indicating what is there." The critic's job, like the hunting-dog's, is to point to "what is there," "to put us on the scent": it is for the poet—the hunter following the baying of the hounds, the graceful and wily trout—to take up "what is there" and "'rehandle it.'"

But the poet has no place in these lines: it is not until "When I Buy Pictures" that we find her getting even an imaginary purchase on something she admires and overtly taking her prize "in hand." "When I Buy Pictures" follows "Picking and Choosing" by more than a year, however, and, more importantly, it postdates Moore's discussion of *The Sacred Wood* by several months as well. A preliminary draft of "Picking and Choosing" begins by complaining that "The half of what is written is not like a play / for enjoyment nor is it rich in material that one can use," but the poem actually has very little to do with the poet's handling and rehandling of what she discovers in her reading. "Picking and Choosing" is instead concerned, as the title makes clear, with the process of selection itself.

It is precisely on this point, though, that the poem is so troublesome. "Picking and Choosing" is most remarkable for the explicitness with which, in the middle stanzas, Moore passes judgment on such writers as Shaw, James, Hardy, Gordon Craig, and Edmund Burke. "Why cloud the fact," she writes in the second stanza,

> that Shaw is self-conscious in the field of sentiment but is otherwise re-
> warding? that James is all that has been
> said of him but is not profound?

Why indeed—but one may ask with equal force why it is necessary to state this "fact" so urgently on this particular occasion. The poem offers its judgments as if to answer some challenge—but the challenge remains unspoken, so there is nothing in the poem to warrant either the belligerent tone or the presence of these lines. They appear to be sanctioned only by the declaration, midway through the poem, that "If he must give an opinion, it is permissible that the / critic should know what he likes"—but since it is not clear why the critic "must give an opinion" here, we are inclined to agree that "the opaque allusion—the simulated flight / upward —accomplishes nothing."

The opinions expressed in "Picking and Choosing" are strikingly similar to those of an unpublished essay called "English Literature since 1914," a survey which Moore completed and sent to *The Spectator* (London) in April 1920—the same month in which "Picking and Choosing" appeared in *The Dial*.[4] With the exception (for obvious reasons) of Edmund Burke, all the writers named in the poem are also discussed in "English Literature since 1914"; and they are discussed according to the same principle—that "If he must give an opinion . . . the / critic should know what he likes." Thus "Picking and Choosing" may well have begun as a survey of contemporary writing, a sort of verse-equivalent to the essay, and it suffers from the same deficiency—that, at least in the opening stanzas, it has no real point to make.

Toward the end of the poem, however, the notion that equates criticism with the expression of opinion gives way to a far more powerful conception of the critical enterprise—a conception belatedly discovered in Eliot's essay "In Memory" of Henry James. As the following comparison of selected passages from "English Literature since 1914" and "Picking and Choosing" reveals, Eliot's essay comes into play at the point where the poem first separates itself from "English Literature since 1914."

Moore writes in "English Literature since 1914" that

> Hardy is an "interpreter of life through the emotions." James has characterized the restlessness and the crafty behavior of the lover but no one has so circumstantially depicted lovers, as Hardy. "Where the Picnic Was," "The Sun on the Bookcase," "Outside the Window," "In the Moonlight," "A Thunderstorm in Town" are testimony. His sentence structure is wrought iron tracery upon

> which one may look or lean; in his fastidiousness he is a prototype of the abbey mason, who "closlier looked and looked again." In conversation, the unintentional rhyme is undesirable and Hardy's intentional rhymes come to one occasionally with a sense of uneasiness, but to attempt to consider separately his prose and his verse is to lose his essential quality.
>
> "drearisome
> Arose the howl of wakened hounds;
> The mouse let fall the altar-crumb,
> The worms drew back into the mounds,"
>
> Is this not one with the description of the baptism in Tess of the D'Urbervilles?[5]

The corresponding lines in "Picking and Choosing" also insist upon the essential complementarity of Hardy's prose and verse, but are so stripped-down as to be enigmatic:

> It is not Hardy
> the distinguished novelist and Hardy the poet, but one man
>
> "interpreting life through the medium of the
> emotions."

Elsewhere, the poem seems blurred and dull where the essay is sharp. The stringency of the latter's verdict on Shaw, for instance—that he "cannot in a straight forward [*sic*], compelling manner, write a love-scene; instead . . . he takes refuge in a quibble or a prank which is intrinsically droll but . . . aesthetically irrelevant"[6]—is missing from the poem's bland remark "that Shaw is self-conscious in the field of sentiment but is otherwise re- / warding. . . ." And where the essay speaks enthusiastically of James's "awareness and . . . unwillingness to compromise, either in technique or in choice of subject,"[7] the poem manages only the ambiguous pronoucement "that James is all that has been / said of him but is not profound. . . ."

Here the difference between "Picking and Choosing" and "English Literature since 1914" becomes more than a matter of phrasing—and given Moore's life-long admiration for James, the ambiguity of these lines is especially disturbing. But the lines on James have nothing to do with "English Literature since 1914": they are the product of an initial misreading on Moore's part of Eliot's essay on James. The *Observations* text has it "that James is all that has been / said of him, if *feeling* is profound," and though the change does not quite resolve the ambiguity, a crucial note at the back of the volume clarifies matters considerably by supplying the provenance of *feeling*: T.S. Eliot; In Memory; The Little Review; August 1918. "James's critical genius comes out most tellingly in his mastery over, his baffling escape from Ideas; a mastery and an escape which are perhaps the last test of a superior intelligence. He had a mind so fine that no idea could violate it. . . . In England ideas run wild and pasture on the emotions; instead of thinking with our feelings (a very different thing) we corrupt our feelings with ideas; we produce the political, the emotional idea, evading sensation and thought."[8]

Direct references to immediate contemporaries are very rare in Moore's published notes; this one has a force that goes well beyond its immediate aim of correcting the misconstruction which Moore had earlier put upon Eliot's account of James's "baffling escape from Ideas," and assuring us that "*feeling*" in James (and in Moore) is indeed "profound." This note is the sign of the prominence which Eliot's work has assumed in Moore's thought by 1924, and it may indicate that she holds the essay on James in special esteem. For it is here that Eliot defines "influence" and "criticism" in ways Moore "can use" as she tries for the first time to break out of the isolation she had imposed on herself in her determination to resist "experience," to "repel influences" (in Emerson's words) as vigorously as possible.[9]

"To be influenced by a writer," says Eliot, "is to have a chance inspiration from him; or *to take what one wants*."[10] It is not, therefore, to allow oneself to be passively "Compelled by experience"—a prospect which, in "Sojourn in the Whale," as elsewhere, Moore had bitterly resented. It now appears that being "influenced" is the consequence of a critical act, an informed picking and choosing which is inseparable from the creative work itself. Thus, according to Eliot, James produces "criticism which is in a very high sense creative"—though not in his "feeble" critical essays, as Eliot unkindly and injudiciously calls them.[11] It is in his fiction that James is what Moore is on her way to becoming in "Picking and Choosing"—"a critic who preys not upon ideas, but upon living beings."[12]

Eliot makes "criticism and creation" not only complementary but simultaneous, and, no less importantly from Moore's standpoint, he makes the thought of being influenced palatable by treating it as a question of deliberate choice on the writer's part. Moore names names in "Picking and Choosing," then, not merely to "give an opinion"—as the poem makes it appear —but rather to signify that she has indeed chosen the writers she names.

Her insistence on having chosen is consistent with the terms of Eliot's essay; it is also important, however, in the context of the letter to Pound in which Moore cites some of the same writers as "direct influences bearing on [her] work."[13] Pound had written her in December 1918, combining an offer of help in getting her work into print with a speculative account of her poetic ancestry,[14] and Moore's reply amounts to a sweeping dismissal of Pound's guesswork. She begins with a curt rejection of his suggestion that her syllabics might represent a conscious elaboration of his own early experiments with metric—"The resemblance of my progress to your beginnings is an accident so far as I can see," she writes—and then goes on to throw out Pound's remaining candidates:

> I have no Greek, unless a love for it may be taken as a knowledge of it and I have not read very voraciously in French; I do not know Ghil and La Forgue [*sic*] and know of no tangible French influence on my work. Gordon Craig, Henry James, Blake, Hardy and the minor prophets are so far as I know, the direct influences bearing on my work.

The list offered here is not precisely identical with that in "Picking and Choosing," and neither may be taken as truly definitive. But "Picking and Choosing" does represent a partial correction by Moore of the account she had given of herself in writing to Pound, and it is at the same time an effort on her part to validate the claims she had made in that letter by bringing the "influences" she had named to bear upon the poem itself in the most direct way possible.

But it is here that the confused, self-vexing character of the poem is most fully exposed. It is evidently the function of the names to declare some of "the direct influences bearing on" Moore's work—but in insisting on her right, as critic, to "give an opinion," Moore actually obscures that bearing in an attempt to retain control rather than let the poem be swayed by the active influence of the writers she has named. (Her tribute to "Gordon / Craig, with his 'this is I' and 'this is mine,'" is very much to the point here.) There is a sense, moreover, in which the names themselves serve a blocking function. While they matter in the general context of Moore's early work, they are rather beside the point, I think, in "Picking and Choosing." This, at least, is what I take to be the significance of an early draft in which Moore clearly contemplates omitting the names altogether and replacing them with algebraic equivalents: the letters *B* and *D* stand in for such names as Shaw and James, for instance, while disyllabic names like Hardy are represented by the combination "BD."[15] More precisely, names work in "Picking and Choosing" much as they do in the letter to Pound, where they allow Moore to write her own history as a poet and put enough distance between herself and Pound to deflect his claim of influence over her. Similarly, "Picking and Choosing" deflects the force of

Eliot's essay on James by giving preference to the names of other, older writers. Once again, Moore erects a barrier between herself and Eliot—not a thick-skinned persona this time, but a wall of names.

II

"Picking and Choosing" thus reveals that Moore's eager responsiveness to Eliot coexists with and is nearly canceled out by her reluctance to grant him full authority. The same tension is manifest in "People's Surroundings" more than two years later.[16] Like "Picking and Choosing," it coincides strikingly at certain points with "English Literature since 1914," but unlike the earlier poem it sustains its concentration on contemporary writers—and on poets in particular—long enough to justify us in calling it a kind of survey of contemporary poetry. It is also—again resembling "Picking and Choosing"—an effort to accommodate Eliot's presence; but that effort, too, is seriously marred by Moore's continuing unwillingness to meet Eliot openly.

The poem begins with a sharply defined initial segment, only five lines long and clearly reminiscent of earlier syllabic stanzas, in which the image of a "deal table compact with the wall" embodies the assured safety of a "simplicity" in which "one's style is not lost." Moore rejects this simplicity, however, as a mere "dried bone of arrangement," a dead and fragmentary thing of no interest to one who insists on "piercing glances into the life of things." And then she embarks on a journey which takes her through a "vast indestructible necropolis / of Yawman-Erbe separable units"—a city of death which is only another version of that "wilderness" she thought she had left "a far cry" behind her.

The long first sentence of the poem, as it appeared in *The Dial*, is divided into six typographically distinct segments that become longer and longer as the sentence proceeds. Demonstrable parallels with Moore's "English Literature since 1914" suggest that each segment is devoted to a discrete "unit" of the poetic environment, and each of these is dismissed in turn as Moore continues her search for a "style" of sufficient power to engage her fully. Thus in the poem's first segment she considers and dismisses Pound and Williams, as, later on in the fifth segment, she takes note of Eliot and dismisses him in order to concentrate on Wallace Stevens.

"There is in Ezra Pound," she writes in "English Literature since 1914," "'a natural promptness,' an energy, an instinct for literature." Again stressing the complementarity of "criticism and creation," Moore notes in Pound's prose "the same momentum that there is in his poems and translations,"[17] thereby to all appearances registering approval of Pound's work. But the opening lines of "People's Surroundings" imply certain reservations:

> . . . a deal table compact with the wall;
> in this dried bone of arrangement,
> one's "natural promptness" is compressed, not crowded out;
> one's style is not lost in such simplicity: . . .

What has been "crowded out" of these lines is the explicitness which in "Picking and Choosing" Moore naively assumes will make clarity of opacity. The allusion to Pound is instead "compressed" in the image of a bare room and the retention from the earlier essay of the quoted phrase. Since neither is associated with Pound in any obvious way, it may seem that we are once again facing an "opaque allusion." Perhaps this is so—but names simply do not matter a great deal in "People's Surroundings"; Moore is not particularly interested in our knowing what she thinks of Pound or any of the other poets to whom the poem privately alludes.

Yet her judgments are integral to the movement of "People's Surroundings" as those put forward in "Picking and Choosing" are not. This first "stanza" looks like praise, a standard by which to judge what follows; and we must take it that way for the time being because no other standard becomes available until we are presented, in the closing lines of the poem, with an ecstatic vision of persons "in their respective places"—a vision of community that exposes the sterile atomism of the poem's first part. That final vision forces us back to reconsider the implications of what we had accepted—forces us to consider more carefully the ironic lengthening-out of the line that seems to celebrate compression, and to take account of the hint of death "in this dried bone of arrangement."

The image of the "dried bone" comes from a letter by William Carlos Williams:

> I cannot object to rhetoric, as you point out, but I must object to the academic associations with which rhetoric is hung and which vitiate all its significance by making the piece of work to which it is applied a dried bone . . . [18]

Williams had always objected to Pound's academicism, and we may take Moore's decision to use his phrase here as indicating at least partial agreement. But whereas Williams tends to treat words like *academic* as synonyms for overinvestment in the European literary past at the expense of the American present, Moore uses his phrase in a very different way—and she uses it in a precisely rhetorical context. "People's Surroundings" has abandoned the overtly rhetorical structures of Moore's earlier syllabic poems, just as it has done away with end-rhymes and syllable-counts; but it has not done away with rhetoric. The poem's implicit argument concerns the relationship between the present and the past—or, more precisely, what Moore by now perceives as the dangerous absence of any such relationship. This is not a nostalgic complaint that the present differs from the past and is therefore worse; the point is rather that the world of the present in "People's Surroundings" is a "vast indestructible necropolis of . . . separable units," a city of isolation and death which has no consciousness of the past at all—and that that consciousness, as the poem's closing lines imply, *is* life. It is in this context that Moore sets Williams against Pound (and maybe against himself as well) and rejects them both.[19] A spare setting may have its advantages, but it is only because "such simplicity" is achieved at the cost of life itself, "in this dried bone of arrangement," that "one's style is not lost." Such a style is not worth keeping; the poet moves on, past "the palace furniture, so old fashioned, so old fashionable," past "landscape gardening twisted into permanence," in search of a living style.

The decisive moment comes in the sixth and final segment of the first sentence, when the poet comes to a place whose gorgeousness and opulence are "quite the opposite" of the "simplicity" of the first image. Having examined and rejected various accommodations along the way, she now enters

> . . . Bluebeard's tower above the coral reefs,
> the magic mouse-trap closing on all points of the compass,
> capping like petrified surf, the furious azure of the bay
> where there is no dust and life is like a lemon-leaf,
> a green piece of tough translucent parchment,
> where the crimson, the copper, and the Chinese vermilion of the poincianas
> set fire to the masonry and turquoise blues refute the clock;
> this dungeon with odd notions of hospitality,
> with its "chessmen carved out of moonstones,"
> its mocking-birds, fringed lilies, and hibiscus,
> its black butterflies with blue half circles on their wings,
> tan goats with onyx ears, its lizards glittering and without thickness
> like splashes of fire and silver on the pierced turquoise of the lattices
> and the acacia-like lady shivering at the touch of a hand,

lost in a small collision of the orchids—
dyed quicksilver let fall
to disappear like an obedient chameleon in fifty shades of mauve and amethyst. . . .

"You'll be reading some French author, or Wallace Stevens," said Moore in 1969, "and for awhile you'll have a touch of that in what you write. Yes, and in your emotions."[20] She may well have been speaking of "People's Surroundings." The lines just quoted include a quotation from the "French author" Anatole France (Moore alludes with characteristic obliquity to France's story "Barbe-bleue" in taking the phrase "chessmen carved out of moonstones" from another of his works),[21] and there is more than "a touch" of Stevens' "hand" in such lines as "where there is no dust and life is like a lemon-leaf"; the latter clause in particular, like "refute the clock" a few lines later, has an elusive but unmistakable Stevensian resonance. Indeed, the whole passage is parodically reminiscent, in its tropical brilliance, of "Sunday Morning"[22]—though here things "Mingle" to intensify, not to "dissipate," the "air of sacrifice" through which "the acacia-like lady" moves to her doom.

The legends on which Anatole France based "Barbe-bleue" told how Bluebeard wooed, married, and murdered seven women; his "hand" is therefore "predatory"—it "can grasp" and it does. Like the "spiked hand," which, in "Marriage," "has an affection for one / and proves it to the bone," its "touch" here ironically rewards the poet's effort to fulfill the promise of her "accessibility to experience" by revealing the extent to which she has adulterated her own "creative power" in marrying her "style" to that of Bluebeard / Stevens. She has been betrayed again into the "sophistication" (mixture, adulteration) which is rejected in "In the Days of Prismatic Colour" as unholy and false—but she has not been betrayed by Bluebeard, or not by him alone. Ironically making her visible to us for the first time, "the touch" of Bluebeard's hand reveals his power, but it also shows us that the lady disappearing "like an obedient chameleon in fifty shades of mauve and amethyst" has been undone by her own helplessly mimetic instincts.

From the moment of her decision to "go in" to "Bluebeard's tower," the poet has been riding "an escalator," moving by virtue of someone else's power—whereas in the passage immediately preceding this one she had been traveling in "straight lines," like the "electricity" of "creative power" in "The Labours of Hercules." She says in that earlier passage that "there is something attractive about a mind that moves in a straight line," and yet that "mind" must know when and how to *stop*. "'[A] good brake is as important as a good motor,'" and unlike "those cool sirs with the explicit sensory apparatus of common sense" who "can like trout, smell what is coming" and apply the "'brake'" in time to avoid a crash, the poet has steered "straight" for trouble.

Here Moore distinguishes herself—not altogether happily—from such "cool sirs" as Eliot, whom she notices and tries to bypass on her way to Bluebeard's tower. Moore has used the simile of the trout at least twice before, both times in prose and both times in reference to Eliot. The closing paragraph of her review of *The Sacred Wood* describes him as moving "troutlike" in his poetry "through a multiplicity of foreign objects"; this is a slight reworking of a phrase from "English Literature since 1914" where Moore speaks of "the facile troutlike passage of [Eliot's] mind through a multiplicity of foreign objects. . . . "[23]

This last phrase was written before Moore had read *The Sacred Wood*, which may account for the faintly pejorative suggestion that Eliot moves a little too easily among all those "foreign objects"; however, the full weight of Moore's phrase is apparent only when we consider the entire sentence in relation to the movement of "People's Surroundings." "The sheen upon T.S. Eliot's poems, the facile troutlike passage of his mind through a multiplicity of foreign objects[,] recall the 'spic torrent' in Wallace Steven's [*sic*] Pecksniffiana."[24] The poem's central encounter takes place in the middle of that "'spic torrent,'" for, according to Moore's published notes, Bluebeard's tower is in the Virgin Islands, in the Carribean setting so often favored by Stevens.[25] And whereas Moore gives Eliot little more than a quick glance in passing, she devotes her full attention to Stevens for twenty lines. She had told Pound in 1919 that she liked Eliot's work,[26] but in "People's Surroundings," as in "Picking and Choosing," she is interested chiefly in Eliot the critic; it is Stevens whose poems demand her response. But criticism and creation are indeed simultaneous here: Moore works mimetically in the Bluebeard's-tower sequence to discover that involvement with Stevens is fatal to her "progress."

Immediately after the lady's disappearance a colon breaks the sentence, and the next three lines—spoken in the coolly sardonic tone which had marked the poem earlier on—assess the damage:

> here where the mind of this establishment has come to the conclusion
> that it would be impossible to revolve about one's self too much,
> sophistication has like an escalator, cut the nerve of progress.

When the poem was reprinted in *Observations*, the simile "like an escalator" was set in quotation marks and attributed, in Moore's notes, to the Reverend J.W. Darr, the minister who had earlier supplied the closing lines of "The Labours of Hercules."[27] There, his words give an express political and social connotation to "the principle of accommodation" Moore has set out "to popularize," for the last of her Herculean tasks is

> to convince snake-charming controversialists
> . . . that one keeps on knowing
> "that the negro is not brutal,
> that the Jew is not greedy,
> that the Oriental is not immoral,
> that the German is not a Hun."

In "People's Surroundings," however, Darr's words are used against "accommodation." The reversion to religious authority signals Moore's recovery from the worldly "sophistication" into which she has "let" herself "fall."

The rapidity of that recovery suggests, however, that this has all been something on the order of a controlled experiment, conceived and executed by a poet who trained in her student years as a biologist and considered going on to study medicine—an experimental surgical procedure which, having ended by cutting "the nerve of progress," has redounded on itself. The poet must therefore devise a new procedure, find a new way "to go in." This time, however, she will work with the aid of what "Those Various Scalpels" calls "more specialized" instruments."[28]

The "eye knows," says the second sentence of "People's Surroundings," what in the first sentence the body does *not* know—"what to skip"; knows, too, that such "personal-impersonal expressions of appearance" as "Bluebeard's tower" do not fully define the spirits that create them. Built as they are on the principle that "the physiognomy of conduct must not reveal the skeleton," they are inevitably "noncommittal." As *Vogue* reminded its readers, offering them a principle of accommodation, "a setting must not have the air of being one."[29] Going in physically, as "the acacia-like lady" has done, is not just spiritually compromising: it is also methodologically inadequate because it can "reveal the skeleton" only at the cost of the life. In order for the poet to discover that "skeleton"—"the fundamental structure" —without resorting to the desperate "simplicity" of the "dried bone," she must employ an "x-raylike inquisitive intensity" that permits "piercing glances into the life of things" while preserving that life. That "x-raylike inquisitive intensity" makes "the surfaces go back" so that, as on a well-prepared slide, "the interfering fringes of expression are but a stain on what stands out." Only by this means will we be able to

> see the exterior and the fundamental structure—
> captains of armies, cooks, carpenters,
> cutlers, gamesters, surgeons, and armourers,
> lapidaries, silkmen, glovers, fiddlers, and ballad-singers,
> sextons of churches, dyers of black cloth,
> hostlers, and chimney-sweeps,
> queens, countesses, ladies, emperors, travellers, and mariners,
> dukes, princes, and gentlemen
> in their respective places—
> camps, forges, and battlefields,
> conventions, oratories, and wardrobes,
> dens, deserts, railway stations, asylums, and places where engines are made,
> shops, prisons, brickyards, and altars of churches—
> in magnificent places clean and decent,
> castles, palaces, dining-halls, theatres, and imperial audience-chambers.

The poem ends by creating a powerful impression of harmony, if not precisely of order, a sense of the rightness of things, or rather—and this is crucial—of people hard at work "in their respective places." There is a great deal of quiet and related activity going forward in these "magnificent places clean and decent," so that the passage as a whole serves to emphasize the atomism of the first sentence, as well as the claustrophobic, deathly silent emptiness of the "separable units" visited there. For in the first sentence there are only places, "people's surroundings" but no people. The only fully human presence is that of the "lady," but her humanity is overwhelmed, first by her "acacia-like" appearance, then by her "conduct," which is no more human than her looks: she behaves "like an obedient chameleon." She is seen, moreover, only that she may be seen to "disappear . . . in fifty shades of mauve and amethyst," so that our final sense of her is that she is not even one of those "lizards glittering and without thickness" of which we had caught sight earlier—she is merely color. (Bluebeard's tower is, in fact, virtually made of color: azure, green, crimson, copper, Chinese vermilion, turquoise, tan, onyx, black, blue, silver, mauve, and amethyst; by contrast, in the final catalogue the only people involved with color are the "dyers of black cloth.")

The fate of "the acacia-like lady" is emblematic; from it we may deduce what has become of the people who seem so strikingly absent from their surroundings in each of the five preceding segments. The lady enters Bluebeard's tower from the outside, at the end of a journey "over . . . great distances": it is not her place, and she is "lost" in trying to accommodate herself to its conditions. Like her, the missing people live in places not—or not fully—their own: composing their "settings" according to notions of "style" derived from sources external to themselves, and perhaps inimical to themselves, they have created a city of death, a "vast indestructible necropolis / of . . . separable units" which have no more to do with one another than do the "separable units" of the sentence that describes them. There "is no dust" where life has been reduced to the sterile artificiality of "landscape gardening twisted into permanence." Bluebeard is worth engaging, however, because he at least has managed to free "a hand" from the edifice in which he has immured himself, and so remains alive and dangerous; but everyone else has disappeared into the walls.

And yet "with x-raylike inquisitive intensity upon it, the surfaces" even of this "petrified" world "go back" until, for the first time in Moore's work, they yield up an ecstatic vision of a living, working community. For six lines we have a kind of antiquarian's *Song of Occupations* in which persons are named according to their functions. Some are "dukes" or "princes," some are "surgeons, and armourers," and each is occupied precisely as the other is, in his own work. Unlike Bluebeard or the lady, each remains fully distinct from yet precisely, formally equal to every other. All have their work, and all have "their respective places" as well, and these, too, are on an equal footing (formally, that is): "prisons" and "palaces," "castles" and "brickyards," all are "magnificent places clean and decent," and all are filled with activity. There is in this ecstatic catalogue of persons "in their respective places" no simple, one-for-one correspondence of persons to places; we see a feudal society, but we see it as it were democratically, so that "there is neither up nor down" to it. All people belong to all places, and all places to all people.

So, too, the present belongs to the past, and the past to the present. There is a distinctly archaic air about this culminating vision, and yet the people here are decidedly alive, just as the "railway stations" and "the places where engines *are* made" (my emphasis)—places belonging to the present—are warped back to an earlier period by virtue of their formal equivalence to the places surrounding them. The past is alive, whereas the contemporary world through which the first sentence passes is dead—dead because, having "come to the conclusion / that it would be impossible to revolve about [itself] too much," it is indifferent to "the fundamental structure," the immanent past.

One may legitimately ask, however, whether this final vision, powerful and attractive as it is, is enough to offset the very different strength of the Bluebeard's-tower sequence. There is no real continuity between the first and second sentences of "People's Surroundings"; in fact it seems to me that the way of seeing which produces the poem's final lines does not really include, as it should and *as the poem says it does*, the way of seeing which produces "Bluebeard's tower" by concentrating on "the surfaces" of things. In the lines introducing the final vision, Moore writes that "we see the exterior and the fundamental structure"; but the poem holds them so far apart that it is impossible to see them together, as we must do if we are to take seriously the possibility that the world envisioned in the final lines is immanent in and accessible to the world that occupies the first two-thirds of the poem.

Eliot insists in "Tradition and the Individual Talent" that "the poet must develop or procure the consciousness of the past,"[30] and this is what Moore has attempted in "People's Surroundings." Writing at first "with [her] own generation in [her] bones," in the poem's second sentence Moore reaches back into the Renaissance to "procure" from Raphael's *Horary Astrology* the "consciousness" of communal labor which is presented in the poem's closing lines as a corrective to the deadening solipsism epitomized in Bluebeard's tower. But there is a considerable difference between developing in oneself a "consciousness of the past" and procuring from the past its consciousness of itself—which is what Moore has literally tried to do in "People's Surroundings." She has had to do it that way, moreover, because in becoming "lost" in Bluebeard's tower she has imprisoned her own consciousness in "the surfaces" of the self-enclosed present.

Ironically, then, the poem's "progress" is cut short just when it most nearly coincides with Eliot's account of "progress" in "Tradition and the Individual Talent." For the poet cultivating "the consciousness of the past," he says, "what happens is a continual surrender of himself as he is at the moment to something which is more valuable. The progress of an artist is a continual self-sacrifice, a continual extinction of personality."[31] Structurally at least, this is precisely what happens to Moore's "acacia-like lady," who becomes visible "at the touch" of Bluebeard's "hand" only to disappear in the next instant "like an obedient chameleon," betrayed by her own mimetic instincts into accommodating herself too readily to alien and hostile—and male—surroundings.

The problem is not that the "self-sacrifice" demanded under Eliot's notion of "progress" is unacceptable to Moore—though at this stage it still makes her acutely uncomfortable. The problem is that a poet interested in developing a consciousness of the past makes a serious mistake in surrendering herself so thoroughly to the present, in sacrificing herself to an "establishment" whose "mind . . . revolves[s]" exclusively about itself. Such a mind is by definition impervious to any suggestion that there might be "something . . . more valuable" than itself, and therefore cannot provide the link to anything beyond itself. Moore had praised Eliot for "opening a door upon the past and indicating what is there," but there is no such door in Bluebeard's tower. It is Eliot—not Stevens—who sets himself explicitly to bring past and present into close conformity; and in "Novices," goaded by the example of *The Waste Land*, Moore reaffirms her commitment to Eliot's conception of progress as "a continual self-sacrifice, a continual extinction of personality." But a brief look at "Tradition and the Individual Talent" is in order before we turn our attention to "Novices."

III

Eliot's essay "In Memory" of Henry James makes being "influenced by a writer" a matter—partly, at least—of taking from that writer "what one wants." His first move a year later, in "Tradition and the Individual Talent," radically extends the scope of that remark by defining "tradition" itself as a body of knowledge rather consciously and actively appropriated than passively or unconsciously received. Nothing is simply handed down the generations; like the weary figures in Yeats's "Adam's Curse," who know that women and poets alike "must labour to be beautiful," Eliot's poet knows that tradition "cannot be inherited, and if you want it you must obtain it by great labour."[32] This is to say that tradition exists, if it exists at all, only by virtue of one's efforts to acquire it; and such efforts will be made only by those possessed already of what Eliot calls the "historical sense"—that which

> compels a man to write not merely with his own generation in his bones, but with a feeling that the whole of the literature of Europe from Homer and within it the whole of the literature of his own country has a simultaneous existence and composes a simultaneous order.[33]

Eliot might well have added here what Emerson had said seventy-five years earlier, near the end of "The Poet": "I look in vain for the poet whom I describe."[34] For certainly no one has ever written, and no one ever will write, with "the *whole* of the literature of Europe from Homer and within it the *whole* of the literature of his own country" in his possession. One may write "with a feeling that the whole of . . . literature . . . has a simultaneous existence and composes a simultaneous order," but it cannot be more than a *feeling*, communicated more or less successfully to others: the "ideal order" cannot, in the nature of things, be set forth. (And Eliot does not try: in *The Sacred Wood* and elsewhere, he limits himself to making notes toward a definition of culture and "indicating what is there.") The "ideal order" cannot be demonstrated, nor can it be apprehended in its entirety: "The existing order is complete before the new work arrives."[35] But because the poet "as he is at the moment" of writing is inevitably not possessed of the whole of literature, his apprehension of the order it composes cannot be anything but incomplete.

In this view of things, however, the apprehension *is* tradition. Thus it is the inevitable failure to grasp the existing order in its completeness that makes "the new (the really new) work of art" possible.[36] Or rather, what counts is the precise quality of the failure: for the "really new" in this context can only mean a new and compelling reformulation of the "tradition" itself. Recording the poet's necessary failure to apprehend the existing order in its totality, the "new work" "fits in" among the "existing monuments" by redefining them in relation to itself[37]—that is, by revealing their apprehensions of order, their "traditions," to be as incomplete as its own, which nonetheless includes theirs. This revelation (a "development, refinement perhaps, complication certainly," but "not, from the point of view of the artist, any improvement") comes about because "the *whole* existing order" is, "if ever so slightly, altered" by the "supervention" of a "really new" work in such a way that "the relations, proportions, values of each work of art toward the whole are readjusted . . . ."[38] It is this readjustment, and not any simple obeisance to established conventions, that makes for true "conformity between the old and the new."

"Novices," published in *The Dial* eight months after "People's Surroundings," responds to the "supervention" of *The Waste Land* in November 1922[39] with the sort of readjustment Eliot discusses in "Tradition and the Individual Talent." Nothing in "Tradition and the Individual Talent" as Moore would have seen it in *The Egoist* in 1919 or in *The Sacred Wood* the following year suggests the sheer scale of the readjustment Eliot effects in *The Waste Land*; the poem itself reveals the subversive possibilities of the argument as a whole, just as the mad babel of the closing lines exposes the dangers inherent in following Eliot's call for "a continual extinction of personality":

> I sat upon the shore
> Fishing, with the arid plain behind me
> Shall I at least set my lands in order?
> London Bridge is falling down falling down falling down
> *poi s'ascose nel foco che gli affina*
> *Quando fiam uti chelidon*—O swallow swallow
> *Le Prince d'Aquitaine à la tour abolie*
> These fragments I have shored against my ruins
> Why then Ile fit you. Hieronymo's mad againe.
> Datta. Dayadhvam. Damyata.
> Shantih shantih shantih[40]

Out of linguistic incoherence Eliot creates an extraordinarily coherent image of emotional, political, and cultural disorder. His lines imply a way of proceeding, if not precisely a method—that is, they are themselves a model for a response in kind. Moore's technique in the last thirteen lines of "Novices" is very much like that which Eliot employs in the eleven lines quoted above; for in "Novices," too, coherence is produced by joining discontinuous phrases together. But it is a very different sort of coherence: here a group of "good and alive young men" are

> . . . "split like a glass against a wall"
> in this "precipitate of dazzling impressions,
> the spontaneous unforced passion of the Hebrew language—
> an abyss of verbs full of reverberation and tempestuous energy,"
> in which action perpetuates action and angle is at variance with angle
> till submerged by the general action;
> obscured by fathomless suggestions of colour,
> by incessantly panting lines of green, white with concussion,
> in this drama of water against rocks—this "ocean of hurrying consonants,"
> with its "great livid stains like long slabs of green marble,"
> its "flashing lances of perpendicular lightning" and "molten fires swallowed up,"
> "with foam on its barriers,"
> "crashing itself out in one long hiss of spray."

We may take these lines—where the "young men" who were so "good and alive" a moment ago are drowned like "Phlebas the Phoenician . . . who once was handsome and tall as you"[41]—as imaging the violence with which *The Waste Land* has shattered prevailing conceptions of literary value and "readjusted" "the relations, proportions, values of each work of art toward the whole. . . ." But the vision Moore's lines serve, with a violence all their own, is very different from that of *The Waste Land*, and a corrective to it. The "fundamental structure" to which "Novices" ultimately refers all its compositional elements stands in radical opposition to Eliot's apprehended tradition. Restoring to the conventional Christian vocabulary of "surrender" and "self-sacrifice" which he uses in "Tradition and the Individual Talent," the Christian significance which Eliot deliberately and provocatively ignores, Moore arrives in "Novices" at a vision of the divine order of creation—an order which, unlike Eliot's "tradition," is not contingent upon its being apprehended at all.

As in *The Waste Land*, Moore's closing lines establish "conformity between the old and the new" by drawing together phrases composed at different times and in different places and (originally at least) in different languages as well.[42] They are drawn, however, into a grammatically continuous sequence, as Eliot's are not, and the difference is revealing. For the "historical sense" at work here is not at all like that informing *The Waste Land*, which has nothing to do with such continuities as Moore's arrangement insists upon. Eliot's guiding principle is simultaneity —which looks like discontinuity on the page because his lineation, like his transcriptions, respects linguistic and temporal differences as Moore's quotations and translations do not. Conformity "between the old and the new" is not an identity for Eliot, but identity is what "Novices" implies, and identity is what Moore asserts when, in 1924, she changes the tentative title "So far as the future is concerned," to an unequivocal declaration: "The Past Is the Present." (See chapter 1 for a discussion of the poem.) Here Moore gives priority to the past, not just in order of time but in order of significance as well; and it is in the closing lines of "Novices" that that priority is decisively established. For what matters there is not conformity between old and new, but rather the conformity *of* "the new" *to* "the old."

The process of conforming the present to the past demands that writers like Eliot and Pound stand in the final lines of "Novices" as both silent presences and active collaborators. This may sound ridiculous; remember, though, that Moore's own presence in these lines is largely a silent one —silent, that is, in the special sense given to that word in "Silence" a year and a half later, where we learn that "'Superior people . . . can be robbed of speech / by speech which has delighted them,'" and that "'the deepest feeling always shows itself in silence— / not in silence, but restraint'": the poem goes forward although the poet is restrained from speaking by the active supervention of someone else's delectable speech. Moore's silence in "Novices"—restraint, rather—is enjoined upon her by her status as a novice, a newcomer to an already-established order, and she places her contemporaries under the same injunction. "Novices" marks both the poet's conversion from the ranks of those writers whose devotion is primarily to themselves, and her initiation into a community of writers dedicated to the observation and exposition of truth. But the title also defines the limits of this new status: Moore's emphasis has changed, but she is still a novice, still a beginner. That limitation is reflected, too, in the closing lines of the poem, where the quotations permit older, more established members of the community to speak while the poet herself holds still. "Novices" asks us to consider that present utterance may be the bearer of the past, but it asks us to consider, too, that the present is born out of that past.

IV

Thus "Novices" succeeds where "People's Surroundings" had failed. As in "People's Surroundings," Moore splits the poem in the effort to achieve community, and again the vision of community erupts in the last thirteen lines of the poem. (Of course, this statistical similarity may be coincidental. I take it, however, as indicating a renewed effort on Moore's part to establish a convincing relation between "the exterior and the fundamental structure"—a necessary reassertion, in the absence of the syllabic pattern, of the principle that "spirit creates form." It also validates and extends her discovery in "People's Surroundings" of a form capable at once of releasing vision and of keeping it recognizably within bounds.) Unlike "People's Surroundings," though, "Novices" sustains itself through the eruption that splits it "'like a glass against a wall,'" and Moore carefully trains the reader to perceive that the visionary mode which dominates the closing lines is an extension of the ordinary way of seeing characterized and condemned in the first part of the poem.

That the closing lines of "Novices" consist almost entirely of quotations suggests that vision, as I have called it, is to be equated with a way of reading. Further, the superiority of vision inheres in the fact that it does not rely exclusively upon the unaided eye of a single individual. The quotations used here represent independent moments of perception on the part of persons widely separated in time and space, both from each other and from the poet. Moore's vision works, then, by juxtaposing these isolated perceptions in such a way that the image they now form has both spatial and temporal dimension.

To the ordinary seeing defined in the first two-thirds of the poem, the sea appears in "'detailless perspective . . . ,' reiterative and naive"; but what appears to one "given over to precise seeing," who "has predominently [*sic*] the scientific attitude of mind in conjunction with spiritual vision,"[43] is a succession of individual details—more sharply seen, more fully realized, and therefore more fully distinct from one another than the persons and places catalogued at the end of "People's Surroundings"—a "'precipitate of dazzling impressions'" fused into a single impression of the sea in motion. By presenting two views of the sea, "Novices" persuades us that vision is continuous with seeing, for "'the detailless perspective of the sea'" ironically frames the very details on which the closing lines focus so tightly, and helps us to retain our sense of the whole. Unaided, the eye sees that the wave is breaking; it takes an "x-raylike inquisitive intensity" to perceive that the wave is composed of materials already extant, and that the rhythm of its movement was laid down at the Creation.

Thus the conversion of Moore's poems to the ends of "truth" and vision demands the renunciation of one way of reading and the substitution of another. The poet—and her readers with her—must learn to read with what Eliot calls the "historical sense," by virtue of which we recognize, in the wave "'crashing itself out'" in the poem's closing lines, poetic speech remembering and marking not just the history of the words it uses, but the origin of the world as well. As Moore puts it in "Bowls," published five months later:

> Renouncing a policy of boorish indifference
> to everything that has been said since the days of Matilda,
> I shall purchase an Etymological Dictionary of Modern English
> that I may understand what is written . . . [44]

Present utterance—"Modern English"—is the bearer of the past—of "Etymology"; quotation has become the form of the "historical sense"; and Moore now speaks *for* experience, not against it.

Like vision, then, what I have called ordinary seeing is also a kind of reading. It is reading that preserves a "boorish indifference" to the past, reading "with a perfect contempt" for the history of "what is written"; and any writing which may be produced by such readers will be like the work "anatomize[d]" in the first thirty-six lines of "Novices"—inevitably and fatally "averse to the antique." Moore's stance in "Novices," then, is diametrically opposed to the one worked out with such passionate care in poems like "Roses Only" and "Black Earth."

Accordingly, "Novices" relies more heavily on quotation than any previous poem of Moore's, and Moore works as never before to educate the reader's attention (by concentrating explicitly on awareness of "the right word," for example) so that we may save ourselves from the fatal consequences of indifference and ignorance. Quotations characterize the novices and define the poet's stance, both directly and by implication; they create a distance, a kind of safety zone, between us and the novices so that we can witness what happens to them without suffering the disaster ourselves. "'We know so much more than they did,'" wrote Eliot, mockingly anticipating objections to his emphasis on the writers of the past: "Precisely, and they are that which we know."[45] The quotations which help us to see what the novices cannot see—that they are familiar types—emphasize that in their self-absorption they are as inaccessible to experience as Bluebeard in his tower, and that inaccessibility is precisely what makes them so vulnerable.

They are also dangerous, however: the novices share not only Bluebeard's remoteness, but also his murderous interest in women. They write "the sort of thing that would in their judgment interest a lady," and their success depends entirely upon their ability to create a "style" or a "setting" to which the "lady" whom they hope to "interest" will accommodate herself "at the touch of a hand." Their work is full of "acacia-like ladies disappearing into "dungeon[s]" disguised as opulent homes.

Of course it is Moore's own work that supplies this particular disappearing lady: the novices' attempts to "interest a lady" thus reflect unflatteringly on Moore's efforts to generate interest in her own work, once more raising the fear that the engagement in "commerce" may come to no more than a scheme to derive profit from flattery. And yet it is precisely the novices' efforts to convince us of their harmlessness that arouse suspicion and make their ignorance so dangerous: the novices "present themselves as a contrast to seaserpented regions 'unlit by the half-lights of more conscious art'"; but for all their self-consciousness, they remain unconscious that they themselves are "Dracontine cockatrices, 'perfect and poisonous from the beginning.'" They are embryonic and deadly versions of the dragon whose image Moore had borrowed from *The Greek Anthology* to discover, in "In the Days of Prismatic Colour," that the monstrous "complexity" of her own verse had carried her far from "Truth": "'part of it was crawling, part of it / was about to crawl, the rest / was torpid in its lair.'"

The novices hold up a mirror to the poet: "the counterpart to what we are," they duplicate and complement her work. In rejecting their claims to "wisdom," then—"What an idea!"—Moore is also repudiating her own past. (Compare the draconian revisions of "Poetry," discussed in chapter 1, and the exclusion from later collections of "Roses Only" and "Black Earth.") Consciously risking both the poem's coherence and the credibility of her attack on the novices' craftsmanship, Moore brings "Novices" to a close with a stunning arrangement of quotations which constitutes a series of reflections on the relationship of her own work to "the antique," and affirms her dedication to vision. As in Augustan satire, these reflections create a mirror which simultaneously reflects an ideal and shows the reader to himself as a distorted image of that ideal. The novices, however, are "deaf to satire" and of course cannot be expected to recognize their "interest" in attending closely to what is said of them. In the words of "Picking and Choosing," the novices are not "afraid of literature" at all; on the contrary, because they approach it "too familiarly," and because Moore identifies herself closely with them, "the situation is irremediable." They have to be destroyed.

But in this miniature (and very polite) *Dunciad*, fools are allowed the dubious privilege of destroying themselves. The novices are so "Accustomed to the recurring phosphorescence of antiquity" that they give it no thought, but embark without even noticing that they are at sea—and so without realizing, either, that their actions recall "the lucid movements of the royal yacht upon the learned scenery of Egypt." Like the "king, steward, and harper seated amidships while the jade and the rock crystal course about in solution," they believe that conditions are stable and that their own positions are secure; but they are only oblivious to their surroundings—how can they know, with their aversion to the antique, what happened when Pharaoh ventured rashly into the sea? They are "blind to the right word," and when, like the royal yacht, "their suavity surmounts the surf," they fail to see "the transparent equation" of "the surf" with the apocalyptic visions of "Isaiah, Jeremiah, Ezekiel, Daniel." Indeed, like the king and his attendants, they see nothing at all, for they are

> bored by "the detailless perspective of the sea," reiterative and naive,
> and its chaos of rocks, the stuffy remarks of the Hebrews . . .

They have been warned twice now—first by "the transparent equation" of the surf and the prophets, and again by the equally transparent linkage of "the stuffy remarks of the Hebrews" with the "chaos of rocks" of which they are about to run afoul. For suddenly, their position is terribly precarious: they and their "royal yacht"—the "suavity" which has brought them so far—are poised at the crest of a huge wave, and when the wave breaks the novices and their shoddy craft are drowned by an accumulation of precisely such details as they have been too "bored" to see.

And when the poet ceases to speak for herself and gives the poem over to the words of others, the wave of speech—in the past so often associated with darkness and, even at its most transparent, in "A Graveyard," with deceit—is no longer "at the antipodes from the init- / ial great truths." For the wave whose breaking brings the poem to its resounding conclusion is "'split like a glass against a wall'" and reconstituted as light. The poem is "'swallowed up'" not by the "opaqueness" which had threatened the poet in "Sojourn in the Whale," but by the "'molten fires'" it has *itself* "'swallowed up,'" by "submerged shafts of the / sun" brought up to the surface to destroy those whose "boorish indifference" to the means and ends of their art makes them irredeemable—and to assert the persistence of an older, more "fundamental" order. This "drama of water against rocks" takes place in an "'ocean of hurrying consonants,'" a sea composed largely of language *about* language—much of it specifically about that biblical Hebrew which to them had seemed "stuffy" and dull, as "reiterative and naive" as "'the detailless perspective of the sea.'"

Of the eight marked quotations in the final thirteen lines of the poem (there are two unmarked ones), five are taken either from A.R. Gordon's *Poets of the Old Testament* or from George Adam Smith's commentary on the book of Isaiah in *The Expositor's Bible*.[46] Each phrase quoted from these sources reflects its author's commitment to the exposition of divine truth; and Moore takes up her new novitiate not only by reconsecrating their words to a vision of that truth, but also by converting the words of secular authors (Boccaccio, Flaubert, Leigh Hunt) to the same end.[47]

In so doing she relies most heavily on Smith's account of Isaiah 17:12–13:

> The phonetics of the passage are wonderful. The general impression is that of a stormy ocean booming in to the shore and then crashing itself out into one long hiss of spray and foam upon its barriers. The details are noteworthy. In ver. 12 we have thirteen heavy M-sounds, besides two heavy B's, to five N's, five H's, and four sibilants. But in ver. 13 the sibilants predominate; and before the sharp rebuke of the Lord the great, booming sound of ver. 12 scatters out into a long *yish-sha 'oon*. The occasional use of a prolonged vowel amid so many hurrying

consonants produces exactly the effect of the lift of a storm swell out at sea and now the pause of a great wave before it crashes on the shore.[48]

This passage supplies far more than a few quotable phrases. Indeed, it provides the model upon which the conclusion of "Novices" is based. The poem moves with assurance and apparent calm for the first thirty-six lines; but as the poet's anger builds to and then passes the breaking-point, the relatively "lucid movements" of the verse are shattered into confusion. Along with the far flimsier craft of the novices, and with a deliberateness of which they are incapable and for reasons they could never fathom, the poem allows itself to be "'split like a glass against a wall'" in the sudden irruption of *ss*, *ts*, *ps*, *shs*, double-*ss*, *gs*, *ks*, and hard *cs* which compose "this 'ocean of hurrying consonants.'" To use Smith's words, in the closing lines "the occasional use of a prolonged vowel amid so many hurrying consonants" contributes to the effect of a momentary lull in the storm's fury. When the novices are "obscured by fathomless suggestions of colour," for instance, the long *u*, the broad *a*, the rounding of the final *o* in *colour*, make the line sound more gently, heightening the effect of a sudden stillness in which the eye looks down for a brief instant into "fathomless suggestions of colour." Those "suggestions" resolve themselves in the harsh sibilants and percussive consonants of the next line into "incessantly panting lines of green, white with concussion," which resume the frenetic pounding of the surf

with its "great livid stains like long slabs of green marble,"
its "flashing lances of perpendicular lightning" and "molten fires swallowed up,"
"with foam on its barriers,"
"crashing itself out in one long hiss of spray."

At first the proliferation of *ls* mingling with harsher sounds makes it seem that the sea is suspended between liquid and solid; then the water liquefies in an even greater profusion of *ls* and immediately boils up in the heat of the "'molten fires'" it has "'swallowed up.'" But in the penultimate line the long diphthong holds the wave "in its essential perpendicularity"[49] so that we may see it rising "'with foam on its barriers,'" creating the effect of "the pause of a great wave before it crashes on the shore." When the wave finally breaks, "the sibilants predominate" as Smith says they do in Isaiah 17:13, so that the final line is filled with the reverberation of the sea "'crashing itself out in one long hiss of spray.'" Thus, in splitting the poem "'like a glass against a wall,'" Moore composes an elaborate and difficult homage to the prophet Isaiah, by arranging her quotations in such a way that they complete the very sentence they interrupt while conforming in their rhythmic progression to Smith's analysis of Isaiah's language.

Smith's words, like those of the other writers she quotes and those of the writers to whom she alludes, are fragments mirroring a greater design for which none of them is responsible and *to* which all of them *are* or must be made responsible. Rearranging Smith's language to make it enact what it describes, Moore honors him for providing access to that greater design, that fundamental structure—for treating his description as prescriptive has enabled her not only to "quote" Isaiah's rhythm but to answer Eliot as well. Moore imitates the compositional methods of *The Waste Land* in order to reconcile the theoretical and practical aspects of Eliot's work; in turn, that reconciliation permits her to approximate the conditions laid down in Smith's analysis of Isaiah and so to fulfill the conditions of Isaiah's prophecy. The prophet exerts a prior claim, and Smith's analysis constitutes the "expediency" which "determines the form" not only of Moore's attempt to come to terms with Eliot, but also of her far more ambitious effort to establish a typological basis for relations between herself, her contemporaries, and their respective predecessors, both immediate and remote.

We have already had occasion to note Moore's displeasure with Eliot's treatment of Swinburne in *The Sacred Wood*. She acknowledges Eliot's superiority as a critic, but she also insists on Swinburne's priority, pointedly remarking that Eliot's treatment of the past "recalls Swinburne's comment" that "'Art knows nothing of death . . . those themes only are dead which never were other than dead. No form is obsolete, no subject out of date, if the right man be there to rehandle it.'" Eliot had been careful to distance himself from Swinburne, but Moore is equally careful in forging a link between them, in effect casting the older poet as the type to the younger's antitype. That relation holds for "Novices" as well.

In the last thirteen lines of "Novices" there is one (and only one) quotation that Moore never acknowledged as such, and that quotation comes from Swinburne's correspondence: "incessantly panting lines of green, white with concussion. . . . "[50] The words are Swinburne's, but the line presses back against Eliot's objection to the "morbidity" of Swinburne's poetic language, its habit of making objects "disappear."[51] He writes in "Swinburne as Poet" that "Language in its healthy state presents the object, is so close to the object that the two are identified"; but he goes on to say that "They are identified in Swinburne's verse solely because the object has ceased to exist."[52] Indirectly at first, Moore rejects this argument, writing that "in [Swinburne's] verse . . . 'you feel the sea in the air at every step'"; then she takes Eliot on more directly:

> As for "the word," however, invariably used by [Swinburne] as a substitute for "the object," is it always so used? "When you take to pieces any verse of Swinburne," says Mr Eliot, "you find always that the object was not there—only the word." What of
>
> "The sea slow rising
> . . . .
> the rocks that shrink,
> the fair brave trees with all their
> flowers at play?"[53]

It does not matter that Moore's question hardly constitutes a crushing reply to Eliot's objection; what matters is the use she makes of Swinburne's words in "Novices." She quotes from Swinburne's prose, not his verse —but it would be a mistake to see this as a concession to Eliot. She uses Swinburne's words, in the context of the poem, precisely to make an object "disappear"—but, operating on the principle that in Swinburne's case as in Hardy's, "to consider separately his prose and his verse is to lose his essential quality,"[54] she does so precisely to affirm the "healthy state" of Swinburne's language, not to deny it. That affirmation is implicit in her turning this bit of casual prose to the high purposes of her poem, employing it not just to pulverize the novices (they are the unhealthy ones, the true objects of her wrath) but also to build up the verbal and visual specificity of "this 'ocean of hurrying consonants'" and, by expanding the temporal range of reference, to persuade us of the continuing power and presence of the transcendent object with which her sea of borrowed language is so closely "identified."

Another correspondence—Flaubert's—stains the sea "with its 'great livid stains like long slabs of green marble'" to impress upon us the urgency of the search for *le mot juste*, "the right word."[55] This phrase, too, works typologically, reminding us of *il miglior fabbro*—Ezra Pound, to whom Eliot dedicates *The Waste Land*, and whose cast-off persona, Hugh Selwyn Mauberley, had taken Flaubert for "His true Penelope . . . ."[56] Moore could not have known, of course, how much of a hand Pound had had in creating *The Waste Land* she read; but she did not need to know that in order to grasp the implication of Eliot's dedicatory phrase—that he and Pound are not the "separable units" she had deprecated in "People's Surroundings" less than a year earlier. They are rather, as "Novices" recognizes, collaborators in a collective enterprise, dedicated, like Moore herself, to the revelation of "the fundamental structure."

Together with the older writers who speak for them, they constitute the new community which Moore envisions in the closing lines. These writers form a second group of novices, who stand in typological relation to the drowned young men. Believing that "Because one expresses oneself and entitles it wisdom, one is not a fool," the hack-writers of the first novitiate prove their folly by showing off their work, taking out copyright "according to the Act of Congress . . . and all the rest of it." The new dispensation which emerges in the final thirteen lines of the poem, however, is one in which individual claims to authorship are honored (by quotation marks in the poem, and by the notes Moore appends to each collection of her work) but at the same time subordinated to a larger purpose: the fulfillment of the writer's promise to deliver "wisdom." This fulfillment is accomplished by the smashing of self-proclaimed idols, by a return from the idolatry of the "letter"—the hacks are "curious to know if we do not *adore* each letter of the alphabet" (emphasis added)—to the proper veneration of the spirit: not "a word" but "the *right* word."

The word is Isaiah's, and it is the spirit of his prophecy that the novices violate:

> At that day shall a man look to his Maker. And his eyes shall have respect to the Holy One of Israel. *And he shall not look to the altars, the work of his hands, neither shall respect that which his fingers have made.* (Isaiah 17:7–8 emphasis added.)

Moore's use of borrowed language, then, is in effect mandated by Isaiah himself: to use her own words would be to make too much of her own handiwork. In this sense, she may be compared with George Herbert: the supreme challenge to Herbert's faith and art is in the attempt to compose a poem which can be completed only by the direct intervention of God, without implying that his own skill as poet and rhetorician can in any way be credited with having brought that intervention about (for such a suggestion necessarily presumes man capable of forcing God to act, thereby denying God's absolute supremacy). Similarly, though on a smaller scale, "Novices" implies that the most rigorous test of the artist's worthiness is to be found not in her ability to establish and preserve the absolute uniqueness of her work, but rather in her capacity to recognize and yield to a force superior to her own.

It might seem, though, that Moore is tempting herself by imitating Isaiah's rhythm—for to replicate his rhythmic effects without the resources of the language that produced them is a far more difficult achievement, from a purely technical standpoint, than direct quotation could possibly be. Indeed, Ezra Pound had suggested ten years earlier that such a replication would be impossible, arguing that "That part of your poetry which strikes upon the imaginative *eye* of the reader will lose nothing by translation into a foreign tongue; that which appeals to the ear can reach only those who take it in the original."[57] Pound implies here that aural effects are specific to particular languages, and therefore not susceptible to translation; but to lose them—and especially to lose rhythm—is to lose a very great deal, for inevitably the poet's rhythm is idiosyncratic, interpreting him and his emotions. "A man's rhythm," wrote Pound in his "Credo," "must be interpretative, it will be, therefore, in the end, his own, uncounterfeiting, uncounterfeitable."[58]

But even as early as 1916, Moore was writing of the ease of "counterfeiting." Her first published essay, "The Accented Syllable," begins by arguing that the skilled writer, working syllable by syllable to make her meaning unmistakable, simultaneously marks her writing indelibly as her own by establishing a "tone of voice," which Moore defines as "that intonation in which the accents . . . responsible for it are so unequivocal as to persist, no matter under what circumstances the syllables are read or by whom they are read."[59] It is not long, however, before she reveals the uneasy awareness that is at the heart of her deliberate effort to establish her own voice through the medium of syllabic verse: "It is true," she notes, "that a distinctive tone of voice employed by one author may resemble that same tone of voice as employed by another author."[60]

Up to this point the essay has concentrated on prose, the principal figures being Poe and Samuel Butler. It is when Moore turns her attention to verse that the implicit justification of her own poetic practice emerges. For in "Rhymed verse" (and it is clear by her examples that she means conventionally *accentual* verse) she says that "a distinctive tone of voice depends on naturalistic effects"; and if, as she immediately goes on to say, "naturalistic effects are so rare in rhyme as almost not to exist,"[61] then it follows that "rhymed verse" must be inadequate as a means of establishing "a distinctive tone of voice." But "free verse" is no better, since Moore sees free verse as tending almost automatically toward the *mimetic*: "So far as free verse is concerned, it is the easiest thing in the world to create one intonation in the image of another until finally one has assembled a bouquet of vocal exclamation points"—a form of punctuation that rarely appears in Moore's early syllabic poems.[62]

We shall see in chapter 7 that an attempt "to create one intonation in the image of another" is central to Moore's purposes in several of the major *syllabic* poems of the mid-1930s, most notably "Virginia Britannia" and "Bird-Witted"; but for the time being our concern is with the mimetic tendencies of her free-verse poems. Those tendencies run away with "the acacia-like lady" of "People's Surroundings," landing her in fatal difficulties, but under the stricter discipline of "Novices" they are the poet's means to salvation. Considering Moore's focus on Poe (who figures prominently in "The Accented Syllable"), she must have been aware of his claim, in "The Philosophy of Composition," to having arrived at the famous refrain of "The Raven" only after he had determined which *sounds* would best suit his purposes—thereby implying that those sounds have an affective force which is virtually independent of semantic considerations.[63] It is hardly surprising, therefore, that Moore—whose training in the biology laboratories at Bryn Mawr would have stressed repeatability as an essential feature of experimental design—should have understood Smith's analysis of Isaiah as implying a repeatable procedure by which she could "approximate the original rhythms" of Isaiah, just as, in translating La Fontaine much later on (1954), she would attempt "to approximate the original rhythms of the Fables."[64]

But Moore accepts this technical challenge only in pursuit of larger aims. The closing lines of "Novices" effect what we have seen Moore trying to avoid in every case: the loss of her "style," of that "distinctive tone of voice" created first in the syllabic poems of the previous decade and maintained with increasing difficulty against an "accessibility to experience" brought on by her own abandonment of protective form. In submitting herself to the discipline of deliberate imitation, however, and in deliberately restraining her own voice to so great an extent, Moore signifies that she is not merely *losing* her style: rather, she is actively "renouncing" it. This is of course no simple matter: if "the rhythm is the person" (as Moore wrote in 1938, restating principles first articulated in "The Accented Syllable"), then the "restraint" which permits the accession of another rhythm demands the surrender of the very self.

V

In "Silence" (October 1924), the celebratory restraint of "Novices" becomes a trickier, more critical posture.[65] Taking stock of her situation as a woman in what "Marriage" calls "this common world"—a world where "men have power / and sometimes one is made to feel it" in the ungentle touch of "the spiked hand / that has an affection for one / and proves it to the bone"—Moore discovers that what men want most from women is silence. As Adam says to Eve about two-thirds of the way through "Marriage": "The fact of woman / is 'not the sound of the flute / but very poison'"—a remark Moore glosses with a note about "Silence on the part of women—'to an Oriental this is as poetry set to music.' . . ."[66]

In "Silence," however, it is not the "unfathered" husband who prohibits speech, as it is in "Marriage": it is the "father" himself who lays down the law. And there is no arguing with him as Eve argues with Adam throughout "Marriage." Thus Moore uses silence itself with "criminal ingenuity," to circumvent the father's authority and appropriate it to herself.

The first voice we hear in "Silence" is the poet's, but she quickly yields the floor:

> My father used to say,
> "Superior people never make long visits,
> have to be shown Longfellow's grave
> nor the glass flowers at Harvard . . ."

This opening sentence is much less straightforward than it looks. The anecdote it seems to be setting up never materializes: what follows is not a story but a monologue spoken by the "father." His speech thus becomes the focal point of the poem, but this is no simple matter, either, for Moore never knew her father. The "father" to whom all but three of the poem's phrases are ascribed is a borrowing from the conversation, and indeed from the life, of another woman. He is the father of a Miss A.M. Homans, professor emeritus of hygiene at Wellesley College, who quoted his remarks.[67]

Moore is a Midwesterner by birth and a New Yorker by choice; but in adopting Miss Homans' father she proclaims herself the spiritual legatee of the New England tradition for which he evidently speaks. She thus demonstrates the extent to which she shares Eliot's conviction that "Tradition cannot be inherited, and if you want it you must obtain it by great labour." But what we see in "Silence" is the self-conscious application of this principle to the specifically American tradition which, like James before him, Eliot had dismissed as too narrowly confined, just as he had dismissed America itself as fundamentally hostile to serious art. And it is within the acknowledged limits of that tradition that Moore seeks to demonstrate her superiority.

But Eliot's assertion is categorical, absolute: "Tradition cannot be inherited"; and Moore cannot take her place within the Emersonian tradition for granted. The burden of her "labour" in "Silence," then, is precisely to *take* her place, to legitimize her claim by establishing her superiority within the terms defined by the "father"—a "great labour," moreover, because the "father" is not at all accommodating. The poet is not a resident of New England but a visitor, a tourist; and since "'Superior people never make long visits'" and never ask for guidance, she must work quickly and alone. The father does not and will not volunteer his services: indeed, he says that visitors should be "'Self reliant like the cat— / that takes its prey to privacy, / the mouse's limp tail hanging like a shoelace from its mouth. . . .'" The extravagant simile betrays the father into his visitor's hands, however. In quoting him, the poet turns the tables on him: playing "cat" to his "mouse," she takes him at and in his word, and so lays violent claim to the Emersonian principle on which his own presumption of superiority is founded.

Here, as in "Roses Only," Moore adopts an Emersonian posture, but she does so far more openly and, unlike the "self-dependent" poet of the earlier work, she is concerned neither to inhibit her own "predatory" tendencies nor to "repel influences." On the contrary: if to be "'Self reliant like the cat'" is to take one's "'prey to privacy,'" so, according to Eliot, "to be influenced by a writer is . . . to take what one wants." The self-reliant, catlike poet of "Silence" "'takes [her] prey to privacy'" not because she fears detection—for, like the cat Peter, she has become "one of those who do not regard / the published fact as a surrender"[68]—but rather because both cats and superior people "'sometimes enjoy solitude,'" as the father says. Betraying both the success of the hunt and the partial ingestion of the prey, "'the mouse's limp tail hanging like a shoelace'" from the cat's mouth allows us to identify the sort of creature she has pounced upon—just as quotation marks publish the fact that the poet has not quite swallowed everything she has found, and help us to determine what she has taken in by marking its boundaries.

While "the published fact" is not in itself "a surrender," it does indicate that a certain "surrender"—albeit a partial one—has indeed taken place. For at the heart of "Silence," "Self-Reliance" shades into "Tradition and the Individual Talent": in that "'solitude'" to which those who are "'Self reliant like the cat'" take what they have seized, they fall victim to their own erstwhile prey and are "'robbed of speech / by speech which has delighted them. . . .'" Just as the cat with a mouse in its craw can do nothing else until it has finished eating, so the poet with a quotation on her lips can say nothing of her own accord until she reaches the end of the phrase she has appropriated—or, to put the matter more broadly, until she discovers the limits of the tradition she has tried to apprehend in its wholeness. This is the other side of superiority as "Silence" defines it: here as in "Novices," Moore accepts Eliot's contention that the highest artistry is that which recognizes and is prepared to yield to "something which is more valuable" than "the poet as [s]he is at the moment." But Moore makes an ironic reservation, or rather revision: that to "obtain" a tradition "by great labour," as Eliot decrees—to adopt a "father"—is to be "robbed" by that "father," that tradition, of one's own capacity for speech.

But even as it limits speech—indeed threatens to choke it off altogether—the voice of the poet's chosen "father," of her elected tradition, grants a (limited) reprieve. The father seems to sign poetry's death warrant when he insists that "the deepest feeling always shows itself in silence," for on this principle the poem, or any utterance for that matter, would have to lapse into silence precisely as it reached its emotional peak. But when he concedes that "the deepest feeling always shows itself . . . not in silence, but restraint," he gives individual talent a little room in which to show itself as well. Tradition sets an a priori limit upon the self and its expression, but it may also work to enable expression. As Eliot puts it, "the best and *most individual* parts of [a poet's] work may be those in which his dead ancestors assert their immortality most vigorously."[69]

But in "Silence" Moore allows her dead ancestor to assert his immortality just long enough to snare him in the straitjacket of his own principles. For once he has defined the limits of expression, the "father" has little choice but to stay within those limits; accordingly, he must bring his remarks to a close. In doing so, however, he renders himself helpless, for it is only in the exercise of "'restraint,'" and "'not in silence,'" that the depth of his "'feeling'" can "'show itself.'" His mere silence is insufficient testimony to the firmness of his belief, therefore, and the poet does not allow it to stand. Instead, seizing the opportunity to demonstrate her own restraint once more, in the penultimate line she affirms for him what it would not otherwise have occurred to us to doubt—his commitment to what he has been saying. But she goes farther than that: as if in all innocence she were afraid we might miss his point, she offers another of his apothegms as a kind of summation: "Nor was he insincere in saying, 'Make my house your inn.'"

The exquisite irony is that the father cannot make himself clear without the aid of those visitors whom he has disdained to assist. It is the poet who transmutes his "'silence'" into "'restraint,'" after all—and it *is* restraint precisely because the father is *quoting* here, as the poet has been doing all along: the phrase comes from James Prior's life of Edmund Burke.[70] But in grasping after Burke's words as a cat pounces on a mouse—to feed his hunger—the father himself becomes a visitor in a house even narrower than his own. Accepting Burke's invitation, he must also pay the price of relinquishing his own speech to a spokesman for the tradition from which he has tried to liberate himself. As the poet wryly declares in the double-edged closing line, "Inns are not residences."

Thus Moore establishes her superiority by doing what Miss Homans—the source of the remark from which "Silence" unfolds—will not do. A woman much older than Moore herself, Miss Homans stands so completely within the tradition from which her father speaks that, like the neighbor of another poet who took New England for his adopted home, she "will not go behind [her] father's saying," will not ask *why* "'Superior people never make long visits.'"[71] She has no need to ask such questions: her father's reasons are her reasons, too.

Like Frost, however, Moore *must* "go behind" what the father says, and for the same reason: to learn what her adopted tradition entails. Just as it is Frost who "let[s his] neighbor know" when it is time to start rebuilding the wall that separates their properties, so it is Moore who in "Silence" initiates the process by which the boundaries of home are redefined: not the male ritual of "Mending Wall," but the female ritual of visiting. Thus, like Frost, she proves her knowledge of what the tradition requires. But if she knows her way around like a native, she knows, too, that the home of Emerson and Thoreau—and Frost—is a male enclave, and that to accept unreservedly the tradition to which its landmarks point is, therefore, to marry oneself to the male dead. "Longfellow's grave" is no place for a living woman poet, nor are "the glass flowers at Harvard"—so strikingly reminiscent of what "People's Surroundings" dismissively calls "landscape gardening twisted into permanence"—the vital signs of flourishing life. Because the tradition is moribund, the father must hark back to Burke and the English past to help out his American inarticulateness—must acknowledge that his house is not, after all, entirely his own. Or rather, since he will not acknowledge it for himself, the poet must do it for him as, in the final couplet of this free-verse sonnet, she does it for herself: if the father is not "insincere in saying, 'Make my house your inn,'" neither is *she* "insincere" in affirming that "Inns are not residences."

But it is precisely by virtue of that acknowledgment that Moore gains her ascendancy. In "Silence," as in "Roses Only," "spiritual facts" have a "native superiority" to such "material facts" as one's place of birth or residence, and it is in recognizing herself as "a citizen of somewhere else" (in Hawthorne's phrase)[72] that Moore situates herself most decisively within the tradition she has elected.

5

Approximating Paradise: "An Octopus" and the Discovery of America

I

Near the end of his essay "The Poet," Emerson catalogued some of the features of American life which had yet to be transmuted into art. "Our log-rolling, our stumps and their politics, our fisheries, our Negroes and Indians, our boasts and our repudiations, the wrath of rogues and the pusillanimity of honest men, the northern trade, the southern planting, the western clearing, Oregon and Texas, are yet unsung," he chanted, and then he announced the central project of American poetry: "Yet America is a poem in our eyes; its ample geography dazzles the imagination, and it will not wait long for metres."[1]

To write the poem of America, Emerson says, will require a "genius, with tyrannous eye," such as we have not yet had, for only such a genius knows "the value of our incomparable materials."[2] Insisting in "An Octopus" that "Bows, arrows, oars, and paddles for which trees provide the wood, / in new countries are more eloquent than elsewhere," Moore responds to Emerson's call by seeking to discover the transcendent significance of America itself in the "incomparable materials" of a specific American landscape.[3] The "ample" and complex "geography" of Mt. Rainier, which Moore calls "Big Snow Mountain" or "Mount Takoma," presents a real challenge to the poet's "tyrannous eye" and "Relentless accuracy." By the same token, the specifically American setting of "An Octopus" implies a challenge to Eliot's insistence on the primacy of the European literary tradition; in "An Octopus" Moore aligns herself not only with Emerson, but also with William Carlos Williams, who thought of Eliot as an archrival.

This is not to say, however, that Moore has turned completely away from Eliot. It is rather that the "great labour" of "Silence"—the effort to take over the stewardship of the American "inn" from the hapless "father"—has become a process of renovation. Moore seeks to expand the Emersonian tradition by bringing it into conjunction with its English parent-tradition; the meeting point is Paradise.

II

Comprehending "austere specimens of our American royal families" (these are fir trees) as well as "the original American 'menagerie of styles,'" "Maintaining many minds," the mountain ultimately becomes not only a synecdoche for America as a whole but also an image of America as Paradise. This is not, however, the "old celestial map" regained through the good offices of the unicorn in the closing lines of "Sea Unicorns and Land Unicorns."[4] As Patricia C. Willis explains in a recent essay, Paradise is the name of a meadow on Mt. Rainier, from which one gains access to the peak; Moore and her brother spent a night at the nearby Paradise Inn in July 1922.[5] Thus the Paradise of "An Octopus" is an ironic, entirely earthbound, and decidedly wintry place, recognizable as Paradise only by those who have learned to interpret those "odd oracles of cool official sarcasm," the manuals and brochures of the National Parks Service on which Moore relies heavily throughout the poem. For Paradise has become a

> . . . game preserve
> where "guns, nets, seines, traps, and explosives,
> hired vehicles, gambling, and intoxicants are prohibited,
> disobedient persons being summarily removed
> and not allowed to return without permission in writing."

According to Christian doctrine, of course, we are all of us "disobedient persons"; once we have learned to read "An Octopus," however, the poem itself becomes the "permission in writing" we need in order "to return." We come back, however, not as residents but as mere tourists, our right to stay contingent upon our continuing submission to the harsh, ascetic discipline which the mountain, like the poem, imposes. "It is self evident," Moore writes, "that one must do as one is told / and eat 'rice, prunes, dates, raisins, hardtack, and tomatoes' / if one would 'conquer the main peak' of Mount Takoma." But what is not so "self evident" is that in thinking of

Mount Takoma as something to "conquer," we misconstrue the nature of the place in which we find ourselves. Our failure to recognize the "official sarcasm" of the "oracle" arouses the mountain's fury:

> "Creeping slowly as with meditated stealth,
> its arms seeming to approach from all directions,"
> it receives one under winds that "tear the snow to bits
> and hurl it like a sandblast
> shearing off twigs and loose bark from the trees."

These "winds" drive us furiously back until, with the trees, we are " 'shrunk in trying to escape' / from the hard mountain 'planed by ice / and polished by the wind' "—but we are not permitted simply "to 'escape.' " Like Adam and Eve, we have proved ourselves unequal to the strain of obedience, and, having lacked the faith to do as we have been told, we must be expelled. Thus the closing lines eject us from the poem, and from

> . . . the white volcano with no weather side,
> the lightning flashing at its base,
> rain falling in the valleys, and snow falling on the peak—
> the glassy octopus symmetrically pointed,
> its claw cut by the avalanche
> "with a sound like the crack of a rifle,
> in a curtain of powdered snow launched like a waterfall."

The "glassy octopus" is not broken by "the avalanche" of our Fall, however. Its "claw" has been "cut," but we have been told already that "this fossil flower" remains "intact when it is cut": Paradise, unlike mere nature, is unaffected by the Fall.

According to Milton, when Eve "pluck'd" and "eat" the forbidden fruit, "Earth felt the wound, and Nature from her seat / Sighing through all her Works gave signs of woe, / That all was lost" (*Paradise Lost*, IX:781–84).[6] This occurs, however, well before the actual expulsion from the Garden in book XII, when Adam and Eve,

> . . . looking back, all th' Eastern side beheld
> Of Paradise, so late their happy seat,
> Wav'd over by that flaming Brand, the Gate
> With dreadful faces throng'd and fiery Arms . . . (XII:641–44)

So, too, in "An Octopus" Earth feels "the wound" of the Fall long before we are forced from the mountain:

Larkspur, blue pincushions, blue peas, and lupin;
white flowers with white, and red with red;
the blue ones "growing close together
so that patches of them look like blue water in the distance:"
this arrangement of colours
as in Persian designs of hard stones with enamel,
forms a pleasing equation—
a diamond outside; and inside, a white dot;
on the outside, a ruby; inside, a red dot;
black spots balanced with black
in the woodlands where fires have run over the ground. . . .

The "Persian designs" of this jeweled landscape recall a moment in "Marriage" when Adam is figured as "a crouching mythological monster / in [a] Persian miniature of emerald mines. . . . " This image in turn prepares the way for Adam to "become an idol," from which posture he is "impelled" to his Fall "by 'the illusion of a fire / effectual to extinguish fire.' . . . " There is a similar "illusion" here as well, though it is produced in this case by "patches" of blue flowers growing so "close togther" that they "look like blue water in the distance." And so the implication of the passage as a whole seems clear: the "fires" which "have run over the ground" of "An Octopus" are the fires of human passion. Ungoverned as they are, those passions, and the scorched earth they leave behind, are at the same time essential, for without them "this arrangement of colours" would be incomplete; like the Fall itself, they are part of the poem's artful "designs."

As in *Paradise Lost*, then, the Fall is foreknown (indeed, from the poet's perspective, it has already happened); but it is nonetheless *our* Fall. It results not from a failure of rhetorical control, as in "Marriage," where Adam is borne to disaster by the "industrious waterfall" of his own eloquence, but rather from a failure of *vision*, a failure to heed or even to recognize the warning signs we are given along the way. The scars of old "fires" and the far more explicit signs "which stipulate 'names and addresses of persons to notify / in case of disaster'" are by no means the only warnings we get. There is a more direct prefiguring of the Fall quite early in the poem, when we come upon the first waterfall. This one is composed of water, not snow; but like the blue flowers, it, too, is involved in an illusion, for what we see is a "waterfall which never seems to fall— / an endless skein swayed by the wind, / immune to force of gravity in the perspective of the peaks." Like the mountain itself, though, the "perspective of the peaks" is "Deceptively reserved and flat": however it may appear, that waterfall is no more "immune to force of gravity" than we are, than Adam is. We are reminded late in the poem that Adam once had "such power" to name things correctly as "we are still devoid of," but that was before his rhetoric had become (in "Marriage") "the industrious waterfall" that bore him so "violently" toward the greater Fall which was "Man's First Disobedience (*Paradise Lost*, I:1).

Our failure of vision is so nearly complete that we do not see where our route might have taken us until it is much too late to do anything about it. A little more than a third of the way through the poem, we are shown "the road 'climbing like the thread / which forms the groove around a snail-shell, / doubling back and forth until where snow begins, it ends.'" This serpentine road is "superintend[ed]" by "the eleven eagles of the west," tutelary spirits "Perched" atop the very signs that tell us whom "'to notify / in case of disaster.'" "They make a nice appearance, don't they," the poem asks sardonically, "happy seeing nothing?" But it is we who are so "happy seeing nothing," who fail to recognize how closely this road, in "doubling back and forth," resembles Donne's description, in the "Satyre: Of Religion," of the way to Truth. "On a huge hill," Donne writes,

> Cragged and steep, Truth stands, and hee that will
> Reach her, about must, and about must goe;
> And what the hills suddennes resists, winne so;
> Yet strive so, that before age, deaths twilight,
> Thy Soule rest, for none can work in that night.[7]

Though the road takes us "about . . . and about" as we make our way through "An Octopus," we never "will / Reach" Truth: we are told early in the poem that progress itself, like the "waterfall which never seems to fall," is an illusion. "Completing a circle," Moore writes, "you have been deceived into thinking you have progressed. . . ." And indeed the poem *does* describe "a circle": like the road, "it ends" "where snow begins"—ends, as we have already seen, "'in a curtain of powdered snow launched like a waterfall.'" We have managed simply to repeat the Fall.

III

As at the end of Poe's *Narrative of Arthur Gordon Pym*,[8] we are faced at the end of "An Octopus" with a "curtain" of white, through which we pass helplessly into terrible knowledge—the knowledge, in this case, that we are "being summarily removed" from the strange Paradise of the poem and returned to an America with which we had thought ourselves familiar and of which we are no longer quite so certain. However, we are not so much like Pym voyaging into the absolute unknown as we are like Prince Amerigo, of James's *The Golden Bowl.* Amerigo, an Italian prince descended from an ancient family with a wicked past, is betrothed to Maggie Verver, the daughter of a fabulously wealthy man named Adam Verver—another American Adam—who has come to Europe in search of art treasures for the museum he plans to build in his hometown, American City. Verver, like the sea in "A Graveyard," is "a collector," and indeed his daughter tells the prince early on that the two of them have been acting "like a pair of pirates—positively stage pirates, the sort who wink at each other and say 'Ha-ha!' when they come to where their treasure is buried." She even tells him, in almost the same breath, that *he* is part of her father's collection.[9] It is with all this in mind that the prince, walking around London to kill time before dining with the Ververs, contemplates the prospect of entering permanently into relation with them, and as he does so he remembers

> to have read, as a boy, a wonderful tale by Allan Poe, his prospective wife's countryman—which was a thing to show, by the way, what imagination Americans *could* have: the story of the shipwrecked Gordon Pym, who, drifting in a small boat further toward the North Pole—or was it the South?—than anyone had ever done, found at a given moment before him a thickness of white air that was like a dazzling curtain of light, concealing as darkness conceals, yet of the colour of milk or of snow. There were moments when he felt his own boat move upon some such mystery. The state of mind of his new friends . . . had resemblances to a great white curtain.[10]

What so bewilders the prince, what makes his "boat" seem to "move upon" a "mystery," is precisely the Ververs' wonderful American innocence—in the face of which his own European knowingness becomes a kind of ignorance. Moreover, his ignorance is the reader's as well: it is essential to James's narrative method that we should be limited, in the first half of the novel, almost entirely to what the prince is able to "make out" for himself, just as in the second half we are restricted to the "register" of Maggie Verver's consciousness.[11] As readers, therefore, we know at any given point only what the registering consciousness knows, see only what that consciousness sees; and there is so much detail, such a wealth of observation, that often we do not realize how little our knowledge really amounts to.

Near the end of "An Octopus" we learn that the mountain has been "damned for its sacrosanct remoteness— / like Henry James 'damned by the public for decorum'; / not decorum, but restraint." Thus reading "An Octopus" is something like reading *The Golden Bowl*: just as James confines us within the limits of the prince's awareness, or the princess's, so Moore confines us within a perspective which is far too limited to comprehend the full significance of the scene it presents in such profuse detail. It is not until the very end of the poem—not until we have been "summarily removed" from it by "the avalanche," in fact—that we realize we have been in Paradise.

The Golden Bowl, however, will not take us all the way. The narrative "restraint" which James exercises in limiting himself to "the consciousness of but two" of his characters, produces what Moore implicitly characterizes as an effect of "neatness" with which the effect of "An Octopus" is very much at odds. The "public," "wor[n] out" by the strain "of doing hard things," is "out of sympathy with neatness," and, for very different reasons, the poet herself finds it both problematic and dangerous. "Neatness of finish! Neatness of finish!" she exclaims immediately after comparing "Mount Takoma" to Henry James, as if to say, "The horror! The horror!" For even as she celebrates that Jamesian "Neatness of finish" she disavows it, implying that the methods by which it has been achieved are at worst unsound, like Kurtz's, or at best incomplete. The exclamation itself, as Laurence Stapleton has pointed out, directs us to a passage near the end of Williams's *Kora in Hell*, which Moore had reviewed in 1921.[12] Mocking the notion that "a work of art" is something to be neatly "wrapped" and packaged, Williams writes:

> Neatness and finish; the dust out of every corner! You swish from room to room and find all perfect. The house may now be carefully wrapped in brown paper and sent to a publisher. It is a work of art. You look rather askance at me. Do not believe I cannot guess your mind, yet I have my studies. You see, when the wheel's just at the up turn it glimpses horizon, zenith, all in a burst, the pull of the earth shaken off, a scatter of fragments, significance in a burst of water striking up from the base of a fountain. Then at the sickening turn toward death the pieces are joined into a pretty thing, a bouquet frozen in an ice-cake. *This* is art, *mon cher*, a thing to carry up with you on the next turn. . . .[13]

"An Octopus / of ice," Moore's poem begins; again, it is only at the very end of the poem, when it has taken what Williams calls here "the sickening turn toward death" and we have begun to Fall, that "the pieces are joined into a pretty thing" which reveals that we have been in Paradise.

The problem with James's sort of "neatness," Moore seems to imply, is not that it is too "hard" a "thing" to pull off, but (astoundingly) that it is too *easy*. We have been told by the time the poem comes to James that

> The Greeks liked smoothness, distrusting what was back
> of what could not be clearly seen,
> resolving with benevolent conclusiveness,
> "complexities which will remain complexities
> as long as the world lasts";
> ascribing what we clumsily call happiness,
> to "an accident or a quality,
> a spiritual substance or the soul itself,
> an act or a disposition or a habit
> or a habit infused to which the soul has been persuaded,
> or something distinct from a habit, a power—"
> such power as Adam had and we are still devoid of.

So much for "Neatness of finish!" The poet's impatient, sardonic interruption neatly finishes off the increasingly desperate eloquence of Richard Baxter, who—having been pressed into service in an effort to attach a more precise name to whatever it was that produced for the Greeks "what we clumsily call happiness"—is made to demonstrate all too neatly the sort of mess we get into without "such power as Adam had." The interruption says all that need be said about the nature of that "power," while it allows the poet to acknowledge that she, too, suffers the lack of "power" to give things their proper names.

"Neatness of finish," then, is like the "smoothness" of which the Greeks were so fond; indeed, it is like Greek itself, "'that pride-producing language'" whose speakers are "'Like happy souls in Hell'"—persuaded that they can resolve the unresolvable. The temptation to speak with such "benevolent conclusiveness" is countered in "An Octopus" by a poetic method which aims rather at a "Relentless accuracy" than at mere "Neatness of finish": as Moore tells us in what amounts to the poem's peroration, "Relentless accuracy is the nature of this octopus / with its capacity for fact." What makes her "accuracy" so "Relentless," though, is precisely her "capacity" to acknowledge that, in a fallen world, *linguistic* accuracy is impossible. Like us, the poet is "still devoid of" the "power" of naming—as she confesses both in acknowledging that when we speak of "happiness" we do so "clumsily" at best, and when, in the closing lines, fleeing with us "from the hard mountain," she asks in comic despair, "Is tree the right word for these strange things / 'flat on the ground like vines'?"

Whether it is or not (and we have no way of knowing), "these strange things" put us back with *Kora in Hell*: "suggesting dustbrushes, not trees," they also suggest the broom with which Williams (or rather his wife; he is watching her clean house) "swish[es] from room to room," digging "the dust out of every corner"[14] before wrapping "the house . . . in brown paper" and sending it off "to a publisher" as a finished "work of art." But the debris of "An Octopus" cannot be swept up: the "winds . . . 'tear the snow to bits / and hurl it like a sandblast'" at us, just as, in Williams's "Coda" to the improvisation quoted above, "the north wind, coming and passing, swelling and dying, lifts the frozen sand [and] drives it arattle against the lidless windows. . . ."[15]

In a letter of 2 September 1924, Moore complains to Scofield Thayer (who would publish "An Octopus" in *The Dial* three months later) of the poem's "undesirable expansiveness"; yet she knows that its "expansiveness" works as a necessary corrective to her own tendency to be—as she puts it in the same letter—"impetuous and perilously summary" in "so vital a matter,"[16] a tendency which, unchecked, leads directly to the falsifying "smoothness" of the Greeks, the "neatness" she so admires and deplores in James. The poem's "expansiveness" (except for "Marriage," it is the longest of Moore's individual works) is the inevitable by-product of the "Relentless accuracy" which it opposes to "neatness" and "smoothness": having lost the Adamic "power" of naming, the poet has no choice but to resort to circumlocution.

If "Relentless accuracy" requires the acknowledgment of that loss, it compels, too, an awareness that loss of the "power" to name things involves (as both cause and effect) the loss of a further "power": the power of *seeing clearly*. According to John Ruskin, that power is even rarer and more crucial than the power of naming. As he puts it, in a passage quoted by Hugh Kenner in *A Homemade World* and more recently by Bonnie Costello in *Imaginary Possessions*: "Hundreds of people can talk for one who can think; but thousands can think for one who can see. To see clearly is poetry, prophecy, and religion all in one."[17]

Perception here is much more than a physical or psychological process; it is specifically made synonymous not only with poetry itself, but also with religious devotion and with the prophetic mode to which, as poems as different as "So far as the future is concerned" (1915), "Poetry" (1919), and "Novices" (1923) attest, Moore has consistently aspired.[18] It is precisely the aim of "An Octopus" to fuse "poetry, prophecy, and religion" in the act of seeing—or, as Moore put it in praising the work of the naturalist W.H.

Hudson, to bring "the scientific attitude of mind [into] conjunction with spiritual vision."[19]

IV

This is a highly complex fusion, for there is nothing simple about seeing, as "An Octopus" reveals in its treatment of Ruskin himself. Early in the poem we see a stand of fir trees, "austere specimens of our American royal families" rising "aloof" from the glacial "manoeuvres" of the mountainside; then, quoting Ruskin, Moore imparts to the trees a paradoxically ethereal solidity—each tree, she tells us, is " 'like the shadow of the one beside it. / The rock seems frail compared with their dark energy of life.' . . . "[20] Twenty lines later, however—having completed one of those circles which deceive you "into thinking you have progressed"—we come upon a lake where the wind, busily " 'obliterating the shadows of the firtrees, . . . makes lanes of ripples.' " The latter quotation is taken from a National Parks Service pamphlet;[21] thus the "odd oracles of cool official sarcasm" have the last word. It is not quite the last word, however, because still later in the poem water itself has become an illusion " 'in the distance,' " one created by "patches" of blue flowers "growing close together."

Thus we have "progressed" from trees to trees like shadows; and from trees like shadows to shadows cast, like reflections (though a reflection is the opposite thing to a shadow), on water and obliterated by wind; and finally to the mere illusion of water. Here, then, we have the method of the poem in miniature: a moment of intense and apparently clear perception leads, by a circuitous route, to another moment which seems to cancel the first and then to be rendered illusory in its turn; yet each image remains "intact" in the mind, like the "fossil flower," the mountain itself, "when it is cut."

As the poem goes on, seeing becomes more complicated, not less. Relying on *ordinary seeing*, "the scientific attitude of mind" generates details in great profusion; those details, however, are isolated from each other by their intense particularity. What we require is a "spiritual vision," in Moore's phrase, capable of integrating discrete particulars so that they form a coherent whole within which each takes on its proper significance. In other words, we need "the poet, who," as Emerson says in "The Poet," "re-attaches things to nature and the Whole" by means of "what is called

Imagination, . . . a very high sort of seeing, which does not come by study, but by the intellect being where and what it sees, by sharing the path or circuit of things through forms, and so making them translucid to others."[22]

The inadequacy of ordinary seeing, and the near-impossibility of seeing "clearly" enough to achieve the fusion of "poetry, prophecy, and religion," are the direct consequences of the Fall. As Emerson writes in "Experience," the essay immediately following "The Poet" in *Essays, Second Series*:

> It is very unhappy, but too late to be helped, the discovery we have made that we exist. That discovery is called the Fall of Man. Ever afterwards we suspect our instruments. We have learned that we do not see directly, but mediately, that we have no means of correcting these colored and distorting lenses which we are, or of computing the amount of their errors. Perhaps these subject-lenses have a creative power; perhaps there are no objects. Once we lived in what we saw; now, the rapaciousness of this new power, which threatens to absorb all things, engages us.[23]

The Fall thrusts us into self-consciousness, into a subjectivity which, insidiously distorting our vision while making it impossible to correct or recognize our mistakes, "threatens to absorb all things" into itself, like "that lady-fingerlike depression in the shape of the left human foot," called "The Goat's Mirror, . . . which prejudices you in favour of itself / before you have had time to see the others . . ."

We come upon this place early in the poem; it is in "the middle lake" of this strange "depression" (itself enclosed by "dumps of gold and silver ore") that the wind erases the Ruskinian "'shadows of the firtrees.'" Here, too, we have a prefiguration of the Fall. For "The Goat's Mirror . . . prejudices you in favour of itself" because, like the savage's looking-glass in "When I Buy Pictures," it shows you what you do not recognize as an image of yourself. The Goat's Mirror is the "clear / Smooth Lake" of the dream Eve reports in book IV of *Paradise Lost*:

> That day I oft remember, when from sleep
> I first awak'd, and found myself repos'd
> Under a shade on flowers, much wond'ring where
> And what I was, whence thither brought, and how.
> Not distant far from thence a murmuring sound
> Of waters issu'd from a Cave and spread
> Into a liquid Plain, then stood unmov'd
> Pure as th'expanse of Heav'n; I thither went
> With unexperienc't thought, and laid me down
> On the green bank, to look into the clear

Smooth Lake, that to me seem'd another Sky.
As I bent down to look, just opposite,
A Shape within the wat'ry gleam appear'd
Bending to look on me, I started back,
It started back, but pleas'd I soon return'd,
Pleas'd it return'd as soon with answering looks
Of sympathy and love; there I had fixt
Mine eyes till now, and pin'd with vain desire,
Had not a voice thus warn'd me, What thou seest,
What there thou seest fair Creature is thyself,
With thee it came and goes. . . .
(*Paradise Lost*, IV:449–69)

There is no telling how long we stand staring into The Goat's Mirror, with "its indigo, pea-green, blue-green, and turquoise, / from a hundred to two hundred feet deep. . . . " No "voice" warns us in any explicit way: instead we hear a question: "What spot could have merits of equal importance / for bears, elk, deer, wolves, goats, and ducks?" This apparently rhetorical question, with its apparently casual allusion to "goats," implies that we have not moved: the scene has only *seemed* to shift with the dissolution of the fir trees' shadows and the cataloguing of the various fauna by whose "ancestors" this "spot" has been "Preempted." This catalogue seems to end with "the bears inspecting unexpectedly / ant hills and berry bushes," and again the poem seems to move on. We have been looking at animals and are now looking at what seems to be a cave, "Composed of calcium gems and alabaster pillars, / topaz, tourmaline crystals, and amethyst quartz" —or at least we *seem* to be looking at a cave. As it turns out, though, this is the bears' "den," and it is "*somewhere else, concealed* in the confusion / of 'blue stone forests thrown together with marble and jasper and agate / as if whole quarries had been dynamited'" (italics added). Still we have not moved: that "den" is "somewhere else"; it is "concealed," and our eyes are still "fixt" on The Goat's Mirror, where what now appears with startling clarity is the image of yet another animal. What *should* it be but the Goat itself?

And farther up, in stag-at-bay position,
as a scintillating fragment of these terrible stalagmites,
stands the goat,
its eye fixed on the waterfall which never seems to fall—
an endless skein swayed by the wind,
immune to force of gravity in the perspective of the peaks.

What we are looking at is an illusion in a mirror; to be more precise, we are looking at the reflected and perhaps illusory image of a creature which, in turn, has "its eye fixed"—like Eve's, like ours—on illusion. The "perspective of the peaks," controlling the latter illusion, is very tricky indeed—and it is about to get even trickier.

In its "stag-at-bay position," the goat is reminiscent of the land unicorn of "Sea Unicorns and Land Unicorns," "rebelling proudly at the dogs / which are dismayed by the chain lightning / playing at them from its horn. . . . "[24] But the goat, if it *is* a goat (and that, too, is open to question, as we shall see) is at best a debased parody of the unicorn, sexual where the unicorn is chaste and undiscriminating where the unicorn is fastidious; no power radiates from it, and even its "position"—patently unnecessary in the absence of pursuing "dogs"—imitates that of another and nobler creature.

The implications of this posture become clearer in the poem's next sentence. In a structurally similar but considerably more elaborate image, it represents the animal in a very different light, as something mysterious, something almost divine. Here, though, we are made to feel what it is to have lost the power of naming, for the "goat" is now called something else:

> A special antelope
> acclimated to "grottoes from which issue penetrating draughts
> which make you wonder why you came,"
> it stands its ground
> on cliffs the colour of the clouds, of petrified white vapour—
> black feet, eyes, nose, and horns engraved on dazzling icefields,
> the ermine body on the crystal peak;
> the sun kindling its shoulders to maximum heat like acetylene,
> dyeing them white;
> upon this antique pedestal—
> "a mountain with those graceful lines which prove it a volcano,"
> its top a complete cone like Fujiyama's
> till an explosion blew it off.

The figure is "engraved on dazzling icefields" as the land unicorn of "Sea Unicorns and Land Unicorns" is "etched . . . on an old celestial map"; but here it is the "icefields" that dazzle rather than the creature itself, and we will do well to remember Adam in "Marriage," "Unnerved by the nightingale / and dazzled by the apple. . . . " Bathed in sunlight which, like a metal sculptor's blow torch, alters its color and renders it at least temporarily malleable to human vision, the animal (whether "goat" or "special antelope") stands "upon this antique pedestal" like the statue of Daniel Webster at the end of "Marriage"—like Adam himself, who in the same poem takes such immoderate and "solemn joy / in seeing that he has become an idol." As Williams writes in *Kora in Hell, "There is nothing the sky serpent will not eat. Sometimes it stoops to gnaw Fujiyama. . . .* "[25] Even the "antique pedestal" is unstable: like Adam's dream of himself as a god, it has already exploded once. When it happens again, it will be our turn to fall.

We may say with Emerson, then, that "Dream delivers us to dream, and there is no end to illusion. Life is a train of moods like a string of beads, and as we pass through them they prove to be many-colored lenses which paint the world their own hue, and each shows only what lies in its focus. From the mountain you see the mountain."[26] He might almost be describing "An Octopus"—except that it is emphatically not the case, in this poem, that "From the mountain you see the mountain." We "see the mountain" only when we are sufficiently removed from it to take it in—nor, though we approach it from a distance, do we manage to take it in at first glance. The opening lines establish an aerial perspective (the first sentence, which includes the title, is derived from the caption to an aerial photograph in a National Parks Service pamphlet),[27] but we are looking through a subjective, a human eye, not the "objective" lens of a camera:

AN OCTOPUS

of ice. Deceptively reserved and flat,
it lies "in grandeur and in mass"
beneath a sea of shifting snow dunes;
dots of cyclamen red and maroon on its clearly defined pseudopodia
made of glass that will bend—a much needed invention—
comprising twenty-eight icefields from fifty to five hundred feet thick,
of unimagined delicacy.

The image is virtually unintelligible. What we see is not a mountain, but a series of things that cannot be: an ocean-creature composed of and frozen into the very medium in which it resides—but we do not think of the ocean as freezing solid; "a sea of shifting snow dunes"—but snow melts when it falls on water; "pseudopodia," false feet, "made of glass that will bend"—but glass is made from sand, the material which ordinarily piles up in dunes beside, not *on*, the sea, and does not bend. The whole exhibits an "unimagined delicacy"—a delicacy, that is, both unforeseen and real; yet it is at the same time an illusion, the product of human "invention." The perspective here is not just aerial; it is also *fallen*. Our vision is bound up in illusion from the outset because—though we have no way of knowing it at first—the poet has already lost the power of naming. We must be reminded, moreover, that we have lost that power as well; and so the poet resorts to the "much needed" faculty of "invention" (quotation is one of its forms) to find the series of rapidly "shifting" analogies and metaphors whose radical incompatibility with one another makes it virtually impossible for us to bring the image confronting us to a satisfactory resolution.[28]

It will take us the whole poem to learn to "see the mountain" with anything like clarity. For what we see "From the mountain" is not the mountain itself but, as I have indicated, a succession of scenes "distinguished by a beauty / of which 'the visitor dare never fully speak at home / for fear of being stoned as an impostor.'" Each scene is so highly particularized that, like The Goat's Mirror, it "prejudices you in favour of itself / before you have had time to see the others"; thus the various scenes become, "as we pass through them," the "many-colored lenses" of which Emerson speaks, "which paint the world their own hue" and conform the world to their own curvature. Successive illusions, however, do not so much cancel each other (as I suggested earlier) as reveal each other. For if "each shows only what lies in its focus," numerous focuses may be combined, as in the closing lines of "Novices," to achieve a greater comprehensiveness of vision. Thus we arrive, finally, at the culminating vision of

> . . . the hard mountain "planed by ice and polished by the wind"—
> the white volcano with no weather side;
> the lightning flashing at its base,
> rain falling in the valleys, and snow falling on the peak—
> the glassy octopus symmetrically pointed,
> its claw cut by the avalanche
> "with a sound like the crack of a rifle,
> in a curtain of powdered snow launched like a waterfall."

Like Adam and Eve, we have been allowed a backward look at Paradise; but, having fallen, we can never be free of the limiting "focus" of analogy and metaphor. Our only hope of "correcting," even minimally, "these colored and distorting lenses which we are" is to invert the methods of the Greeks, in whose "'pride-producing language,'" Moore tells us (she is quoting Cardinal Newman now), "'rashness is rendered innocuous, and error exposed / by the collision of knowledge with knowledge.'"[29] For in a fallen world where "there is no end to illusion," "error" may only be "exposed / by the collision" of error with error and illusion with illusion.

V

In his journal for 5 July 1632, John Winthrop, governor of the Massachusetts Bay Colony, recorded the following incident for posterity:

> At Watertown there was (in the view of divers witnesses) a great combat between a mouse and a snake; and, after a long fight, the mouse prevailed and killed the snake. The pastor of Boston, Mr. Wilson, a very sincere, holy man, hearing of it, gave this interpretation: That the snake was the devil; the mouse was a poor contemptible people, which God had brought hither, which should overcome Satan here, and dispossess him of his kingdom. . . .[30]

The reverend Mr. Wilson (who badgers Hester Prynne in the opening scenes of *The Scarlet Letter*) could offer what seems to twentieth-century readers an outlandish interpretation, and Winthrop could set it down as part of the historical record, confident that no one who heard it would find it arbitrary or would laugh at the idea that a mouse might represent the "poor contemptible people" of New England. Winthrop's concern is not to justify Wilson's interpretation of the event, but rather to assure his future readers that this "great combat" did in fact take place: hence the careful reference to the presence of "divers witnesses."

Most of us, upon watching such a struggle, would probably remark on the unusual outcome and leave it at that; but Winthrop and Wilson were leaders of a community whose raison d'être consisted in a shared framework of interpretation which not only made their reading of this event possible, but virtually demanded it. What we call "nature" did not exist to be described for the sake of its manifest beauties, and indeed for these men the beauties of nature were *not* manifest at all: nature made it abundantly clear that God wanted men to form covenanted communities for the purpose of keeping nature at bay. As Winthrop himself said in a speech to the General Court in 1645, "There is a twofold liberty, natural (I mean as our nature is now corrupt) and civil or federal. The first is common to man with beasts and other creatures. By this, man . . . hath liberty to do what he lists; it is a liberty to evil as well as to good. . . . The exercise and maintaining of this liberty makes men grow more evil, and in time to be worse than brute beasts. . . ."[31] Even Jonathan Edwards, writing a hundred years later and far more appreciative of things natural than his predecessors had been, could say that "Children's coming into the world naked and filthy and in their blood, and crying and impotent, is to signify the spiritual nakedness and pollution of nature. . ."[32] What distinguishes Edwards from earlier

American Puritans, however, is that a text like *Images or Shadows of Divine Things* examines the more ordinary phenomena of nature; Winthrop would not have thought the "great combat" worth recording had it turned out differently.

Moore, a devout Presbyterian and a theological descendant of Winthrop and Wilson and Edwards, may be said to share their attitudes toward the natural world at least to the extent that for her, as for them, nature is never simply *there*. It is always a highly symbolic realm in which the workings of God are made manifest and the order of things is made clear. That order is always moral; and in Moore, as in the Puritan writers, it is most often the special, the complicating case which reveals that order most fully.

As time goes on, though, Moore's interest in the "special" increasingly declines into a fascination with the merely peculiar—a fascination, that is, with objects which do not so much force the order of things to disclose itself in relation to them as they force the poet to declare their significance with respect to an order which is evident *only in the objects themselves.* In other words, in Moore's best poems, the order of things remains hidden until the poet discovers it dialectically, through observation of a given object—a mountain, say, or some other landscape—in relation to other objects. In the later poems, by contrast, the *object* is obscured, lost in the increasing *dis*order of things; the poet plucks it out, holds it up for our approval, and—often—begs us to "save it."[33] For Moore is also a post-Romantic writer, to whom nature is a source of positive rather than negative value: man, not nature, is the agent of moral "pollution."[34]

Like Ruskin before her and Emerson before *him*, Moore takes the ability to see nature clearly as a positive virtue in itself. The act of perception is one combining "poetry, prophecy, and religion" in a way that would have been as inconceivable to the Puritans—even Puritans like Edwards and Cotton Mather, who took an active and (by the standards of the day) scientific interest in natural philosophy—as "the scientific attitude of mind" which is conjoined "with spiritual vision" in the work of W.H. Hudson.

Moore also shares with Emerson and Ruskin the conviction that, as Emerson puts it in *Nature*, "few adult persons can see nature. . . . At least they have a very superficial seeing."[35] Emerson's initial response to this problem is to present himself as a mediating figure, "a transparent eyeball" through which we may look upon nature with clarified sight while remaining so far as possible unaware of his action as mediator.[36] He must also seek, therefore, to make his *language* as nearly "transparent" as possible—to "fasten words again to visible things" so that we may the more readily perceive the "natural facts" of which "Words are signs," and, perceiving them, recognize also the "particular spiritual facts" they symbolize, and so be led at last to understand nature in the aggregate as "the symbol of spirit."[37] But the "tyrannous eye" of the "genius" is subject to grievous and incalculable error,[38] for the Fall has made all of us into "colored and distorting lenses." To pass our own vision, however imperfect it may be, through a mediating form which is itself not only "distorting" but invisible as well is to compound the difficulties forced upon us by our fall into subjectivity and, at the very least, to double the amount of our error.

Unlike the Puritans, both Moore and Emerson address themselves to an audience whose members, far from sharing the interpretive framework which makes of nature something that demands interpretation, do not consider the natural object as requiring interpretation at all. "An Octopus," like *Nature,* is concerned to correct the "very superficial seeing" with which most "adult persons" seem to be content, but Moore works more analytically than Emerson does. Emerson simply states as given fact that "few adult persons can see nature," and then explains as best he can how nature should ideally be seen. Moore makes no such statement, however, nor does she put herself forward as "a transparent eyeball"; instead, she attempts to show us how "To see clearly" by making us look through a succession of "these colored and distorting lenses which we are," and by making us do so consciously. It is the succession that matters: as image follows image, each makes us aware of the limits which had been imposed, imperceptibly or nearly so, by the previous one.

Thus Moore has discovered, in "An Octopus," a new method for revealing, gradually and dialectically, the significance of the observed world, a method for placing a given object within a network of relations within which, in turn, it acts and is acted upon, and by which its significance is not only revealed but constituted as well. This is not the gradual filling-in, the patient layering of detail upon detail by which, in a novel like *The Portrait of a Lady,* James transforms an initial "sketch" into a finished "picture."[39] Moore's method is effectively the inverse of James's: she begins by breaking up before our eyes what we sense to be a finished image hovering just outside the field of vision, multiplying the perspectives from which we look at it, as a cubist portrait gives us a face from several angles simultaneously.

The multiplication of perspective is accomplished by a variety of means, of which quotation is by no means the least significant. There are more than fifty marked quotations (and many more unmarked borrowings) in

"An Octopus," and one of their functions is to serve, like the scenes they help to constitute, as "lenses"—or lenses-within-lenses, actually—through which the poem and the reader are made to pass, and by which vision is, if only slightly, distorted. The inverted commas are like the frames of eyeglasses, holding the lenses in place and letting us know they are there. The result is that in the course of the poem we see both the mountain and *the problem of seeing the mountain* from a number of different vantage points, no one of which is sufficient—as when in the closing lines of "Novices" we see the ocean, another natural phenomenon too complex to be apprehended by a single pair of eyes. But in "Novices" the inverted commas around the individual phrases comprising "this 'ocean of hurrying consonants'" stand surety for both the accuracy of the perception and the precision of the language that reports it; in "An Octopus," they often indicate just the reverse. Yet if the local effect is one of distortion, the cumulative effect is corrective: strong lenses distort vision only for those who know already how to "see clearly."

VI

Williams and Eliot rarely see eye-to-eye on anything, but "when they do agree, their unanimity is great";[40] and since they do agree in their estimates of the quality of Moore's work, I want to look for a moment through the lenses their commentary provides. Eliot can think of only "five contemporary poets"—he does not name them—"whose work excites [him] as much as, or more than, Miss Moore's"; for Williams she is, simply, "the best."[41] Eliot had promised to review Moore's *Poems* for *The Dial* in 1921, but had been unable to do so; the publication of "Marriage" in 1923 gave him another—perhaps a better—opportunity to judge her earlier work. "Up to the present time," he writes, "Miss Moore has concerned herself with practising and perfecting a given formation of elements; it will depend, I think, on her ability to *shatter* this formation and painfully reconstruct, whether Miss Moore makes another invention equal in merit" to her discovery of the "quite new rhythm" which is "the most valuable thing" in *Poems*.[42] Eliot does not mention "Marriage," except of course to say that it has been published, and he cannot have seen "An Octopus"; but the latter poem corresponds uncannily to his prescriptions, shattering our perception at the outset and then reconstructing it, slowly and "painfully."

For a clearer sense of how that process works we may turn to Williams, who puts before us, in an essay celebrating Moore's receipt of the Dial Award for *Observations*, "the geometric principle of the intersection of loci: from all angles lines converging and crossing establish points." Now "carry it further," he urges us, and consider how "apprehension perforates at places, through to understanding—as white is at the intersection of blue and green and yellow and red. It is this white light," Williams insists, "that is the background of all good work. . . . Local color . . . is merely a variant serving to locate [an] acme point of white penetration."[43] We could describe Moore as working prismatically, breaking up the image to reveal its smaller and more variously colored constituents, as a prism refracts what appears to the eye as white light and shows it to contain the entire spectrum. In the end the prism is removed, and "the white volcano" stands revealed—but only for a moment: it, too, is finally obscured by the descent of a great "'curtain of powdered snow launched like a waterfall'"—the white curtain of knowledge.

But the process of shattering and reconstructing which Eliot calls for in 1923 has already been anticipated by Moore, and on a much larger scale than that of "An Octopus." We have seen her abandon the syllabic patterns of her earlier poems, shattering the "given formation of elements" to which her work owed its identity; what remains to be seen is how, in the coming years, she manages the painful process of reconstruction, of fusing the multiplied perspectives of "An Octopus" into a single, complex vision of America.

6

A Reason for Living in a Town Like This

Now we must take note of a long hiatus, a seven-and-a-half-year poetic silence, which in its own way is as much a part of Moore's career as her poems. And just as the significance of Moore's syllabic patterns is most decisively revealed by her decision to abandon them in favor of free verse, so the significance of her silence is most clearly indicated by her return to speech and her renewed effort to articulate her increasingly complex vision of America.

Moore's silence was finally broken in June 1932, when "The Steeple-Jack," "The Student," and "The Hero" appeared in *Poetry* under the collective title "Part of a Novel, Part of a Poem, Part of a Play."[1] With these new poems—the first since "The Monkey Puzzler" in January 1925—Moore resumed the elaborate syllabic patterns which had characterized her verse in the 1910s, as if to say that her career had now come full circle; as if to say that the poetic identity she had begun to define with such rigor in 1915, and which she had had to smash "like a glass against a wall" in her search for community, had now been reconstituted so as to include and fuse the multiple perspectives of "An Octopus"; and as though the process of reconstructing that identity, which seemed to have come to a halt in 1925, had only gone underground, to run its course more or less invisibly until Moore could present it to the world as an accomplished fact.

It was a stunning fact, too, a triumph, as the response of Moore's contemporaries attests. In 1935 Eliot placed "The Steeple-Jack" and "The Hero" (without "The Student," which Moore had decided not to reprint) at the head of *Selected Poems*; and when Wallace Stevens called Moore "A Poet That Matters" (in his review of *Selected Poems*), he based his case on a discussion of "The Steeple-Jack."[2] Williams fired off a congratulatory letter soon after receiving his copy of *Poetry* in June 1932. The letter hails Moore upon the resumption of a great career, and acclaims her return as a triumph not only for Moore but for Williams as well, in his running battle with Eliot. It got lost for a few days in the Moores' elaborate filing system, but on 26 June 1932, Moore reported to her brother Warner that

> W.C. Williams' letter was *found*—in the post-card drawer. I will give you some of it. He starts out, "The first poem especially . . . is reward enough for any waiting. Why should I not speak in superlatives: there is no work in verse being done in any language I can read which I find more to my liking and which I believe to be so thoroughly excellent. . . . Your words have an immediate quality which only comes when the intelligence matches the acuteness of the perception to which you add an aimed heat of the emotions. . . . And to me especially you give besides a sense of triumph in that it is my own scene, without mistaking the local for the parochial."[3]

Moore had spent four of those silent years, from July 1925 to July 1929, as acting editor and then editor of *The Dial*—hardly an invisible position given the magazine's prominence as "America's only complete magazine of the creative and the critical arts."[4] In 1927 the editors of *The New Republic* expressed their regret that the only difference between *The Dial* under Scofield Thayer and *The Dial* under Moore was that Moore's poems no longer appeared in the magazine,[5] but Moore's time as editor was by no means wasted. There is a basic continuity between Moore's poetic practice and her practice as editor, as William Wasserstrom argues in *The Time of "The Dial"* (she was, says Wasserstrom, "a critic whose poem was *The Dial*"),[6] and we are in a position to see what Moore could not have known when she accepted the editorship: that just as her work as editor would be a significant extension of the poetic work in which she had been engaged, so her subsequent poetic career would represent a significant extension of her work as editor of *The Dial*.

The editorial policies Moore inherited from Scofield Thayer were intended to accomplish nothing less than the moral renovation of America through the medium of artistic excellence;[7] Moore was already moving in that direction when she took over the magazine. Her time at *The Dial* served not so much to interrupt her career as to consolidate and sharpen her sense of her artistic mission and to train her prophetic vision. Having established her authority within the artistic community, she could now strive to transform that community into a moral force working on and for

America as a whole. She could use her art to define the ground for moral action—or so it seems now, in retrospect, and so perhaps it seemed to Thayer and his partner, James Sibley Watson, Jr., when they decided in July 1929 to discontinue publication of *The Dial* at least partly, Moore believed, so that she could get back to her own writing. But though she recognized the "chivalry" of their decision, Moore was apparently not quite ready.[8]

Soon after *The Dial* ceased publication, Moore and her mother gave up their apartment at 14 St. Luke's Place in Greenwich Village, where they had been living since coming to New York in December 1918, and moved to quieter surroundings at 260 Cumberland Street, Brooklyn; Moore would remain there until 1965. The move seems to have been made for the sake of a certain decorum. In "An Octopus," Moore compares herself implicitly to the figure of "Henry James 'damned by the public for decorum'; / not decorum but restraint," and the opening paragraph of her late reminiscence of "Brooklyn from Clinton Hill" (1960) sounds a similar note. "Decorum marked life on Clinton Hill in the autumn of 1929 when my mother and I came to Brooklyn to live," she writes. "An atmosphere of privacy with a touch of diffidence prevailed, as when a neighbor in furred jacket, veil, and gloves would emerge from a four-story house to shop at grocer's or meat-market. Anonymity, without social or professional duties after a life of pressure in New York, we found congenial."[9]

It may seem odd that a poet who had so assiduously courted recognition should have begun cultivating "Anonymity" just at the height of her success, but Moore was desperately tired, as her reference to her "life of pressure in New York" makes clear, and she needed rest. The only way she could regain the sense of "privacy" on which so much in her poetry depends was by remaining silent, at least for a time, until something should happen to spark her interest again. In 1960 she said that she had "never intended to write poetry" in the first place, that she was always trapped into it by "some fortuity," and she added, significantly, "I think each time I write that it may be the last time."[10]

Moore closes her account of "Brooklyn from Clinton Hill" by saying that "Someone" should do for the Brooklyn of 1960 what she has just finished doing (again) for the Brooklyn of 1929: "Someone," she writes, "should delineate the Hill, the Heights, the center—doing justice to landmarks and losses."[11] Something like that is what Moore does in "Part of a Novel, Part of a Poem, Part of a Play," and does pre-eminently in "The Steeple-Jack" —although she does it in a way much tougher minded, less literalistic, less patently nostalgic, and more widely ramifying. She takes up her pen again in 1932 with considerable "diffidence," and she acts precisely in order to defend the "atmosphere of privacy" she has come to cherish against another manifestation of the "pressure" she had felt in New York. "The Steeple-Jack" marks the beginning of Moore's effort to "do justice" to those "losses" with which she becomes increasingly preoccupied in the latter portion of her career.

Moore's diffidence appears quite clearly in her title, "*Part* of a Novel, *Part* of a Poem, *Part* of a Play." It is as if she really were turning to verse as being "the next best thing" to the fiction she had always admired. "Didn't I write something one time, 'Part of a Poem, Part of a Novel [*sic*], Part of a Play'?" she asked Donald Hall. "I think I was all too truthful. I could visualize scenes, and deplored the fact that Henry James had to do it unchallenged."[12]

"The Steeple-Jack" owes much less to James than it does to Hawthorne—but James owes a great deal to Hawthorne, too, and we have seen that Moore typically challenges a writer by reverting to one or more of his predecessors, acknowledged or otherwise. But she does not rely on Hawthorne alone to make her challenge effective. She also turns to a visual artist, Albrecht Dürer, to discover new methods of visualizing scenes. Thus, under the combined tutelage of Dürer and Hawthorne, Moore's diffident challenge to James takes shape, in "The Steeple-Jack," in the composition of a scene with the near-hallucinatory quality of Dimmesdale's midnight vigil or a Dürer etching. Ambiguously dominated by the figure of the steeple-jack, this markedly American scene presents itself as a field for heroic action; the nature of that action, and the attitude requisite to it, are explored in the subordinate poems "The Student" and "The Hero," as Moore seeks to define a mode of action that will allow her to "let go" of her anonymity if necessary and to "give [her] opinion firmly," without betraying herself or her community into the very "Danger" she is trying to warn against.

II

"Part of a Novel, Part of a Poem, Part of a Play" presents a clear instance of the extension of Moore's work as editor of *The Dial* into her subsequent poetry. In the late winter or early spring of 1928, as she was preparing to write an editorial "Comment" for the July issue dealing with an exhibition of Dürer's work at the New York Public Library,[13] Moore came upon a passage in the artist's correspondence in which he explains his plans for a triptych called *The Assumption of the Virgin* (1508–9) to a patron named Jacob Heller; this passage would provide the basic outline for the tripartite structure of "Part of a Novel, Part of a Poem, Part of a Play," just as George Adam Smith's analysis of Isaiah had provided the model for the closing lines of "Novices."

In a letter dated August 1508, Dürer explains to Heller that he will soon begin work on the triptych, and Moore recorded parts of this in her reading diary:

> . . . In a fortnight I
> shall be ready w Duke Friedrich's
> work; after that I shall make a
> beginning w yr work, and as my
> custom is . . . I will not paint
> any other picture till it is finished.
> I will be sure carefully to paint the
> middle panel with my own hand.
> Apart from that, the outer sides of the
> wings are already sketched in—they
> will be in stone-colour.
> The middle panel (Das Caput)
> I have outlined with the greatest care
> & at cost of much time. . . .
> No one shall paint a stroke
> on it except myself. . . .[14]

Dürer reveals his commitment to perfection even more strikingly in a letter about the finished painting:

> . . . I have painted it with great care
> as you will see. It has also
> been done with the best colours I could get.
> It is painted with good ultramarine under
> & over, & over that again some 5 or 6
> times, & then after it was finished
> I painted it again twice over so that
> it may last a long time. If it be kept
> clean I know it will remain bright
> & fresh 500 years, for it is not done
> as men are wont to paint. . . .[15]

Dürer's insistence that the central panel will be his work and his alone is especially significant with respect to "The Steeple-Jack." Just as the middle panel is entirely his own work, so the poem contains no quotations, and may fairly be described as being entirely the work of Moore's "hand." It is, thus, the centerpiece of "Part of a Novel, Part of a Poem, Part of a Play"; like "the wings" Dürer mentions in the excerpt quoted above, "The Student" and "The Hero" complement and explain the central "panel" of Moore's poetic triptych.

Moore's awareness of Dürer's career informs "The Steeple-Jack" in other ways as well. Sometime between 22 November and 3 December 1520, Dürer wrote in his journal:

> At Zierikzee, in Zeeland, a whale has been stranded by a high tide and a gale of wind. It is much more than 100 fathoms long, and no man living in Zeeland has seen one even a third as long as this is. The fish cannot get off the land; the people would gladly see it gone, as they fear the great stink, for it is so large that they say it could not be cut in pieces and the blubber boiled down in half a year.[16]

Fascinated, Dürer undertook a difficult sea passage, which eventually ruined his health, in hopes of seeing the huge creature, but on 9 December he acknowledged that his efforts had been in vain: "Early on Monday we started again by ship and went by the Veere and Zierikzee, and tried to get sight of the great fish, but the tide had carried him off again."[17]

Moore noted the failure of Dürer's adventure in her reading diary and again in her "Comment" in *The Dial*, where she presents this incident, along with another in which Dürer traveled from Venice to Bologna "to learn the secrets of the art of perspective" from someone who was "willing to teach" him, as evidence that Dürer's "mere journeyings are fervent. . . ."[18] Four years later, the same incident would give her a starting point for "The Steeple-Jack": "Dürer would have seen a reason for living / in a town like this, with eight stranded whales / to look at. . . ." In telling us that "Dürer would have seen a reason for living / in a town like this," however, Moore does not call attention to Dürer's failed adventure; rather, she invites us to identify our perspective with Dürer's, and with her own, and by suggesting that we, too, should "see a reason for living" here, she makes a subtle appeal to our vanity, to our sense of ourselves as critics and connoisseurs.

Based in part on Moore's memories of summers spent on Maine's Monhegan Island, "The Steeple-Jack" seems at first sight to provide ample confirmation of Eliot's judgment that Moore's poetry is essentially "'descriptive' rather than 'lyrical' or 'dramatic.'"[19] In the little "seaport town" of the poem,[20] there are exotic creatures "to look at," there is "the sweet sea air coming into your house / on a fine day," there are sea gulls, a town clock, a lighthouse, boats, flowers, elegant summerhouses, and a white-washed church whose storm-damaged steeple is being repaired by the steeplejack of the title. It is a pretty place—so pretty, in fact, that it sounds almost as though the description had come from a travel agent's brochure. Even the apparently casual opening remark is reminiscent of the travel agent's strategic hyperbole:

> Dürer would have seen a reason for living
>   in a town like this, with eight stranded whales
> to look at; with the sweet sea air coming into your house
> on a fine day, from water etched
>   with waves as formal as the scales
> on a fish.

This seems very pleasant until we stop to consider that the "reason for living" offered here consists in a vision of creatures out of their element, a vision of death on a truly massive scale. Yet the image does not immediately strike us as a terrible one, perhaps because of the speaker's calmly detached, even cheerful tone—and perhaps, too, because she moves so lightly from looking at the whales to what is, on a casual reading, the pleasant olfactory image of "sweet sea air coming into your house / on a fine day." And then, before we have had time to realize that that "sweet . . . air" is tainted with the stench of decaying flesh, the poem has moved on to the striking and elegant image of "water etched / with waves as formal as the scales / on a fish."

These last lines may tell us more about why the image of the whales seems so much less unpleasant at first than it might. The rhyme on "whales" and "scales," besides setting the rhyme scheme for the entire poem, also serves in an important way to diminish the whales: it "scales" them down to the size of mere "fish." By the end of the stanza, then, the whales have been reduced to "formal" elements and firmly subordinated to a larger verbal and visual composition. That composition, moreover, is self-contained, an effect secured by what is for Moore the relatively rare device of a fully end-stopped stanza. Thus the reader may be tempted to view the whales not as creatures grotesquely dead, but as parts of a rather pretty (and rather distant) picture, over which Dürer seems to preside in a purely "formal," a purely technical sense.

But Dürer provides more than a technical model. A few months before the publication of "Part of a Novel, Part of a Poem, Part of a Play," Moore wrote in a review of two recent books by Conrad Aiken that

> Art . . . is not an overture to a neighbor. One's work would not be the potent and accomplished thing it is, if it were done for any reason but to fulfill the instinct of technical mastery. . . . There is no pleasure subtler than the sensation of being a good workman; and in work there is consanguinity—unconscious as a rule, but sometimes conscious.[21]

Considered from this perspective, the opening stanza of "The Steeple-Jack" clearly reveals that Moore is "conscious" of her "consanguinity" with Dürer. They are bound by a common enthusiasm for rare and exotic animals; they are bound by a shared commitment to "technical mastery"; and they are united by a common moral and religious sensibility. Moore writes in *The Dial* that "There is danger of extravagance in denoting as sacrosanct or devout, an art so robust as to include in it that which is neither," but she is willing to risk that "extravagance": she goes on to say that "Dürer's separately perfect media do somehow suggest the virtues which St Jerome enumerates as constituting the 'hous of cryste.' . . . "[22]

Moore's devoutness, like Dürer's, expresses itself most clearly in "the instinct of technical mastery." And her admiration for Dürer—an "Appreciation which is truly votive and not gapingly inquisitive," as she puts it in *The Dial*—expresses itself in an attempt to emulate what she describes in the same essay as "the effort of experts to recover mutilated originals, to repudiate 'copies,' and to recognize Dürer's many priorities."[23] Thus "Part of a Novel, Part of a Poem, Part of a Play" makes restitution for the lost "original" of Dürer's *Assumption of the Virgin*, which was destroyed by fire in 1729.[24] And in much the same way, though on a smaller scale, the opening stanza of "The Steeple-Jack" makes up for Dürer's failure to see that beached whale by offering us the verbal equivalent of a Dürer etching—of such an etching, that is, as Dürer might have made had he reached Zierikzee in time. For in giving us not one but "eight stranded whales / to look at"—a "reason for living" indeed—Moore seizes upon and magnifies Dürer's lost opportunity.

This effort is entirely in keeping with the spirit of Moore's "Comment" in *The Dial*, where she writes that "liking" for Dürer's work "is increased perhaps when the concept is primarily an imagined one—[as] in the instance of the rhinoceros, based apparently on a traveller's sketch or description."[25] The "concept" in "The Steeple-Jack" is "an imagined one," too, not only because Moore has to imagine an etching Dürer never actually made, but also because her own vision of stranded whales relies on a description of an event she herself had not witnessed. Moore wrote to a Mrs. Barbara Kurz in 1961 that she still had "somewhere" a "newspaper clipping" referring to "eight whales" that had been "stranded" either in Brooklyn Harbor or in Sheepshead Bay—she was no longer certain which.[26]

The Dürer of "The Steeple-Jack" is not entirely "an imagined one," however, nor does Moore spend all her energy in trying to "recover mutilated originals." For the third stanza—a sudden burst of color which shocks us into the belated recognition that, like an etching, the first and second stanzas are drawn in black and white—celebrates another of "Dürer's separately perfect media." We are led to it by the apparently aimless movement of the sea gulls flying "back and forth" through the second stanza, thus:

> One by one, in two's, in three's, the seagulls keep
>   flying back and forth over the town clock,
> or sailing around the lighthouse without moving the wings—
> rising steadily with a slight
>   quiver of the body—or flock
> mewing where
>
> a sea the purple of the peacock's neck is
>   paled to greenish azure as Dürer changed
> the pine green of the Tyrol to peacock blue and guinea
> grey. . .

The effect of richness here is produced in large part by the sudden movement out of black-and-white which I have already mentioned, and by a corresponding change in the poem's rhythm—a clustering of difficult consonants which forces us to slow our reading considerably in order to articulate the words clearly. And these changes in turn result from the sudden confrontation of the poet's attempt to imagine what "Dürer would have seen" with the reality of his art.

For if the first stanza is the verbal equivalent of an etching Dürer might have made, the third stanza draws an analogy between its sea and a completed painting which Moore describes in *The Dial* as "a small Turner-like water-colour of the Tyrol"—one of several paintings which, she says, "tempt one to have favorites."[27] The painting in question, in which the deep green of a pine-covered mountain in the middle distance pales gradually but dramatically as we move toward the foreground, is called the *Wehlsch Pirg*; painted about 1494, it is part of a series of "amazing watercolors" that Dürer made while traveling between Nuremberg and Italy in the mid-1490s.[28] The *Wehlsch Pirg* is an unusual painting for Dürer, and it might seem a somewhat unusual choice for Moore, too, because it lacks the closely observed detail that characterizes so much of the work of both artists. But given Moore's immediate interest in the sea, Dürer's medium is probably more important to her than his subject-matter; and the manner in which Moore indicates the change in the sea's color tells us even more clearly why she found this particular painting so appropriate.

By making an analogy between her sea and Dürer's landscape, Moore insists that we regard the sea-change not as a natural phenomenon but as an artistic one. Note the change from passive to active voice as she writes, the "sea *is* / *paled* to greenish azure as *Dürer changed* / the pine green of the Tyrol . . . " (italics added). Dürer, the conscious, skilled artist, changes the landscape for reasons of his own. Similarly, it is Moore, the skilled poet who is so "conscious" of her "consanguinity" with Dürer, who "pales" the sea for reasons of *her* own. And the rhyme scheme makes it clear that this "changed" scene has indeed been carefully "arranged."

III

It is in the fourth stanza of "The Steeple-Jack" that we begin to see the purpose these arrangements serve, for the poet now brings on a carefully orchestrated storm that seems to come out of nowhere and to end almost before it has begun. There is, I think, no way we could have seen it coming; even if we had been paying closer attention to the movements of the sea gulls in the second stanza, we would have had no way of knowing then that we were only riding out the calm before the storm.

We see the birds "flying back and forth over the town clock, / or sailing around the lighthouse without moving the wings," and think nothing of the fact that they are moving between two different measuring devices —neither of which, as it turns out, is answerable to our need. The "town clock" measures time, of course, but measured time is of no consequence in a poem that can treat a fifteenth-century artist as if he were a virtual contemporary; nor can local time—clock time—define the duration of an event that occurs in cosmic time, as I think this storm does.[29] The lighthouse warns approaching ships that they risk tearing out their hulls on submerged rocks, an especially crucial function in stormy weather, but it cannot tell them that a storm is coming. Only the "slight / quiver of the body"—and of the poem—just before the gulls "flock / mewing" to the "changed" sea, gives notice of the impending change in the poem's weather. But then the explosion of color blinds us, and before we have had time either to consider what it means when a purplish sea changes to a "greenish azure," or to haul in the "fishnets" which have been "arranged / to dry," the

> whirlwind fifeanddrum of the storm bends the salt
>   marsh grass, disturbs stars in the sky and the
> star on the steeple. . . .

And when it is over, the poet laughs delightedly: "it is a privilege to see so / much confusion." The confusion in which the poet takes such unconcealed delight affects the town, and it affects us; the poet herself is untouched by it, except that in celebrating it she reveals her own position more clearly than she has yet done.

The vantage point from which she can say "it is a privilege to see so / much confusion" is closely analogous to that of the narrator in Hawthorne's "Sights from a Steeple."[30] The narrator is perched in a steeple high above a New England town which, though nameless, is presumably Salem; from that privileged position he watches the movements of the citizens. At one point, he sees a band of red-coated British soldiers marching up the street to the loud tune of the fife and drum; they are followed by a gaggle of small boys who mimic their every movement so expertly that the narrator playfully wonders how to distinguish the mimics from their models. For a few moments he looks elsewhere, but after a brief interval his attention again turns to the soldiers, whose proud marching has come to a sudden halt, as has the blare of martial music: the parade has encountered a funeral procession. The troops' confidence seems to vanish as they and the narrator watch the coffin being lowered into the grave, and when a thunderstorm bursts over their heads (its approach has already been noted by the narrator), the scene is plunged into disarray. All except the well-protected narrator abandon their dignity in their haste to get out of the rain.

The story obliquely prefigures the dismay of the British colonial forces as they read their defeat in the symbolic coffin and in the storm that routs them. The storm in "The Steeple-Jack" is also an agent of disturbance, and in the "whirlwind fifeanddrum" of its music the poem, too, carries the faint note of a revolution which is more explicitly recalled in "The Hero," where the hero is manifest in one form as the "decorous frock-coated Negro / by the grotto" who

> answers the fearless sightseeing hobo
>   who asks the man she's with, what's this,

> what's that, where's Martha
> buried, "Gen-ral Washington
> there; his lady, here"; speaking
> as if in a play—not seeing her; with a
> sense of human dignity
> and reverence for mystery, standing like the shadow
> of the willow.

But revelation comes more slowly in "The Steeple-Jack," because the storm creates its "confusion" by affecting the topography of the town and, more importantly, by clouding our vision as well. It "disturbs stars in the sky and the / star on the steeple," and in the "fog" which follows in its wake as if to assure us that our "confusion" is only natural, the "sea- / side flowers and / trees" are "disguised," are

> . . . favoured by the fog so that you have
> the tropics at first hand: the trumpet-vine,
> fox-glove, giant snap-dragon, a salpaglossis [*sic*]
> that has spots and stripes; morning glories, gourds,
> or moon-vines trained on fishing-twine
> at the back
>
> door . . .

None of these flowers is native to North America. All derive originally from tropical or subtropical regions, although they have since become widely domesticated in coastal areas of the eastern United States. Carefully "trained on fishing-twine / at the back / door," they belong to the realm of nature as controlled by art: we "have / the tropics at first hand" only because some artistic "hand" has brought them here to beguile us, as it earlier "paled" the sea. Like the whales earlier on, then, the flowers are out of their element, albeit in a more immediately colorful and apparently less troublesome way (they have survived transplantation, after all); and just as the "etched" and "formal" sea of the opening stanza gives way, under the conjoined artistry of Moore and Dürer, to the vividly colored and violent sea of the third stanza, so now the little garden "at the back / door" blossoms almost imperceptibly into something wilder, and then shrinks back again within its borders.

The poem now unfolds a list of wild plants—that is, weeds—at least one of which, the spiderwort, should be "vigorously rooted out" of any garden in which it appears, lest it take over completely.[31] There are "cat-tails, flags, blueberries and spiderwort, / striped grass, lichens, sunflowers, asters, daisies—the yellow and the crab-claw blue ones with green bracts —toad-plant. . . ." An uncontrolled, "cruel" nature (the second adjective is Moore's)[32] is never very far away from the seemingly idyllic, controlled version represented by the garden and by the town itself, and indeed the garden is not immune to that cruel power. We return to the list of garden flowers for another two lines, but now the rhythm has become abrupt and unsettling, and the quiet, peaceful garden is suddenly infected with a hint of the wildness and grasping, "crab-claw" savagery of nature unrestrained: "petunias, ferns; pink lilies, blue / ones, tigers; poppies; black sweet-peas." Suddenly there are "tigers" burning bright among the flower-beds, as in a painting by Henri Rousseau or a poem by Blake; the fire turns the sweet peas "black," as in "An Octopus" the jeweled wilderness of Paradise is outlined by the "scars of old forest fires."

Not that the village environment is entirely hospitable to tropical plants: now we are told that "The climate / is not right for the banyan, frangipan, the / jack-fruit tree; nor for exotic serpent life." The absence of "exotic serpent life" should not fool us into thinking we are in Paradise: for one thing, the phrase excludes certain forms of "serpent life"—the common garden snake, for instance; also, we see that while "there is nothing" in this town "that / ambition can buy or take away," it is possible to buy "Ring-lizard and snake-skin for the foot if you see fit." Of course, those who "see fit" to buy put themselves at hazard.

There are, besides, other nasty little creatures to spoil our composure: "here they've cats not cobras to keep down the rats"—which means, of course, that there are rats here as well as cats. Like the flowers, the cats are imported—but they have been brought in to control a distinctly unpleasant, highly prolific, and rapacious nature (which is the gardener's job as well). Moreover, the banyan tree is conventionally included in representations of paradise, so it is fair to say that its specific exclusion from the poem—"The climate / is not right" for it—makes it quite certain that this garden is an earthly one.

This is no ordinary garden, as we have already begun to see, and here again we may resort to Hawthorne for an analogy. The center of the lush garden in "Rappaccini's Daughter" is a brilliant purple shrub, the jewel of Rappaccini's perverse botanical experiments.[33] This plant, the most beautiful in the garden, is also by far the most dangerous: its scent is fatal to all except Rappaccini and his daughter, Beatrice. Moore herself had a passionate dislike for heavily scented flowers,[34] and we must wonder whether her garden is not perhaps *too* beautiful, *too* brilliant to be trusted. For "foxglove" is another name for Digitalis, a plant whose leaves are poisonous —although the deadly heart stimulant it produces is used, in carefully measured doses, for medicinal purposes. We must also consider that in association with Nightshade, another deadly plant and one which is symbolic of pride, foxglove is emblematic of punishment—and the "salpaglossis that has / spots and stripes" is a member of the Nightshade family.[35]

The most likely source for this unassumingly venomous garden, however, is not "Rappaccini's Daughter" but a painting of which Moore copied a description into her reading diary on 30 January 1932:

> A Satanist Picture? Infernal
> details of the Triptych of Aix. At
> Burlington House. . . . "The artist
> in malefic endeavor has inverted
> the objects Christian symbolism reserved
> for attributes of the divine, & his skill
> in insinuating hell into every detail
> while preserving the pious appearance
> of the picture. (writer in the Times)
> . . . In the vase beside the lily stand
> 3 evil herbs, basil, foxglove, &
> belladonna—malefic gesture
> wh Spanish wizards termed *bacer*
> *figa* (Thumb bet 3rd & little finger)
> The announcing angel has owls' wings.[36]

The presence of foxglove and belladonna (the specific name for the Deadly Nightshade) in this account, and of foxglove and the salpiglossis in Moore's garden, can hardly be coincidental, as the reference to "inverted . . . Christian symbolism" makes clear; nor is it insignificant that at least some of the components of Moore's garden have evidently been taken from the description of a triptych which, like Dürer's, Moore had not actually seen. The full significance of these details will become apparent most clearly, however, in relation to "the college student / named Ambrose," who is out of his element in this scene as the flowers are—though in his own way, he, too, has been domesticated.

IV

Given that "The Steeple-Jack" is set in a village, it seems odd that up to this point the only living things we've seen have been plants and animals, and it is odder still that when we do finally come upon a man, *he* should be the one who seems out of place. This is partly because the poem has kept us so busy with details that there has been neither time nor occasion to notice that there don't seem to be any people around. Ambrose's sudden appearance onstage, then, brings the paucity of human beings home with the force of belated recognition. Paradoxically, though, it is also because Ambrose is so firmly insisted upon, so squarely placed, that he seems out of place.

The garden, for instance, is built up in considerable detail, but we are never even told that it is a garden. We simply follow along as the poet piles flower-name upon flower-name, and not until she finally locates them for us "at the back / door" do we have a plot to set them in. By contrast, Ambrose seems overdefined: we know what he is, who he is, and where he is; we know what he has with him; and we know what he does. The wealth of information lifts him off the page:

> The college student
> named Ambrose sits on the hill-side
> with his not-native books and hat
> and sees boats
>
> at sea progress white and rigid as if in
> a groove.

With his slightly odd, slightly foreign name, with his "not-native books" and his funny hat, Ambrose is at once a foreigner (but later we are told that "in his way" he is "at home" here) and a pleasant image of relaxed and thoughtful contentment:

> Liking an elegance of which
> the source is not bravado, he knows by heart the antique
> sugar-bowl-shaped summer-house of
> interlacing slats, and the pitch
> of the church
>
> spire, not true, from which a man in scarlet lets
> down a rope as a spider spins a thread . . .

Suddenly, in the space of eleven lines we have been presented with two figures where there were none before. The presence of the "man in scarlet" poses a very complex problem, for it is by no means clear how we are to account for it, and we will not be able to say who he is until we have established who it is that sees him; and this effort will require a closer look at Ambrose.

Ambrose, we know, is sitting "on the hill-side," although we do not know whether he is looking out over the town or facing away from it. We do know, however, that he "sees boats / at sea progress white and rigid as if in a groove," and this tells us something extremely important. There is a special trick to Ambrose's vision: he "sees . . . *as if*." This "college student" is perhaps a bit poetical; he "sees" by analogy and comparison. (There is, too, a distinct similarity between his view of "boats / at sea" and the view of the ocean presented by the poet in the first stanza.)

That Ambrose "sees . . . as if" is crucial, for it implies either a critical awareness of important discrepancies between things as they are and as they appear to be, or a blindness (equally critical, though in a different sense) to such differences. But Ambrose is capable of far more than pretty but empty analogies; he is capable, too, of precise observation, and he has a devastatingly accurate memory (". . . he knows by heart the antique / sugar-bowl-shaped summer-house of / interlacing slats, and the pitch / of the church / spire . . .").

If Ambrose is a poet, he is a good one—and the suggestion that he is a poet is confirmed when we learn that "The Student" is, in explicitly Emersonian terms, a heroic figure in his own right. He

> "gives his opinion
> firmly and rests on it"—in the manner of the poet;
> is reclusive, and reserved; and has such
> ways, not because he has no feeling but because he has so much.

In its stillness, Ambrose's posture resembles the rapt intensity of "the base- / ball fan, the statistician" of the much earlier "Poetry": what appears as his detachment from the town is in fact a reserve which derives from his passionate involvement in the scene it presents to his eye and to his memory.

Sitting "on the hill-side / with his not-native books and hat," "Liking an elegance of which / the source is not bravado," Ambrose is what Emerson calls "Man Thinking." (The phrase comes from "The American Scholar," to which Moore alludes in "The Student" when she tells us that "Emerson said," "One fitted / to be a scholar must have the heroic mind.")[37] Ambrose can perform "the office of the scholar" in "showing [us] facts amidst appearances," for he knows that it is not only books that must be read properly, but the world as well—knows that "Particular natural facts are symbols of particular spiritual facts," as Emerson wrote in *Nature*.[38]

"The American Scholar" poses as an urgent task the discovery of "a right way of reading." Emerson insists that

> One must be an inventor to read well. As the proverb says, "He that would bring home the wealth of the Indies, must carry out the wealth of the Indies." There is then creative reading as well as creative writing. When the mind is braced by labor and invention, the page of whatever book we read becomes luminous with manifold allusion. Every sentence is doubly significant, and the sense of our author is as broad as the world.[39]

Moore's vision of this nearly deserted village takes on a new and significant moral authority in passing through the twinned vision and memory of "the college student / named Ambrose," for Ambrose is the reader Emerson describes. In taking the figure of this Emersonian student, "this schoolboy under the bending dome of day,"[40] as authority for her own analogic and symbolic vision of a world in which appearances "dramatize a / meaning always missed / by the externalist,"[41] Moore points out for us the "right way of reading" "The Steeple-Jack." Its "page is luminous with manifold allusion," and its "Every sentence is doubly significant"; Ambrose's name has been planted as carefully as those flowers "at the back / door."

In A.D. 374, a man called Ambrose, who had been a lawyer before being appointed a Roman provincial governor, was named bishop of Milan. He was to become one of the four great Latin doctors of the Roman Catholic church, and would eventually be canonized, but as bishop he faced a number of extremely delicate situations. Christianity was on the increase at the time of Ambrose's ordination, but paganism was still widespread, and in Rome a group of senators tried to restore the altar of the goddess Victory to the Senate chamber; in Milan the empress-regent demanded that the Arians be given a building for use as a church. Ambrose mounted successful opposition in both cases, thus securing a reputation as a vigorous defender of the church against heresy from within and without. He also became a figure of punishment, and is frequently represented as holding a scourge which symbolizes the public penance he imposed on Emperor Theodosius I after the massacre of several thousand persons at Salonika in 390.

Moore writes in "The Student" that "we are / as a nation perhaps, undergraduates not students," and we must bear this distinction in mind when considering Ambrose, who is anything but a simple "undergraduate." For Ambrose is especially qualified as an arbiter of truth in church affairs, and he is something of a political figure as well; moreover, he possesses a special competence as a judge of "pitch," for St. Ambrose is known as the father of Catholic hymnology.[42] It is thus entirely appropriate that Ambrose should be the one to recognize that the "pitch / of the church / spire" is "not true," and it becomes still more appropriate when we consider the logic of "The Steeple-Jack" more closely.

Although Ambrose seems clearly set apart from the town, and particularly from the garden "at the back / door," I have suggested that the intensity of his contemplation involves him intimately with the scene; the symbolism of punishment associated with both the garden and St. Ambrose joins them more firmly together, and also helps to account for Ambrose's vision. When he is first introduced, we are told that Ambrose "sees boats / at sea progress white and rigid as if in / a groove," and now, with the help of the rise and fall of the speaker's voice as we follow the lineation of the stanza and "the pitch / of the church / spire," we see that the church itself is all "at sea": it may be "white and rigid," but its "progress" is by no means smooth, its direction by no means clear. Ambrose's vision is very precise indeed.

But it is just at this point that the poem becomes most treacherous, for *Ambrose is not looking at the church*: he "knows [it] by heart," he is *remembering* it. It cannot be Ambrose, then, who looks on as "a man in scarlet lets / down a rope as a spider spins a thread." He—that is, the "man in scarlet"—"might be part of a novel," a character in one of Ambrose's "not-native books," but they are not novels, and anyway,

> . . . on the sidewalk a
> sign says C. J. Poole, Steeple-Jack,
>   in black and white; and one in red
> and white says
>
> Danger.

It must be the poet who sees him. Having employed the figure of Ambrose as a means of establishing an apparently independent standard of judgment, a point of view other than her own, the poet joins him briefly in order to note that the "pitch" of the "spire" is "not true"—in order to give her opinion "firmly" and then "rest on it" as "the poet" is supposed to do; then she turns away from him, to consider the fascinating and somewhat alarming figure of the "man in scarlet," whom she sees already embedded in an analogy, just as Ambrose "sees boats."

Before we come to the "man in scarlet," however, we must look carefully at the church atop which he stands—for something has gone terribly wrong. Not only is "the pitch / of the church / spire, not true," but

> The church portico has four fluted
> columns, each a single piece of stone, made
> modester by white-wash

That these "columns" are "fluted" links them firmly not only to the "pitch" of the "spire" but also to the "whirlwind fifeanddrum of the storm," while their whiteness links them to the "boats / at sea," making it clear that none of these things is quite "true." The columns have been "made / modester by white-wash," and the clause carries with it the same implication of a deliberate artistic decision that is present when, much earlier in the poem and just before the storm, the sea is "paled to greenish azure as Dürer changed / the pine green of the Tyrol. . . ."

Now, however, that aesthetic decision, the artist's necessity and prerogative, is seen to have serious moral implications: "white-wash" suggests unmistakably that the church itself is guilty of pride, and that it is attempting to hide its sin behind a facade of purity. It is a pathetic effort, though, for the columns are only "made / modester": no mere paint job can make them modest. The church may be built of stone, but its foundations are water, and its white-washed, fluted columns represent "an elegance of which / the source" *is* "bravado": the poet likes it no better than St. Ambrose would have.

Thus, when she remarks (of the town as a whole) that

> This would be a fit haven for
> waifs, children, animals, prisoners,
> and presidents who have repaid
> sin-driven
>
> senators by not thinking about them,

the weight of the poet's judgment of the spiritual inadequacy of the church falls equally on the recently retired President Coolidge, whose strategy for weathering the scandals he had inherited from the Harding administration, including Teapot Dome, consisted primarily in allowing the storm of patriotic rhetoric blown up by antiadministration forces in the Senate to exhaust itself in its own excessive zeal. The strategy may have been politically successful (that time), but an early draft of "The Steeple-Jack" has it that "This would be a fit haven for . . . presidents who can *condone* / sin-driven /

senators by not thinking about them" (italics added).[43] The statement suggests that Moore thought Coolidge had at the very least failed to grasp the moral significance of his inaction. Edmund Burke, one of Moore's favorite writers,[44] wrote that all that is required for evil to flourish is that good men do nothing; by doing nothing, by "not thinking about" those whose own ambitions drove them to threaten the stability of the nation, "good men" like Coolidge tacitly "condone" wrong actions. This little town, with its poisoned garden "at the back / door" and its proud church, would indeed be "a fit haven" for such as he.[45]

All this further tarnishes the already-"disturbed" but "solid- / pointed star, which on a steeple / stands for hope," making it all too evident that the steeplejack—the "man in scarlet" who is busy "gilding" the star—is implicated in the same sort of aesthetic process as that which "can condone" corrupt political behavior by ignoring it, or that which attempts to cover the pride of the church with a glittering coat of "white-wash." But the implication that the steeplejack is a corrupt and corrupting presence is deeply disturbing: when we first see him he is an arresting, indeed an astonishing figure, but he seems to give an entirely unambiguous warning. As we follow the course of the "rope" that the "man in scarlet lets / down" from the spire, we are led inevitably to the "red / and white" sign that fairly screams "Danger"; the sign seems to tell us that the "Danger" can be avoided, and thus distracts us. We try to skirt the "Danger" and move on, but we do so without considering that the "Danger" is posed by the steeplejack himself.

Clothed in scarlet, standing atop the spire, the steeplejack "lets / down a rope as a spider spins a thread"—to catch something; but we do not think of ourselves as flies to wanton boys and do not think that he spins his web for us. We are told that the steeplejack "might be part of a novel," and if he were, we should know how to interpret his presence—and, more importantly, we should understand that his presence requires interpretation; but in the next breath the poet brings us down to earth. He "might be part of a novel, but on the sidewalk a / sign says C. J. Poole, Steeple-jack"—"says" it, moreover, "in black and white," as if to assure us that this is the cold print of unambiguous reality: this sign "in black and white" is all we need to account for the startling, scarlet-clad figure. It is worth remembering, though, that the absence of color in the "etching" presented in the first stanza reduces another terrifying vision to black and white, and so misleads the unwary. For there is another sign, this one in "red / and white," and the prominence which the stanzaic pattern assigns to its warning of "Danger"—the word stands alone on the first line of a new stanza—warns us not to trust what is said "in black and white." The colors of the new sign are those of the steeplejack's costume and of the "four fluted columns" which have been "made / modester by white-wash": there is something deeply false about the steeplejack.

V

Just how dangerous the steeplejack really is begins to appear in the following passage from Harold Donald Eberleis' *Little Known England*, in which Eberleis quotes John Leland:

> . . . there is the spire and choir of St. Alkmund's where "in the year 1533, upon Twelffe daye, in Shrowsburie, the Dyvyll appeared . . . when the Preest was at High Masse, with great tempeste and darknesse, so that as he pasyd through, he mounted upp the Steeple in the sayd churche, tering the wyers of the clock, and put the prynt of his clawes uppon the 4th bell, and tooke one of the pinnacles away with him, and for the Tyme stayde all the Bells in the churches within the sayd Towne, that they could neither toll nor ringe."[46]

This anecdote was transcribed from Moore's published notes to *What Are Years?* (1941), where it is used to account for a phrase in "Walking-Sticks and Paper-Weights and Water-Marks," a poem first published in November 1936. I have taken it from *What Are Years?* only for the sake of accuracy in transcription (Moore copied it into her reading diary in the fall of 1931, well before "The Steeple-Jack" was published) and use it here because this passage informs Moore's vision of the "man in scarlet," and identifies him as none other than "the Dyvyll."

In Leland's account, the devil climbs the steeple, just as the steeplejack does; more importantly, in Leland's narrative it is the devil himself who damages the steeple and brings on the "great tempeste." It is for this reason that I contended earlier that the storm, which in "The Steeple-Jack" precedes the appearance of the "man in scarlet" by a considerable margin, actually takes place in "cosmic" rather than "local" time, in a moment whose duration cannot be measured by the "town clock" because the devil has torn out its "wyers" and stopped its motion, as he has "stayde" the bells which might have warned us. Thus the storm only seems to precede the appearance of the "man in scarlet"; as in "The Fish," however, we have been shown the effects before being led to the cause.

It may appear that Hawthorne's "Sights from a Steeple," offered earlier as a possible source for Moore's steeplejack and for the "whirlwind fifeand-drum" of her storm, has now been disqualified. I am reluctant to dismiss it from consideration, however, not only because the poem is "luminous with *manifold* allusion"—in Emerson's phrase—but also because it seems to me that Hawthorne is entirely necessary to "The Steeple-Jack."

For in order to balance two such formidable antagonists as St. Ambrose and the devil, who are of necessity locked in permanent struggle, the poem requires yet another figure—a hidden one, capable of balancing good and evil in extremely complex situations, and of juxtaposing allegorical and literal interpretations of the "same" event or figure. This is what we have to do with the steeplejack, who "might be part of a novel" (so that Dürer cannot help us) but who is also a man with a name, part of the everyday world. Hawthorne, the author not only of "Sights from a Steeple" and "Rappaccini's Daughter" but also, and more importantly, of *The Scarlet Letter* (which is so nearly named in the lines that tell us how "a man in *scarlet lets* / down a rope as a spider spins a thread"), is entirely appropriate in such a role. He might indeed be "*part* of a novel."

The unobtrusive presence of Hawthorne—whom Moore somewhat grudgingly described as "a bear but great"[47]—explains much more than the steeplejack's shocking costume. One of the central episodes in *The Scarlet Letter* unfolds as the Reverend Arthur Dimmesdale, unacknowledged father of the child whose existence has made it necessary for Hester Prynne to wear the scarlet "A" on her bosom for seven agonizing years (the period of Moore's silence), delivers the Election Day sermon to a packed church. Hester stands outside with Pearl, listening intently though she is unable to make out the minister's words.

> Muffled as the sound was by its passage through the church-walls, Hester Prynne listened with such intentness, and sympathized so intimately, that the sermon had throughout a meaning for her, entirely apart from the indistinguishable words. . . . Now she caught the low undertone, as of the wind sinking down to repose itself; then ascended with it, as it rose through progressive gradations of sweetness and power. . . . Still, if the auditor listened intently, and for the purpose, he could detect the same cry of pain. What was it? The complaint of a human heart, sorrow-laden, perchance guilty, telling its secret . . . to the great heart of mankind . . .[48]

At the height of his career, Dimmesdale stands at the center of his theocratic community, knowingly submerging his corruption in his congregation's desire to interpret his physical weakness as a sign of his spiritual strength (when in fact the state of his soul is accurately imaged in his physical condition). Hester stands apart, as always, but her stillness, like Ambrose's, is only the sign of the deep "feeling" with which she listens while the pitch of Dimmesdale's voice reveals the sin he has never been able to confess openly. As she listens, her attitude resembles that of Moore's hero, who "doesn't like" "standing and listening where something / is hiding," but does it anyway—and what Hester hears is very much like what "The Hero" hears:

> The hero shrinks
> as what it is flies out on muffled wings, with twin yellow
> eyes—to and fro—
>
> with quavering water-whistle note, low,
> high, in basso-falsetto chirps
> until the skin creeps.

But the hero's shrinking is inward; it does not betray itself outwardly.

It may well be Hawthorne, too, who authorizes the introduction of "presidents" into "The Steeple-Jack." In "The Custom-House," the prefatory sketch affixed to *The Scarlet Letter*, Hawthorne details the story of his three-year career as a United States customs officer, a patronage post to which he was appointed by one president and from which he was turned out—"guillotined,"[49] as he rather chillingly puts it—by the next. Far from simply expressing his bitterness at having been removed from office, however, Hawthorne seizes the occasion to investigate the nature of the writer's relation to the state. He concludes that inasmuch as it was his dismissal from the moribund Custom-House which restored to him his life as a writer—for in the Custom-House his imagination had become "a tarnished mirror"—his abrupt "change of custom" has been for the best.[50] In thus accepting his forced retirement, Hawthorne makes himself "a citizen of somewhere else," a self-appointed and more than half-willing political exile like Hester Prynne, and he carefully points a number of analogies between himself and his character.

As "a tolerably good Surveyor of the Customs,"[51] Hawthorne was deeply enmeshed in the process of regulating trade; as editor of *The Dial*, Moore was similarly employed in regulating the day-to-day flow of literary commerce. Hawthorne found the Custom-House so moribund as to make writing impossible, and although *The Dial* was anything but moribund, the effect on Moore was practically the same: she, too, found it impossible to write during her tenure in office. Hawthorne made up his mind to welcome the change in his status once it had been forced upon him by the change in administrations; so, too, Moore seems to have accepted Thayer and Watson's decision to close *The Dial*, and indeed to have welcomed it as providing an opportunity to become quite literally "a citizen of somewhere else."

As if deliberately exiling herself from the literary community she had aspired to lead, Moore moved to Brooklyn soon after the last issue of *The Dial* had been released; almost two years went by before she published anything at all (a review of *Sweeney Agonistes* appeared in *Poetry* in May 1931, testifying to her continuing interest in Eliot's work),[52] and it would be another year before she was ready for poetry again. And, indeed, she might never have gone back to writing poetry had she not been trapped by the fortuitous discovery that, despite having gone "somewhere else," and despite finding "Anonymity" so thoroughly "congenial," she was in fact more nearly "a citizen" of Brooklyn than she had ever felt herself elsewhere.

VI

"The Hero" contains the names of several figures, both real and legendary, whose careers were marked, like Moore's, by a pattern of retirement and emergence:

> And
> Joseph was vexing to some.
> Cincinnatus was; Regulus; and some of our fellow
> men have been, though
>
> devout, like Pilgrim having to go slow
> to find his roll; tired but hopeful—
> hope not being hope
> until all ground for hope has
> vanished. . . .

These lines suggest the strength of Moore's attachment to her "anonymity," her sense of "privacy." For what is most notable here is the implicit celebration of the virtues of retirement. Bunyan's Pilgrim, of course, is "vexing" to those who plead with him to remain at home with his family rather than abandon all worldly attachments in his quest for the Celestial City; Regulus was "vexing" to the Carthaginians in choosing continued imprisonment and certain death at their hands rather than save himself by persuading the Roman Senate to surrender the city. But while Regulus made his personal exile the instrument of his nation's freedom, it was only with great reluctance that Cincinnatus allowed himself to be persuaded to leave his farm to act as leader of Rome, and after a mere sixteen days he returned to his plough, having given up his retirement only long enough to ensure the survival of the republic.

Cincinnatus thus bears a strong resemblance to "Gen-ral Washington," whose grave is visited in the quiet dramatic scene near the end of the poem. Washington assumed the presidency reluctantly, and in his First Inaugural Address made it clear that if he could not in good conscience avoid "going where he did not wish / to go," he had no intention of "suffering and not / saying so":

> . . . I was summoned by my Country, whose voice I can never hear but with veneration and love, from a retreat which I had chosen with the fondest predilection, and, in my flattering hopes, with an immutable decision, as the asylum of my declining years: a retreat which was rendered every day more necessary as well as more dear to me, by the addition of habit to inclination, and of frequent interruptions in my health to the gradual waste committed on it by time. . . .[53]

What all this suggests is that for Moore at forty-five as for Hawthorne at the same age (and they resemble each other, too, in having no significant claim to recognition beyond a narrow circle of readers), the prospect of retirement from the demands of a writer's career was by no means unattractive. It is hardly insignificant, then, that "Part of a Novel, Part of a Poem, Part of a Play" was published in an election year less than three years after the stock market crash of 1929. Indeed, "The Hero" alludes typologically to the Depression in referring to a portion of the biblical story of Joseph which follows shortly after the account of his efforts to store up food against the seven-year famine he had predicted for Egypt—a famine which eventually affected the family from which he had so long been separated. That allusion, together with the presence in the poem of such figures as Regulus, Cincinnatus, and Washington, justifies the further inference that Moore perceived the exchange of her retirement and her anonymity for the difficult and paradoxically public isolation of the poet as a heroic act with political implications—that it was, in effect, mandated by a national emergency.

"Part of a Novel, Part of a Poem, Part of a Play" thus takes on the dimensions of political and religious allegory, as might be expected in a work that alludes explicitly to Dürer and Bunyan, and more obliquely to Hawthorne and St. Ambrose. Yet for Moore, as for Hawthorne—who worried openly about the persistently allegorical twist of his imagination—the mode poses grave moral questions. "Rappaccini's Daughter," for instance, may be read as an allegorical representation of the artistic process in which Rappaccini functions as a dark version of the author, creating artifacts whose beauty betrays the unsuspecting reader into moral danger, just as, in the story itself, Rappaccini uses his daughter to ensnare the young Giovanni.

The guilty knowledge which infuses the story is even more tellingly exposed in "Fancy's Show-Box," where Hawthorne writes:

> A scheme of guilt, till it be put in execution, greatly resembles a train of incidents in a projected tale. The latter, in order to produce a sense of reality in the reader's mind, must be conceived with such proportionate strength by the author as to seem, in the glow of fancy, more like truth, past, present, or to come, than purely fiction. The prospective sinner, on the other hand, weaves his plot of crime, but seldom or never feels a perfect certainty that it will be executed. There is a dreaminess about his thoughts; in a dream, as it were, he strikes the deathblow into his victim's heart, and starts to find an indelible bloodstain on his hand. Thus a novel writer, or a dramatist, in creating a villain of romance, and the villain of real life, in projecting crimes that will be perpetrated, may almost meet each other halfway between reality and fantasy.[54]

This passage bears equally on Moore. Hawthorne wrote in the preface to *Twice-Told Tales* that his stories appeared to him in retrospect as "his attempts, and very imperfectly successful ones, to open an intercourse with the world,"[55] and for all Moore's contrary insistence that "Art . . . is not an overture to a neighbor," the opening lines of "The Steeple-Jack" lure us into the world of the poem just as surely as Rappaccini's daughter tempts Giovanni into the fatal garden. Moreover, like Rappaccini, Moore works hard to keep us within a strange and deadly realm "halfway between reality and fantasy."

"The Student" is "Part of a Poem" because the student speaks "in the manner of the poet," who is necessarily a "part" of the poem; and "The Hero" is "Part of a Play" because, like an actor, the hero speaks his familiar lines without actually "seeing" his audience. "The Steeple-Jack," however, is "Part of a Novel" because it is in a very important sense a fiction—a fiction "conceived," in Hawthorne's words, "with such proportionate strength . . . as to seem . . . more like truth, past, present, or to come, than purely fiction." Like most art—like "The Custom-House" and *The Scarlet Letter*—the poem is based on details of real people, real places, real things (late in August 1932, for instance, Moore wrote to her brother that she had shown Mrs. Moore "the summer house of slats and the iron door beside it").[56] Those details, however, are realigned, transformed, and charged with significance under the pressure of what Moore called, in her brief essay on Dürer, "the conjunction of fantasy and calculation."[57]

The town which seems to be so carefully and lovingly described in "The Steeple-Jack" does not exist on any map. It is not a single place but a composite, most of whose elements are drawn from "various New England seacoast towns . . . visited" over the years by the poet;[58] but it is really an image of Moore's new home.

The church that stands at the troubled moral center of the poem is not in New England. It is, according to Moore,[59] the Lafayette Avenue Presbyterian Church in Brooklyn, which she and her mother had been attending regularly since leaving Manhattan in 1929—a church which Moore describes in "Brooklyn from Clinton Hill" as exercising a "revolutionary force in the neighborhood," and a place of considerable significance in the context of the Moore's family history as well. In the same essay Moore tells a brief anecdote about her grandfather, a Presbyterian minister in St. Louis, who, upon being "urged by his congregation to take vacation, said h e needed none, merely wished to visit Brooklyn sometime and hear Dr. Cuyler preach in the Lafayette Avenue Church."[60]

The link between the Lafayette Avenue Church and the poet's grandfather is absolutely crucial. Moore was raised in her grandfather's house from the time of her birth in 1887 until his death in 1894; he was, in effect, the only father she ever knew. But now that "father" has been betrayed. The "pitch / of the church / spire" is "not true" after all; the "four fluted columns" of the church portico—"made / modester" by a coat of "whitewash," which does nothing to subdue the pride of the church but rather exposes that pride in the very process of trying to conceal it—makes a mockery of the Reverend Warner's unassuming desire to "visit Brooklyn," and perhaps of the poet's desire to live there.

Tired, longing for "Anonymity" and "privacy" and rest, Moore moved to Brooklyn seeking refuge from her "life of pressure in New York." For a time she found that refuge, helped perhaps by the proximity of a building whose mere presence must have evoked powerful memories of childhood security. And now that sanctuary is at risk. The danger comes in part from within —as in "Black Earth," where "external poise . . . / has its centre / well nurtured—we know / where—in pride"—but it comes from without as well, and it comes from the direction of Manhattan.

The threat is manifest in the figure of the steeplejack, the most striking instance of the "conjunction of fantasy and calculation" which Moore admires in Dürer. A healer and a destroyer, like Apollo (or like foxglove), the steeplejack unites in a single figure the "Dyvyll," who in 1533 "tooke one of the pinnacles away with him" from the church at Shrewsbury, and one C.J. Poole, a Brooklyn steeplejack who was employed, four hundred years later, in removing the steeple of the Lafayette Avenue Church after it had been rendered unsafe—not as a result of storm-damage, but because construction of a new subway line from Manhattan into Brooklyn had undermined the foundation.[61]

Moore had always felt deeply ambivalent about New York. It was the Statue of Liberty, and it offered freedom and "accessibility to experience" —but it was also Babylon, the whale's belly, a "vast indestructible necropolis" in which one led a "life of pressure." Moore had left Manhattan in the hope that in Brooklyn she would be safe. But now the city has subtly and invisibly extended itself, made its pressure felt in her life once more, and this time it has struck very deep: it has undermined the foundation of a building closely associated in the poet's mind with the image of "home."

If it is dangerous to enter Rappaccini's garden, it is no less "dangerous to be living / in a town like this," and Moore knows it. It is especially dangerous because it does not seem to be, because Brooklyn seems so much more remote from New York and its pressure than it really is. But it is not only dangerous for the poet: it is dangerous for us as well, and it is so precisely because its suddenly discovered proximity to New York has startled the poet into wakefulness. For if Moore cannot escape New York, neither can she escape herself: as in "In the Days of Prismatic Colour," she cannot slough off the conviction that she is the one who introduces a dark and "pestilential" complexity into the world, a complexity which has only been lying "'torpid in its lair.'"

So consistently does Moore mediate her vision through that of other figures—through Dürer and Ambrose and Hawthorne—that, as in "A Graveyard" eleven years earlier, her willingness to submerge herself allows her to conceal the guilty pride she has always taken in her own "technical mastery." She remains as nearly invisible as she had been in the earlier poem—and as dangerous. "The hero, the student, / the steeple-jack, each in his way, / is at home," she tells us in the penultimate stanza. We have seen the student and the steeplejack, and have tried to identify them. The hero can only be the poet, hiding, like "the unconfiding frigate-bird" of "The Frigate Pelican,"[62] in what Moore knows to be "the height and . . . the majestic / display of [her] art"—hiding, that is, in the "majestic / display" of the steeplejack on his great height just as she had earlier sunk herself in the less ostentatious brilliance of the student. She is "not out / seeing a sight": she is, as she puts it in "The Hero," "the rock / crystal thing to see": the poet and the steeplejack are one.

Even as Moore accuses a president and a religious institution of "gilding" corruption by illicit artistic means, of betraying the revolutionary promise of America, she herself is practicing the art of deception. She says what she does not mean in affirming that

> It could not be dangerous to be living
>   in a town like this, of simple people,
> who have a steeple-jack placing danger signs by the church
> while he is gilding the solid-
>   pointed star, which on a steeple
> stands for hope.

We should have learned by now that we cannot put much faith in what is merely set down "in black and white"; but in these final lines we must supply the proper coloring for ourselves. To read them ironically, however, is to acknowledge that we have found ourselves a "home" with "The hero, the student, / the steeple-jack"—in short, with the poet—and thus to acknowledge that, whatever we may have been when we began, we are no longer "simple people." It is to acknowledge, too, that if we have become complex it is only because the poet herself has taught us.

For the lie of the closing stanza only cements the far more subtle and elaborate one to which Moore has been committed throughout the poem. Despite her very real piety, she has been engaged in emulating the "malefic endeavor" that created the "Triptych of Aix": "Insinuating hell into every detail while preserving the pious appearance of the picture," the poet who had turned to free verse in an effort to come "closer to the truth" has discovered upon returning to her preferred form that the only way to "Tell all the Truth" is "to tell it slant— / Success in circuit lies. . . ."[63]

7

Advancing Backward in a Circle: The Poet as (Natural) Historian

"*Festina lente*," Moore writes in "The Frigate Pelican": "Be gay civilly." But then she stops to wonder, "How so?" and in its quiet way the poem explodes. In the first place, she is asking why the Latin word *lente*, "slowly," should take the very different word *civilly* as its English equivalent in this case. But this is the sort of problem in translation that raises more general questions of linguistic and especially poetic propriety, of how one is to know what is appropriate in a given context. The English phrase itself requires similar knowledge. To "be gay civilly," politely, is to occupy a certain position with respect to the *polis* in which one lives and in which one has a civil part to perform. The question for Moore is how to make poetry (which the Provençal poets called *gai saber*, "the gay science") a civil art—how to write freely without sacrificing her sense of community.[1]

The problem is not a new one for Moore, though it has never before emerged so clearly. By the time "The Frigate Pelican" appeared in Eliot's *Criterion* in July 1934, she had been working for two years to extricate herself from the duplicity of "The Steeple-Jack" and to define an art that would be at once responsible and free. "The Jerboa" (October 1932) begins with a section headed "Too Much," in which Moore assembles a collection of objects that had "passed for art" in ancient Rome and Egypt—emblems of what is most valued in societies where a privileged few have, "everywhere, / power over the poor."[2] Then, in the poem's second section, "Abundance," she moves out into the uninhabited desert, where "Jacob saw . . . steps of air and air angels," to discover a visionary alternative to the "hired" art of cities and kings. The poem begins by describing a grotesque conical fountain made for a fee by a Roman "freedman" and then "Placed," ironically, "on / the Prison of St. Angelo"; however, this huge object is offset by the tiny jerboa, which enters the poem near the end of the first section as a counterweight most immediately to "Pharoah's [*sic*] rat, the rust-backed mongoose" whose "restlessness was / its excellence."

The king "feared snakes" and "tamed" the mongoose, but the jerboa is not made to serve such purposes. A "free-born" creature which cannot be caught (even to pursue it is to be "cursed"), it "honors the sand by assuming its color," and the poem in turn honors the jerboa not only by assuming its name but also by tuning its own movements to those of the animal.

> By fifths and sevenths,
> in leaps of two lengths,
> like the uneven notes
> of the Beduin [*sic*] flute, it stops its gleaning
> on little wheel castors, and makes fern-seed
> foot-prints with kangaroo speed.
>
> Its leaps should be set
> to the flageolet;
> pillar body erect
> on a three-cornered smooth-working Chippendale
> "claw"—propped on hind legs, and tail as third toe,
> between leaps to its burrow.

The jerboa does not actually appear until well past the middle of the poem, but its invisible presence informs the poem from the outset. Every stanza begins with a line of five syllables and ends with a line of seven, so that each one works "By fifths and sevenths," and indeed the whole poem moves "in leaps of two lengths." The first section occupies ninety lines and takes up "Too Much" room; "Abundance" gets its job done in sixty.

Even as Moore returns to the syllabic verse formerly used to guard against imitation, she displays a renewed interest in the mimetic possibilities of verse. However, rather than use her syllabic patterns to secure her own distinctiveness, as she had in the 1910s, she is now using those patterns mimetically, to celebrate and preserve the distinctiveness of her *subjects*—as if by imitating a creature which knows nothing of society's rules she could gain for herself and her community a measure of that freedom and innocence. The closing lines of "The Jerboa" bring the animal within the pale of society—indeed, they make it a piece of living-room furniture, a "three-cornered smooth-working Chippendale / 'claw'" resting "on little wheel castors" so as not to scar the floor—but then they let it go. It has only been glimpsed as it paused "between leaps to its burrow."

"Be gay civilly." The jerboa is perhaps not quite gay enough to serve Moore's purposes completely. As the analogy with Chippendale furniture suggests, it is a bit too polite—like the delicate hothouse flowers of "Camellia Sabina"[3]—to satisfy the need for models of poetic freedom, and it lives too close to the ground to provide an adequate vantage point from which to observe the world. And so, in "The Frigate Pelican," Moore goes to the opposite extreme.

We are not dealing with a "simplified creature" like the jerboa this time. This bird goes under a variety of suggestive names—"hell-diver, frigate-bird, hurricane- / bird; unless swift is the proper word / for him"—but whatever he may be called, "he is not a pelican" and he is "dishonest" to boot. He "should be seen / fishing" but rarely will be, since "he seems to wish / to take, on the wing, from industrious cruder-winged species / the food they have caught, and is seldom successless." He is a thief, a vagabond; there is nothing domestic about him. "This is not the stalwart swan that can ferry the / woodcutter's two children home; no."

The frigate pelican, then, is a model of gaiety, of freedom, of the secret commitment to art:

> As impassioned Händel—
>
> meant for a lawyer and a masculine German domestic
> career—clandestinely studied the harpsichord
> and never was known to have fallen in love,
> the unconfiding frigate-bird hides
> in the height and in the majestic
> display of his art. He glides
> a hundred feet or quivers about
> as charred paper behaves—full
> of feints. . . .

This tricky height seems a perfect vantage point for observation:

> . . . It is not retreat but exclusion from
> which he looks down and observes what went
> secretly as it thought, out of sight
> among dense jungle plants.

The poet, too, would like to be "an eagle / of vigilance," would like to claim for herself "the high bird's-eye view / of the expert for whom" all those on the ground below are merely "ants / keeping house all their lives in the crack of a / crag with no view from the top"—for then she could enjoy the privilege of observing without being observed. But just as she is about to soar, to kick herself free of the earth, she puts a brake on her enthusiasm. "Be gay civilly," she admonishes herself, implying that to keep pace with the bird would be to abandon civility altogether—and suddenly she begins speaking in the plural, as if to assure us that she has taken her stand with us and not with "this most romantic bird." "We watch the moon rise / on the Susquehanna," but the bird is indifferent to the spectacle: flying off to "the mangrove swamp," he "wastes the moon" and goes to sleep.

When he rises again we see him as part of a community, for he has been joined by a flock of "others"; but his community is not ours. The birds, "though flying, are able to foil the tired / moment of danger, that lays on heart and lungs the / weight of the python that crushes to powder," but "We" are caught with the poet in the downdraft from Bryant's "To a Waterfowl" and dragged earthward, toward death.[4] "The tune's illiterate footsteps fail," and when the birds, "unturbulent, avail / themselves of turbulence to fly," they leave us standing flatfooted, sobered into civility.

What that civility really is, however, "The Frigate Pelican" does not and cannot say, except in the sense that the bird's behavior implies a kind of antithetical definition. For "the high bird's-eye view" of the frigate bird proves to be as inadequate to the purposes of civility as the desert-bound perspective of the jerboa is to the task of defending liberty within the bounds of society. "It is not retreat but exclusion" from which the bird "looks down" at the earth, but condescension is incompatible with civility, and civility—at least the American variety—is to Moore's mind the very opposite of "exclusion."

This chapter is an attempt to describe the process and the consequences of Moore's discovery that she shares with Henry James the complex fate of the "Characteristic American," whose civility depends not upon "exclusion" but rather upon "the instinct to amass and reiterate" which Moore finds in James and shares with him—an instinct which, for both writers, goes dangerously hand in hand with what James called "the rapture of observation."[5] This crucial discovery comes slowly, unfolding in four poems which were first published separately in the course of a year and then gathered into a coherent and powerful sequence which represents a critical juncture in Moore's career.

These poems are "Half Deity" (January 1935), "Smooth Gnarled Crape Myrtle!" (October 1935), "Virginia Britannia" (December 1935), and "Bird

Witted" (January 1936). Instead of treating them in the order of publication, however, we shall look at them in the order Moore designated in *The Pangolin and Other Verse* (1936), where they appear under the collective heading "The Old Dominion" and are arranged as follows: "Virginia Britannia," "Bird Witted," "Half Deity," and "Smooth Gnarled Crape Myrtle!"[6] This reordering is purposeful and highly significant. The sequence is designed to reveal, by gradual stages, the extent to which both the peculiar historical shape of America and the anguished, compromised civility of Moore's poetry are produced by the collaboration between "the rapture of observation" and "the instinct to amass and reiterate."

Moore makes James her spokesman when, in "Henry James as a Characteristic American" (April 1934), she quotes him as saying that "one's supreme relation . . . was one's relation to one's country."[7] In the poems of "The Old Dominion" we see Moore writing as one who is, like James, fully conscious of belonging to a particular place and a particular people, and of belonging in ways that have little to do with formal declarations of citizenship. Like James, she is conscious of embodying within herself and in her work the peculiar relationship which has obtained between America and its inhabitants since the first Europeans set foot on the continent. She writes as one who knowingly and openly participates in a tradition and a history, and she consciously takes her identity from that participation. In this respect, too, she is like James, of whom she writes that "Often he is those elements in American life—as locality and as character—which he recurrently studied and to which he never tired of assigning a meaning."[8]

And yet the identity Moore derives from that participation amounts finally to a negation of identity. The history of America is for her, as for many other American writers, a circular process of loss, a search for redemption which ends, inevitably, in yet another recapitulation of the Fall and thus implicates the American self in the irrecoverable lapse from innocence into experience and guilt and complexity. For James that lapse marks the beginning of identity, as in a different way it does for William Carlos Williams;[9] for Moore, however, it is an end point, beyond which the only possible movement is a regressive one that sets the whole cycle in motion again and confirms the enormity of the loss.

That loss becomes increasingly intolerable with each repetition, and by 1940 Moore's consciousness of herself "as a Characteristic American" has become a prison from which she cannot free herself—and from which she no longer even tries to escape. Her sense of history virtually collapses with the outbreak of the Second World War, to be replaced by a deepening, simplifying nostalgia for a world and a self gone beyond all hope of recovery, and the proud, critical intelligence takes to itself a shield of humility. "Humility is armor," Moore writes in 1948, because "it realizes that it is impossible to be original" and makes it unnecessary—in fact illegitimate—to try.[10] Nostalgia and humility combine forces to simplify not only Moore's vision of America and of her own relation to it, but her poems as well. And it is just at this point that she becomes a popular poet and an estimable public character—a writer admired for the delicacy with which she goes about gilding the cage of her civility and ours.

II

The history of "Virginia Britannia" itself exemplifies the process of simplification I have just outlined. The nostalgia which overpowers the late poems also wrecks "Virginia Britannia" in revision, reducing the complex, ironic vision of the original to an impotent and pious hope. The effects of Moore's revisions are most evident in the closing stanza, which is printed here as it originally appeared in the English magazine *Life and Letters Today* in December 1935. The stanza presents a highly detailed visual image of a landscape whose central figure, a child, is clearly identified by an allusion to Wordsworth's "Ode: Intimations of Immortality" as a figure for the innocence which cannot survive the advent of temporal and historical—and economic—consciousness:

> . . . The live-oak's moss-draped
> undulating massiveness, the white
>   pine, the English hackberry—handsomest vis-
> itor of all, the
>   cedar's etched solidity,
>   the cypress, lose identity
> and are one tree, as
>   sunset flames increasingly
>   over the leaf-chis-
> selled blackening ridge of green.
> Expanding to
> earth size, igniting redundantly
> wind-widened clouds, it can
>   not move bothered-with-wages
>   new savages,
> but gives the child an intimation
>   of what glory is.[11]

The allusion to Wordsworth is usually direct for Moore, and certainly she "would never have used allusion . . . in this way" earlier in her career, as Bonnie Costello says.[12] Moore herself acknowledges as much in the following statement, taken from a lecture she prepared for delivery at Sarah Lawrence College in May 1940:

> I did not care to use the word "intimation" because it suggested to me Wordsworth's Ode, INTIMATIONS OF IMMORTALITY and one naturally respects first rights, but after rejecting it a number of times, I still came back to it and felt I must, so I finally kept it. This in itself is of no importance, but it suggests to me what does seem to me important—that one must overcome a reluctance to be unoriginal and not be worried too much about possible comparisons and coincidences.[13]

The allusion is deliberate, then; and it is integral to the significance of the poem, serving a number of functions. First, it acknowledges the influence of Wordsworth's Ode upon the whole of "Virginia Britannia," and not just the final stanza. Second, it gives the final point to the carefully sustained analogy between the poet's deliberate, historically conscious construction of the poem and the equally deliberate and no less historically minded construction (by other hands) of the landscape with which all the poems of "The Old Dominion" are concerned. (The landscape of Colonial Virginia is not a natural one: it is a human artifact, a carefully constructed, reconstructured, and preserved historical record.) Finally, the allusion places "Virginia Britannia" in a complex and ironic relationship to the tradition of the Romantic ode, to which the other peoms of the sequence belong as well.

The allusion to Wordsworth is crucial not only to a full reading of "Virginia Britannia" and "The Old Dominion," but also, in a very real sense, to a reading of Moore's career. As we have seen it developing thus far, that career is best understood as a product of the tension between Moore's powerful "reluctance to be unoriginal" and the desire to "overcome" it. The publishing history of "Virginia Britannia" encapsulates that struggle and its outcome: as the poet's "reluctance to be unoriginal" lessens, the poem's strength diminishes, and Moore attempts to compensate for that loss rhetorically.

Accordingly, the allusion to Wordsworth occupies a very different place in the final version of the closing stanza (1951). Changes in grammar and syntax, and in the image itself, show a pronounced tendency toward simplification and abstraction, and the focus shifts away from the natural elements of the scene. The tone deepens, and the language becomes less concretely visual as the center of moral gravity is displaced—first onto the town, which does not figure at all in the original version, and finally onto the child:

> The live-oak's darkening filagree [*sic*]
> of undulating boughs, the etched
> solidity of a cypress indivisible
> from the now agèd English hackberry,
> become with lost identity,
> part of the ground, as sunset flames increasingly
> against the leaf-chiselled
> blackening ridge of green; while clouds, expanding above
> the town's assertiveness, dwarf it, dwarf arrogance
> that can misunderstand
> importance; and
> are to the child an intimation of what glory is.[14]

The natural elements of the scene have been redisposed and altered in such a way as to deprive them of their power: what had been, in the original version, a force acting upon consciousness, has now become a fixed image upon which consciousness must work—if it can, that is. Why this should be in question will become clearer if we recall the original version for a moment. What counts there is what we see, and to begin with we see five trees, each firmly planted by the definite article. "The live-oak" lends its "moss-draped / . . . massiveness" and its "undulating" motion to "the white / pine" and "the English hackberry," as "the cedar" imparts its own "etched solidity" to "the cypress": thus each tree is a felt, substantial, and active presence. They "are one tree" by the time we raise our eyes to the sunset flaming "over the leaf-chis- / selled / blackening ridge of green," but we carry with us an afterimage of each tree as a separate entity which persuades us both that something real is lost when all five "lose identity" before our eyes, and that something real is gained. The image of five trees becoming "one tree" has a dynamic strength which partakes of, and is greater than, that of any of the individual trees forming it.

The blazing sunset which brings the trees together also dominates the original stanza, and it is characteristic of Moore at her best that we should be made to feel its power most in a negative assertion:

> Expanding to
> earth size, igniting redundantly

wind-widened clouds, it can
　　　　　　not move bothered-with-wages
　　　　　　new savages,
but gives the child an intimation
　　of what glory is.

In the very movement back to earth, the lineation of the stanza discovers, against the pressure of its own expectancy, not what this splendid sunset can do, but what "it can / not" do. This sudden negation, however, does not cancel the sunset's power—for what "can / not move bothered-with-wages / new savages" nonetheless "gives the child an intimation / of what glory is"—but rather marks the adults' diminished capacity for response, a loss we share to the extent that we are more nearly kin to those "new savages" than we are to "the child."

Moore's confidence in our capacity for response has very nearly vanished by 1951, however, for in the revised text she virtually responds for us. What counts here is not so much what we see as what can be said of what is seen—and, in any case, what can be seen is much less than it was. The number of trees has been reduced from five to three (the white pine and the cedar have been cut away), and the remaining trees have been substantially altered. The live-oak, for instance, has been etherealized: the "moss-draped / undulating massiveness" has lost both its "moss" and its "mass" as well, and what we see now is a "darkening filagree / of undulating boughs," a delicate tracery of interwoven limbs. The previously unadorned "cypress," moreover, has taken to itself what had been "the / cedar's etched solidity," so that we find ourselves considering "the etched / solidity of a cypress. . . ." Furthermore, Moore transposes the modifying phrase and replaces the definite with the indefinite article, changes which downplay the importance of the tree itself (and so lessen its "solidity") while playing up, with the help of the new lineation, its appearance as an "etched" figure—a work of art in two, not three, dimensions. The line that names the cypress also moves us quickly past it, leading us to regard the tree not in itself but as part of a larger image consisting of "the etched / solidity of a cypress indivisible / from the now agèd English hackberry. . . ."

The trees seem nearly to disappear behind their attributes in this final version. No longer discrete entities that "lose identity" in coming together, they are treated now as subordinate elements of a scene already composed —a scene, moreover, to which their "identity" has already been "lost." They were central to the scene that was forming itself throughout the original version of this stanza, but they are no longer so: they simply "become with lost identity, / *part of the ground*" (emphasis added), and serve as backdrop to a drama which has nothing to do with them. Nor is this the Wordsworthian drama of the sunset which dominates the last ten lines of the original version, fusing the five trees into one, "igniting" the clouds, and working on the spirit of the child. For in the revised text, the sunset has been reduced to little more than a brief, dazzling spectacle. Though it now "flames against" the "blackening ridge of green" instead of simply rising "over" it as before, the dynamic of opposition implied by the changed preposition is evident only in this single moment. The sunset no longer "Expand[s]"; it no longer "ignit[es]" the clouds; and it now "gives" no more to "the child" than it does in the original version to the adult figures whom "it can / not move. . . ." The significant action—and indeed significance itself—appear to have been removed from the sunset to the clouds: "expanding above / the town's assertiveness," they

> . . . dwarf it, dwarf arrogance
> that can misunderstand
> importance; and
> are to the child an intimation of what glory is.

But in fact the clouds, no less than the sunset, have been rendered symbolically inert.

For all the delicately "etched" pictorial quality of the stanza thus far, Moore's visual thinking fails her when she needs it most. Because the figures of the trees have "lost identity" and "become . . . part of the ground," they are blotted out—as the sunset itself is virtually overshadowed—by the sudden "assertiveness" of a new element in the composition. The town has taken over entirely, occupying the whole field of the poet's vision and subsuming the "bothered-with-wages / new savages" into itself so completely that they no longer appear as discernible figures in the landscape. Like the trees, then, the "new savages" have "lost" their "identity," and the poem suffers for it.

Importing the "black savage" as a slave, killing off those other "savages" who were "subject to the / deer-fur crown" of the Indian chieftain "We-re-wo-co-mo-co"—in "colonizing as we say—" the original settlers of Virginia "were not all intel- / lect and delicacy," but their heirs are "new savages" in their own right. Their status is doubly ironic because they are not the backwoods louts of Crèvecœur's "What Is an American?" (1782)—men and women who slough off the restraining and civilizing influence of the agrarian settlements in the dangerously "unlimited freedom of the woods," and, "degenerat[ing] altogether into the hunting state," become "both Europeans and new made Indians," with "the vices of both" and the virtues of neither.[15] Moore's "new savages" are the nearest thing America has to an aristocracy: direct descendants of those who made Jamestown a place of elegant refinement, they count among their number the present

> . . . mistress of French
> plum-and-turquoise-
> piped chaise-longue; of brass-knobbed slat front door
> and everywhere open
>   shaded house on Indian-
>   named Virginian
> streams, in counties named for English lords! . . .

Moore's revision blunts the sharp historical irony of the original version against her monolithic vision of "the town's assertiveness"—a change emblematic of the shift in her thinking over the years since 1935, for she has increasingly come to identify the city as an agent of moral decay. And it is "the town's assertiveness," both visual and verbal, that drives Moore now to the rhetorical "assertiveness" of a repetition that cannot "dwarf" the town as the poem says the clouds do, but in fact does just the opposite. Forcing us to dwell on the twinned "assertiveness" and "arrogance" of the town, the repetition confirms its "importance" even in the attempt to deny it, thus establishing the town's presence all the more firmly.

Marie Borroff argues that the repetition of "dwarf" marks the upward limit of the poem's rhetorical movement; after this point

> the rhetorical intensity of the [stanza] diminishes noticeably. . . . The . . . description of arrogant behavior as capable of "misunderstanding importance" is surely a charitable understatement for [the] centuries of exploitation and prejudice [with which the preceding stanzas are concerned]. Even the allusion to Wordsworth comes wrapped in a prosy syntax. . . . The sunset continues to flame as the last words of the poem are spoken, but the colors of the language have faded.[16]

Borroff does not take the earlier version of the stanza into account, however. What we hear when we measure the final text against the original is not a diminishing of "rhetorical intensity" at all, but rather a deliberate elevation of tone. Combining the two sentences of the original version into one, eliminating many of the more awkward syntactic constructions—and many of the harsher consonants with them—Moore's revisions give more prominence to the quiet vocalic modulations which take us from "oak" to "boughs" to "now," from "now" to "ground" to "town's," and finally to "glory." Even the sibilants are softer, at least until we come to the sudden harshness of "the town's assertiveness" and its "arrogance / that can misunderstand / importance. . . ."

Not only this deliberate heightening of tone but also the repetition of "dwarf" which contributes to it and the very slight downward modulation following that repetition may be explained in part as the result of Moore's effort to "overcome [her] reluctance to be unoriginal." The effect of these revisions is to bring the tone of the stanza as a whole more nearly into harmony with that of the final strophe of Wordsworth's Immortality Ode. Here, too, a repetition drives the poem toward closure:

> . . . The innocent brightness of a newborn Day
> Is lovely yet;
> The clouds that gather round the setting sun
> Do take a sober colouring from an eye
> That hath kept watch o'er man's mortality;
> Another race hath been, and other palms are won.
> Thanks to the human heart by which we live,
> Thanks to its tenderness, its joys, and fears,
> To me the meanest flower that blows can give
> Thoughts that do often lie too deep for tears.[17]

The last two lines are quieter than the pair immediately preceding them, but there is no lessening of intensity; if there were, the poem would have failed. The repetition of "Thanks" quickens our reading; the quietness of the following lines slows it again, making us feel the emotional pressure which has been accumulating throughout the strophe much as stepping on the brake makes us feel the weight of the car. Moore's closing lines work in a similar way: the speed built up by the repeated "dwarf" is checked by the percussives and sibilants—and the brevity—of the following lines. We feel the fury with which Moore excoriates "arrogance / that can misunderstand / importance," and then the poem moves on, consonants softening and vowels lengthening, to discover with Wordsworth that the clouds "are to the child an intimation of what glory is."

But the similarity of Moore's tone to Wordsworth's both masks and compensates for what is now an evident dissimilarity of conception, for there is a different, more powerful harmony at work in the original version of "Virginia Britannia." There, the natural world is an active force which "*gives* the child an intimation / of what glory is," just as, for Wordsworth, "the meanest flower . . . can *give* / Thoughts that . . . lie too deep for tears" (emphasis added). Wordsworth has only "relinquished one delight / To live beneath the more habitual sway" of "Fountains, Meadows, Hills, and Groves," but these are precisely the "delights" which Moore has relinquished. Now that the town has imposed itself on the scene, the "sway" of nature can no longer be said to be "habitual." The natural elements of the landscape have lost their power to act, and consciousness must therefore assume the burden of acting on them it they are to retain their significance. But the consciousness upon which that burden falls cannot bear the weight: the Wordsworthian "child" is by definition incapable of the sort of conscious recognition which the stanza now requires of her.

The stubborn assertiveness of the town's presence destroys the visual logic of the stanza and threatens its visionary conclusion as well. No "intimation" will be vouchsafed if the "clouds" are obscured; but there is nothing left to look at except the town. The only way to avoid being entirely thwarted by its "assertiveness," therefore, the only way to secure the "intimation" upon which the poem depends, is to avoid looking. Moore accomplishes this by redefining "the town's assertiveness" in abstract moral terms, as a manifestation of "arrogance." She thus removes it from the visual plane in which it is now the dominant feature, to the safer plane of thought; but this critical transposition puts the very existence of "the child" in jeopardy.

The logic by which Moore arrives at the vision of the child in the original version is both visual and syntactic. The gaze travels upward from the trees to the "leaf-chis- / selled / blackening ridge of green," and on into the sky, where it finds the sunset "Expanding to / earth size" and "igniting redundantly / wind-widened clouds. . . ." Having widened the scope of vision as far as possible, it is visually and pictorially natural that the poet should now contract it, and the transitive movement of the sentence provides the means of doing so. The sunset itself, in its inability as grammatical agent to "move bothered-with-wages / new savages," brings the poem back to earth and forces vision to adjust to the human scale. At the same time, the antithetical structure of the sentence makes possible the further narrowing of focus by which the poet finds the child: the sunset "can / not move bothered-with-wages / new savages, / but gives the child an intimation. . . ."

In the final version, however, there is no way, visually speaking, to get to the child. The poem must come to a full stop, then resort to the crudest of conjunctions and the weakest of verbs:

> . . . clouds, expanding above
> the town's assertiveness, dwarf it, dwarf arrogance
> that can misunderstand
> importance; and
> are to the child an intimation of what glory is.

These lines claim for the clouds a mastery over human assertion that the earlier version does not grant to the sunset, the limits of whose revelatory power are reached in and defined by its failure to "move" the adults. Despite that failure, however, the sunset retains sufficient force to bring the child into harmony with nature, "igniting" the clouds and inspiring the child in the same extended movement. The effort in the final version is rhetorically to suggest the same continuity of vision and action, and so to imply a similar consanguinity between the child and the landscape; but the effort is belied by the interruption of the sentence and, more importantly, by the shift from the transitive "dwarf" which precedes the semicolon to the intransitive "are" which follows it. The poet's effort to overcome "the town's assertiveness" by making the "clouds . . . dwarf it" has instead rendered the clouds—and, by extension, the whole of nature—inert: they do not act upon the child at all, and cannot, of themselves, yield up their significance. The poet must therefore tell us what they "are." Abandoning the visual in an attempt to save the visionary, Moore has been forced to substitute for the authority of her own vision that of a more nearly Wordsworthian tone of voice; in doing so, however, she denies the intimation upon which the poem is founded and by which it must prove itself.

The original version anticipates and justifies the introduction of the child by focusing first upon the adults who are presumably her parents and to whom, in turn, according to the Wordsworthian conception, "The child is father"—though we should say "mother" here. To be "bothered-with-wages" as these "new savages" are is to be opposed to the process by which the child gains "an intimation / of what glory is," but it is not necessarily to oppose that process knowingly. It is, if anything, to be entirely oblivious to the transaction, as the child herself is ignorant (intellectually, at least) of nature's operations upon her spirit. The relationship between the enlightened child and the financially concerned "new savages" is not antagonistic, then, nor—since both occupy the stage at the same time—is it mutually exclusive: it is, rather, mutually generative. The child is mother of the woman, and the woman into whom the child has grown, though unable fully to apprehend the "glory" to which the child is privy, engenders in her turn the child to whom such an "intimation" may be given. The one requires the other: the presence of the child is authenticated for us because we know where she has come from and what she must become. Similarly, the "intimation" rings true not only because we know it to be necessarily transitory, but also because the word itself tells us that whatever the immediacy of the child's experience, it is for the poet who employs it with such knowing precision no more and no less than a memory. In this, too, Moore's original conception accords with Wordsworth's. The world is beautiful, says Wordsworth, "The sunshine is a glorious birth; / And yet I know, where'er I go, / That there hath past away a glory from the earth."

The final version of Moore's closing stanza, however, brings the child prematurely into the world, removing her from the generative relations she enjoys in the original text. Without parental figures to justify her presence, there is nothing to engender the child but the pressure of the poet's voice, acceding to the need for a vision to counter "the town's assertiveness" and urged by the memory of Wordsworth. For if in the Immortality Ode we enter the world "Not in entire forgetfulness, / And not in utter nakedness, / But trailing clouds of glory," in "Virginia Britannia" both "glory" and "the child" herself are mere cloud-born memories. The poet must tell us what the clouds "are to the child" because the world as it is can "give" nothing (nothing but impetus, that is) to our already-formed memory of the world as it was; but in doing so she breaks the circuit which, in the earlier version, binds the child to nature, and substitutes for it a bond between herself and the child as joint interpreters of the world. Bringing the child into the sphere she inhabits—a sphere in which such experiences as the child's are impossible—the poet imposes on her the burden of her own conscious antagonism to the world, forces the child to join her in crying out against "arrogance." Thus pitted against "the town's assertiveness," the child is simply dwarfed, rendered as inert as the clouds; the "intimation" of "glory" has been reduced to a pious wish.

Ironically, that reduction is most tellingly revealed by the fact that the word itself has been removed from its original place at the end of the penultimate line and repositioned at the center of what is now the final line. This might be construed as an indication that Moore's struggle against her own "reluctance to be unoriginal" is over at last—that her memory of Wordsworth has by now been so comfortably assimilated that the word "intimation" may be accorded the central position it deserves. But in fact the opposite is true. Moore has had to interrupt the movement of the sentence in order to turn it away from the "arrogance" of the town toward the child; and in order to tell us what the clouds "are to the child," she has had to conflate the child's experience with her own memory. What the repositioning of the word "intimation" intimates most clearly, then, is Moore's failure to maintain the fine, edgy balance—so nicely registered in the way the word had originally been poised—between her own articulate and historical knowledge and what Donald Wesling calls in *Wordsworth and the Adequacy of Landscape* the child's "wordless unity with the forms of nature."[18]

"Our birth," says Wordsworth, "is a sleep and a forgetting"—though our "forgetfulness" is not "entire": we are born "trailing clouds of glory . . . / From God, who is our home." The child does possess a kind of memory, but not one to be confused with the worldly knowledge that allows the poet to recognize "the town's assertiveness" as a manifestation of "arrogance"—a spiritual debility of which the child is (as yet) innocent. We must bear in mind especially that while the child's silent receptivity to intimations depends upon her innate, rudimentary memory of "home," that memory has nothing to do with *time*. It is rather our assurance that the child is innocent of the historical consciousness that not only determines the poet's use of the word "intimation" to name an experience of which the child cannot speak, but also informs the whole of "Virginia Britannia" and the "Old Dominion" sequence.

III

To demonstrate that the presentation of landscape in "Virginia Britannia" is shaped by Moore's sense of the historical forces at work in the formation of the landscape itself, it may be best to begin by setting this landscape against that of an earlier attempt to characterize the American Scene. The first sentence of "England" covers a great deal of ground before reaching its ultimate destination:

England

with its baby rivers and little towns, each with its abbey or its cathedral;
    with voices—one voice perhaps, echoing through the transept—the
criterion of suitability and convenience; and Italy with its equal
        shores—contriving an epicureanism from which the grossness has been

extracted: and Greece with its goats and its gourds, the nest of modified illusions:
and France, the "chrysalis of the nocturnal butterfly" in
whose products, mystery of construction diverts one from what was originally one's
object—substance at the core: and the East with its snails, its emotional

shorthand and jade cockroaches, its rock crystal and its imperturbability,
all of museum quality: and . . .

And so, finally, we arrive in

. . . America where there
is the little old ramshackle victoria in the south, where cigars are smoked on the
street in the north; where there are no proof-readers, no silk-worms, no digressions;

the wild man's land; grassless, links-less, language-less country—in which letters are written
not in Spanish, not in Greek, not in Latin, not in shorthand
but in plain American which cats and dogs can read![19]

To land in such a place is to land in the middle of a parody of what is already parody. For this place, this America, "where there are no proof-readers, no silk-worms, no digressions," this "grass-less, links-less, language-less country," is Moore's answer to Henry James's celebrated catalogue of those crucial "items of high civilisation, as it exists in other countries, which are missing from the texture of American life. . . ." There is, says James in his study of Hawthorne,

> No State, in the European sense of the word, and indeed barely a specific national name. No sovereign, no court, no personal loyalty, no aristocracy, no church, no clergy, no army, no diplomatic service, no country gentlemen, no palaces, no castles, nor manors, nor old country-houses, nor parsonages, nor thatched cottages, nor ivied ruins; no cathedrals, nor abbeys, nor little Norman churches; no great Universities nor public schools—no Oxford, nor Eton, nor Harrow; no literature, no novels, no museums, no pictures, no political society, no sporting class—no Epsom nor Ascot![20]

In granting to "each" of England's "little towns . . . its abbey or its cathedral," Moore seems to grant James's argument as well—especially as she makes her own contribution to his list of "absent things."[21] By the end of the poem, though, she has turned the Jamesian tables: in effect she accuses him of having "misapprehended" America's true cultural condition because he has assumed that "high civilisation" must exist in America "as it exists in other countries," and has therefore sought only the conventional signs, the visible "flower and fruit of all that . . . superi- / ority" which he has "noted" so readily in England and on the Continent. "To have misapprehended the matter," however, "is to have confessed / that one has not looked far enough"—a sin to Moore, as to James. It may well be that "one" has not, in one's American travels, "stumbled upon" such proofs of "high civilisation" as "The sublimated wisdom / of China, Egyptian discernment, the cataclysmic torrent of emotion compressed / in the verbs of the Hebrew language." But, Moore demands, "must one" therefore "imagine / that it is not there?" Civilization and superiority, she reminds us tartly, have "never been confined to one locality."

"Virginia Britannia," like "England," examines the question of what we bring to the vision of America, but poses that question in a very different way. Here, too, we approach America from the vantage point of the early settlers and the subsequent travelers whose negative visions James's parody both reinforces and deprecates: we approach from the sea, and from the past. But we arrive at a very different place from the America of "England": we begin where

> Pale sand edges England's old
> dominion. The air is soft, warm, hot,
>   above the cedar-dotted emerald shore
> known to the redbird,
>   the redcoated musketeer,
>   the trumpet-flower, the cavalier,
> the parson, and the
>   wild parishioner. A deer-
>   track in a church-floor
> brick and Sir George Yeardley's
> coffin tacks and
> tomb remain. The now tremendous vine-
> encompassed hackberry
>   starred with the ivy-flower,
>   shades the church tower.
> And "a great sinner lyeth here" un-
>   der the sycamore.

This looks like a conventional landscape—but not like a conventional American landscape. "Virginia Britannia" makes landfall in what should, by long-standing convention, be an empty new world in which the sights offered to the eye are instantly overwhelmed by the traveler's memory of what he has left at home, as in Bradford's account of the Pilgrims' arrival on Cape Cod:

> Being thus passed ye vaste ocean . . . they had now no freinds to wellcome them, nor inns to entertaine or refresh their weather-beaten bodys, no houses or much less townes to repaire too, to seeke for succoure. It is recorded in scripture as a mercie to ye apostle & his shipwraked company, yt the barbarians shewed no smale kindnes in refreshing them, but these savage barbarians . . . were readier to fill their sids full of arrows. . . . Besids, what could they see but a hidious & desolate wildernes, full of wild beasts & willde men? . . . which way soever they turnd their eys (save upward to ye heavens) they could have little solace or content in respecte of any outward objects. For . . . all things stand upon them with a wetherbeaten face, and ye whole countrie . . . represented a wilde & savage heiw. If they looked behind them, ther was ye mighty ocean which they had crossed, and was now as a maine barr & goulfe to seperate them from all ye civill parts of ye worlde.[22]

Two hundred years later, and more, American artists are still complaining about the absences in American life, though they no longer mourn the missing comforts of home and friends, and for them there is more to see than "a hidious & desolate wildernes." What they miss are the historical markers which abound in the European landscape. Washington Irving writes in 1819 that while no American "need . . . look beyond his own country for the sublime and beautiful of natural scenery . . . Europe [holds] forth all the charms of storied and poetical association. . . . Her very ruins [tell] the history of times gone by, and every mouldering stone [is] a chronicle."[23] Irving cannot imagine a fiction without ruins, and he goes to considerable lengths to remedy the defect—with startling results. In "Rip Van Winkle," which transposes a German folk tale called "Peter the Goatherd" to an American setting, Irving discovers a mechanism which transforms America itself—that brand-new country—into what is already a ruin:

> [Rip] hastened to his old resort, the village inn—but it too was gone. A large rickety wooden building stood in its place, with great gaping windows, some of them broken and mended with old hats and petticoats, and over the door was painted, "the Union Hotel, by Jonathan Doolittle." Instead of the great tree that used to shelter the quiet little Dutch inn of yore, there now was reared a tall naked pole, with something on the top that looked like a red night-cap, and from it was fluttering a flag on which was a singular assortment of stars and stripes. . . . He recognized on the sign . . . the ruby face of King George . . . but even this was singularly metamorphosed. The red coat was changed for one of blue and buff, a sword was held in the hand instead of a sceptre, the head was decorated with

> a cocked hat, and underneath was painted in large characters, GENERAL WASHINGTON.[24]

The landscape painter Thomas Cole also felt the deficiency of ruins, just as he shared Irving's appreciation for the glories of America's "natural scenery." Writing in 1835, shortly after his own European tour, Cole acknowledges that America affords no signs of "antiquity," but he goes on to instruct his readers (and prospective buyers of his work) on the specific virtues of the American landscape:

> There are those who . . . maintain that American scenery possesses little that is interesting or truly beautiful . . . that being destitute of those vestiges of antiquity whose associations so strongly affect the mind it may not be compared with European scenery. . . . But I would have it remembered that nature has shed over *this* land beauty and magnificence, and although the character of the scenery may differ from the old world's, yet inferiority must not therefore be inferred; for though American scenery is destitute of many of those circumstances that give value to the European, still it has features, and glorious ones, unknown to Europe.[25]

Cole's most ambitious series of paintings, *The Course of Empire* (1836), reveals a double preoccupation with "American scenery" and the missing "vestiges of antiquity" which, like Irving, Cole feels impelled to supply. He superimposes on the "glorious" features of the American landscape a set of bizarre buildings, each of which borrows different elements from different European and classical models, somewhat in the manner of the "composite" architecture of Fenimore Cooper's Templeton; successive paintings show these buildings (and the civilization they represent) in progressive stages of decay, until at last there is nothing left but moldering ruins.[26]

Cooper himself displays a certain desperate ingenuity in his effort to discover traces of "antiquity" even in the fastnesses of the American wilderness. *The Last of the Mohicans*—on which Cole based several paintings—was composed in 1826, but it is set in 1757, early in the French and Indian wars that are part of the prehistory of the United States. Setting the novel in the comparatively remote American past, Cooper both solves part of the problem of furnishing himself with a history whose forces are still at work and creates a further difficulty for himself: the landscape in which the action is staged is even less settled than that of Cooper's own day, and therefore even less likely to afford objects of archaeological interest. Cooper's solution can hardly help seeming ludicrous, but in its way it works: he has Leatherstocking lead a bewildered group of settlement-dwellers past the decaying remains of a wooden hut built by Leatherstocking himself during a previous campaign:

> The recollection of the scout did not deceive him. . . . he entered an open space . . . which was crowned by the decayed block-house in question. This rude and neglected building was one of those deserted works, which, having been thrown up in an emergency, had been abandoned with the disappearance of danger, and was now quietly crumbling in the solitude of the forest, neglected, and nearly forgotten, like the circumstances which had caused it to be reared. Such memorials of the passage and struggles of man are yet frequent throughout the broad barrier of wilderness which once separated the hostile provinces, and *form a species of ruins* that are intimately associated with the recollections of colonial history, and which are in appropriate keeping with the gloomy character of the surrounding scenery.[27]

Moore has no need for such desperate contrivances, no need to fabricate the "vestiges of antiquity" on which her predecessors depended so heavily and whose absence they felt so keenly. Someone has already done it for her—someone who, like Bradford and Irving and Cole and Cooper, had evidently found the landscape of the New World too starkly "destitute" of historical markers for comfort. The result is that in the opening stanza of "Virginia Britannia" we find ourselves in a "known" landscape whose elements are familiar and firmly fixed, a landscape in which we are comfortable because we know, or think we know, what to think and how to respond. For this is so much a "typical ivied-bower-and-ruined-tower churchyard," as Moore later called it,[28] that we half expect to hear how

> . . . from yonder ivy-mantled tow'r
>   The moping owl does to the moon complain
> Of such as, wand'ring near her secret bower,
>   Molest her ancient solitary reign. . . .[29]

But the ease with which this setting can be accommodated to such well-"known" landscapes as that of Gray's *Elegy* is deceptive. We do not in fact hear "The moping owl," and though the resemblance is very close, it is not quite perfect:

> . . . The Old Dominion has
> all-green grass-hoppers
>   in all-green, box-sculptured grounds;
>   an almost English green surrounds
> them. . . .

The landscape has been carefully "box[ed]" and "sculptured" to look "almost English"; but as the stanza continues we find that the pursuit of resemblance tends only to the discovery of difference. Thus

> . . . Care has formed, a-
> mong unEnglish insect sounds,
> the white wall-rose. As
> thick as Daniel Boone's grape-
> vine, the stem has
> wide-spaced great blunt alternating os-
> trich-skin warts that were thorns. . . .

Set "a- / mong unEnglish insect sounds, / the white wall-rose" falls a little too heavily on the ear: the carefully modulated but decidedly "unEnglish" prosody, spreading an iambic pentameter across three lines, leads us straight into the "white wall" of a trochee and comes to a dead halt. The plant strikes the eye awkwardly as well, for "the white wall-rose" is no delicate English bloom: as if the soil of this "Rare unscent- / ed, provident- / ly hot, too sweet, inconsistent flower- / bed" were too rich for it, it has grown unchecked into an American grotesque, with a "stem" as "thick as Daniel Boone's grape- / vine" and covered with ugly "warts."

Whoever the gardener may have been, he was no American Adam planting his garden in all innocence, and "the white wall-rose" bears the scars of its troubled origin in its very grotesqueness. The "wide-spaced great blunt alternating os- / trich-skin warts that were thorns" are the heraldic marks of its lineage: they place it in the direct line of descent from that "able / string-ray-hampered pioneer," the "incessantly / exciting Captain Smith" who, "with ostrich, Latin motto, / and small gold horseshoe" for his coat of "arms," explored and mapped and fought—and wrote—both for England's sake and for his own glory and profit. But the anonymous gardener may have had other concerns than money and fame: besides building "the white wall-rose," his "Care has formed walls of yew"—walls meant to conceal from the troubled eyes of people far from home what "Jamestown was" when the first settlers arrived: the "narrow neck of / land" that "Indians knew" long before America's mere existence had become "known" either to "the cavalier" or to "the redcoated musketeer" who came in his wake to secure English supremacy and ended by losing it.

English "dominion" ends and exploration of the new American dispensation begins in the crucial fourth stanza, immediately following the revelation of what the gardener's "Care" has wrought. Having discovered the "wall-rose" and the "walls of yew" which have been "formed" as barriers against what "Jamestown was," we must now begin to penetrate the screen; and to that end we are peremptorily directed to

> Observe the terse Virginian,
> the mettlesome gray one that drives the
> owl from tree to tree and imitates the call
> of whippoorwill or
> lark or katydid—the lead-
> gray lead-legged mocking-bird with head
> held half away, and
> meditative eye as dead
> as sculptured marble
> eyes. Alighting noiseless-
> ly it muses
> in the semi-sun, on tall thin legs,
> as if it did not see,
> still standing there alone
> on the round stone-
> topped table with lead cupids grouped to
> form the pedestal.

Moore's treatment of the mockingbird here and in "Bird Witted" makes it the central figure of "The Old Dominion" sequence, and its significance is manifold. Driving the "owl from tree to tree" without giving it a chance to "complain," the mockingbird evokes the memory of Gray's *Elegy* in the very act of dispelling it, and so ambiguously ushers in the new era: "still standing there alone / on the round stone- / topped table," the mockingbird—not an English import like "the white wall-rose" but a native "Virginian"—persists in sole possession of the field, signaling the end of England's "ancient solitary reign" over her "old / dominion." (Later the poem will remind us that "The rattlesnake soon / said from our once dashingly / undiffident first flag, 'don't tread on me.' . . . ")

But even as the indigenous figure of the mockingbird enters the arena to "drive" off the foreign invader, it is apparently possessed by the very forces which have already "formed" the scene with such "Care." For just as "The Old Dominion has . . . all-green, box-sculptured grounds," so the mockingbird has a "meditative eye as dead / as sculptured marble / eyes," and by the end of the stanza it has become—to all appearances, at least—a leaden statue upon a "stone- / topped table with lead cupids grouped to / form the pedestal." Like the trees in the final version of the poem's closing stanza, the mockingbird seems to have been subordinated to an image which has already been composed, and whose completion has depended only upon the presence of the bird itself. The bird has succeeded in displacing a specific intruder, but it cannot undo that intruder's previous work.

Or at least it cannot undo that work entirely; but it may alter, or even perhaps pervert, its effects. For we may "Observe" of the mockingbird what we "Observe" in the Immortality Ode when Wordsworth instructs us to "Behold the Child, among his new-born blisses"—that it seems "As if [its] whole vocation / Were endless imitation." As though the bird had no "vocation," no "call" of its own, it "imitates the call / of whippoorwill or / lark or katydid. . . . " But it is "As if" the "whole vocation" of Jamestown, too, had been "endless imitation," for we have seen with what painstaking "Care" those "new-born" Americans "formed" the Virginia landscape in the image of the English one they had left behind. There are, then, two quite distinct mimetic projects going on simultaneously in this stanza, projects which proceed from very different and indeed conflicting motives—though, as Moore writes in "Sea Unicorns and Land Unicorns," they may "be combined in concert such / that when they do agree, their unanimity is great. . . . " The Jamestown settlers imitate the forms of home in order to reduce what they can only regard as foreign elements (which is to say, native ones) to familiar terms; they are like the Puritans of Williams's "The American Background" (1934), who "*saw birds with rusty breasts and called them robins . . . . But at a cost. For they were not robins.*"[30] By contrast, the mockingbird "imitates the call" of other creatures not in order to assimilate them more comfortably but rather in order to "drive" its enemies away and to establish its own "dominion."

"Virginia Britannia" thus confronts us, in the figure of the mockingbird, with the possibility that what is most distinctively "American" in American art—whether it be the art of landscape or of poetry—may be precisely that "endless" capacity for "imitation" which has so often been denounced, by writers from Poe and Emerson to Williams and Pound, as a foreign habit detrimental to American expression. The figure of the mockingbird suggests that mimesis is a native—indeed an instinctive—tendency. But its name implies that American mimesis must take a specific form. In order to guard against the deadening effects of mere slavish imitation, of foreign "dominion," it must turn to parody, as Poe had done a century before in the effort to establish America's cultural independence from Europe. For "the lead- / gray lead-legged mocking-bird with head / held half away, and / meditative eye as dead / as sculptured marble / eyes," is a reincarnation, prosodically and imagistically, of the Raven—the macabre creature of that "terse Virginian," Poe, whom Williams had celebrated in the brilliant penultimate chapter of *In the American Grain.*

"It is the New World, or to leave that for the better term, it is a *new locality* that is in Poe assertive," Williams had written; "it is America, the first great burst through to expression of a re-awakened genius of *place.*"[31] The mockingbird is precisely that "re-awakened genius of *place*": "still standing there alone / on the round stone- / topped table with lead cupids grouped to / form the pedestal," just as Poe's Raven "still is sitting, still is sitting / On the pallid bust of Pallas just above [the] chamber door," the mockingbird brings on the American Revolution—driven, as Williams said Poe had been, by the conviction that "all 'colonial imitation' must be swept aside."[32]

IV

Aptly, "Bird Witted" takes its title from the writings of Sir Francis Bacon, whom Moore admired both as a literary stylist and as a scientist credited with a major role in the development of modern scientific methods based on careful, empirical observation of natural phenomena—a development which coincides with the settling of Virginia in the late sixteenth and early seventeenth centuries.[33] The poem invites us once more to "Observe the terse Virginian," the mockingbird to which we are introduced in the fourth stanza of "Virginia Britannia," and to do so with an exact and scrupulous eye. But we are no longer to "Behold" it as a static image, as we do in "Virginia Britannia" and in the case of Wordsworth's "child," that "six months darling of a pigmy size!" The invitation here is implicit: instead of being commanded to "Observe," we are shown a triad of young mockingbirds awaiting their mother at feeding time. The careful observation of this family of birds in action gives an ironic twist, however, to Bacon's concern over what might happen "If a boy be bird-witted,"[34] for Moore is interested not only in the empty-headedness of the young (whose sex is of no concern to the poem) but also in the mother-wit of the adult female who has to feed and protect them.

With innocent wide penguin eyes, three
        grown fledgling mocking-birds below
the pussy-willow tree,

stand in a row,
wings touching, feebly solemn,
till they see
their no longer larger
mother bringing
something which will partially
feed one of them.

The youth of these three birds is crucial: the first thing we learn about them is that their "eyes" are "innocent"—innocent, it will turn out, of that power of observation which would enable them to identify their enemies, and of the capacity for imitation which their mother possesses (though she does not exercise it here), and which depends in turn upon accurate observation.

The young birds are evidently capable of recognizing their mother, but the poet's powers of observation are considerably sharper. As Hugh Kenner has noted, the cries of the "fledgling mocking-birds" are caught in the reiterated double *ee*s of the stanza, though for a moment "their cry is muted to the final syllable of 'partially'" when "they see" their mother coming with food.[35] As the feeding begins, their voices are "raised with a new urgency" in the rhyming "squeak" and "meek" and "beak" of the second stanza[36] —decidedly unmusical sounds attesting to their inability to "imitate the call" of anything but broken machinery:

Towards the high keyed intermittent squeak
of broken carriage-springs, made by
the three similar, meek-
coated bird's-eye
freckled forms she comes; and when
from the beak
of one, the still living
beetle has dropped
out, she picks it up and puts
it in again.

This goes beyond careful attention to detail: as Kenner says, "there is affectionate mimesis in the awkward 'dropped / out' and the businesslike 'she picks it up and puts / it in again.'"[37] The poem is similarly mimetic when, at a crucial stage later on, it stumbles slightly, with one of the birds, then regains its footing and proceeds:

A dangling foot that missed
its grasp, is raised
and finds the twig on which it
planned to perch. . . .

On a casual reading, it may seem that these birds are the objects of a scrupulously neutral (if sympathetic) attention, of the sort empiricism is supposed to demand. But the eye which initially perceives the young birds' eyes as "innocent" is informed by a moral sense, a knowledge which is by definition not available to innocence itself; and such judgments are specifically disallowed by empirical procedures. The poet's status as observer is in fact the central issue in "Bird Witted"—though we have no way of knowing this until the fourth stanza, where Moore turns her whole attention to the mother:

What delightful note
with rapid unexpected flute-
sounds leaping from the throat
of the astute
grown bird comes back to one from
the remote
unenergetic sun-
lit air before
the brood was here? Why has the
bird's voice become

harsh? . . .

As Kenner notes, the mother's song "echoes without effort" in the stanza's alternating rhymes, and then "drops into harshness" as the poem moves into the new stanza and enters a critical new phase.[38] But there is a considerable difference between the mimetic effort we have observed so far and the imitative work being performed here.

Uniquely, the stanza just quoted provides no visual data at all; it is entirely devoted to sound. Furthermore, in other stanzas the poem keeps time with the birds; but the "delightful note . . . leaping from the throat / of the astute / grown bird" is not being sounded now: it only

. . . comes back to one from
the remote
unenergetic sun-
lit air before
the brood was here. . . .

It is, then, a "note" sounding not in the ear but in what Wallace Stevens later called "the delicatest ear of the mind,"[39] reminding us of a moment of apparently innocent ecstasy now past, and deliberately recalled—not by the bird, of course, but by the poet. And Moore's act of recall here is no more innocent than the one which, in the closing lines of "Virginia Britannia," balances the full burden of the poem on a single, carefully poised word out of memory.

Again Kenner alerts us to a crucial aspect of the poem when he suggests that the technical inspiration for "Bird Witted" may be found in Pound's *ABC of Reading,* which had been published just over a year before "Bird Witted" appeared in January 1936.[40] Pound writes that for the troubadour poets the "'whole art'" of poetry "consisted in putting together about six strophes of poetry so that the words and tune should be welded together without joint and without wem"; the poet whose work best exemplified that art, he says, was "the best smith, as Dante called *Arnaut Daniel,* [who] made the birds sing IN HIS WORDS . . . for six strophes WITH the words making sense."[41] This is exactly what Moore has sought to do in "Bird Witted," and she has done it in a way that both confirms and extends Kenner's hypothesis. For she has used Pound's discussion of Daniel very much as she had earlier used Smith's discussion of Isaiah—as a technical prescription which enables her to give formal, mimetic expression to the interest in Provençal poetry which her reading of Pound's *Cantos* had engendered five years ealier. (She even follows Pound's description of the "perfect strophe" in Daniel "where the bird call interrupts the verse."[42]) Reviewing *A Draft of XXX Cantos* for *Poetry* in October 1931, Moore had written:

> If poetics allure, the Cantos will . . . show that in Provençal minstrelsy we encounter a fascinating precision; the delicacy and exactness of Arnaut Daniel, whose invention, the sestina form, is "like a thin sheet of flame folding and infolding upon itself." *In this tongue . . . is to be found pattern.* And the Cantos show the troubadours not only sang poems but *were* poems. . . .
>
> Mr. Pound brings to his reading, master-appreciation; and his gratitude takes two forms; he thanks the book and tells where you may see it. "Any man who would read Arnaut and the troubadours owes great thanks to Emil Levy of Freiburg," he says in *Instigations*. . . . He sings of this in Canto XX. . . .
>
> And as those who love books know, the place in which one read a book or talked of it partakes of its virtue in recollection; so for Mr. Pound the cedars and new-mown hay and far-off nightingale at Freiburg have the glamour of Provence. . . .[43]

Moore's syllabic reinvention of the sestina in "Bird Witted" is much more than a technical tour de force. It is a kind of homage to Pound and, as we shall see, it serves a specific function with respect to Moore's own complex "recollection" in "Bird Witted" (and in "Smooth Gnarled Crape Myrtle!" as well) of another "far-off nightingale." First, however, it is best to take up the question of memory in a more general way.

For in Moore's poems of the 1930s the art of memory seems to function as a prelude to, a warning of, and a shield against danger. In "The Steeple-Jack," for instance, Moore relies on the devastatingly accurate memory of the "college student / named Ambrose" to aim her own perception of dangerous untruth at the heart of a community so firmly convinced of its own innocence that its "simple people" are unable to read even the most blatant "sign" of "Danger." And just as she calls on Ambrose's memory in "The Steeple-Jack," so in "Virginia Britannia" Moore calls upon her own poetic memory for "intimation" as the poem reaches its crisis—when the forces which are to carry out the moral renovation of America have met with resistance. Memory fuels resistance to danger in "Bird Witted," too, for here the adult bird's voice has "become / harsh" because, as the present overtakes the lilting rhymes of memory, "A piebald cat" has been "observing" her young, and it is now climbing toward them. She must act *now*:

> The
>
> parent darting down, nerved by what chills
> the blood, and by hope rewarded—
> of toil—since nothing fills
> squeaking unfed
> mouths, wages deadly combat,
> and half kills
> with bayonet beak and
> cruel wings, the
> intellectual, cautious-
> ly creeping cat.

The urgency of the situation is underscored by the fact that the creatures in Moore's poems are rarely so violent, even in self-defense. The jerboa, for example, conceals itself from predators by "assuming [the] colour" of the sand; the plumet basilisk is also hidden by its coloration, that "octave of faulty / decorum"—at least until "nightfall, which is for man the basilisk whose look will kill; but is / for lizards men can / kill, the welcome dark. . . ." The frigate pelican "hides / in the height and in the majestic / display of his art," while the pangolin, an "armoured animal," either "draws away from / danger unpugnaciously, / with no sound but a harmless hiss," or "rolls himself into a ball that has / power to defy all effort to unroll it.

. . ."[44] But the mockingbird cannot do as the frigate pelican does: "the majestic / display" of her mimetic "art" will not hide her now, nor will it protect her young; so she must change her tune and go on the attack in order to defend her home ground—as in "Virginia Britannia"—against an invader more coldly calculating, more "intellectual" than herself.

For the mother bird, then, to be "Bird Witted" is to mobilize instinct against a natural antagonist, to hazard her own life in defense of her young. For the poet, however, it is deliberately to mobilize remembered emotion through the formal resources of the past, against an "intellectual . . . c r e e p i n g " figure which preys upon "innocent wide penguin eye[d]" children: it is to imitate innocence in order to defend it, and to do so in full awareness that the deliberateness of poetic mimesis belies the apparent innocence of her posture. Of course, the poem cannot literally protect these or any other birds against attack by a marauding cat; it can, however, mobilize its resources in a parodic defense of the mockingbird against the kind of treatment Keats accords the nightingale in his famous ode.

Moore writes in "Smooth Gnarled Crape Myrtle!"—the fourth and final poem in "The Old Dominion" group—that

> "The legendary white-
> eared black bulbul that sings
> only in pure Sanskrit" should
> be here—"tame clever
> true nightingale." . . .

The "'tame clever / true nightingale'" is not "here," of course, but to a considerable extent Moore behaves as if it were. Keats asks in the second strophe of the "Ode to a Nightingale" for "a draught of Vintage! . . . Tasting of Flora and the country-green, / Dance, and Provençal song,"[45] and Moore obliges him, in "Bird Witted," with a poem about a mockingbird (syllabically equivalent to the nightingale) which imitates the Provençal "pattern" of Arnaut Daniel. And she goes farther: her situation as listener, in the crucial fourth stanza where the bird is invisible, closely parallels the situation in which Keats finds himself in the fifth strophe of his "Ode." He "cannot see" either his surroundings or the bird; lying in "embalmèd darkness," he can do nothing in the following strophe but listen:

> Darkling I listen; and, for many a time
> I have been half in love with easeful Death,
> Called him soft names in many a musèd rhyme,

To take into the air my quiet breath;
Now more than ever seems it rich to die,
To cease upon the midnight with no pain,
While thou art pouring forth thy soul abroad
In such an ecstasy!
Still wouldst thou sing, and I have ears in vain—
To thy high requiem become a sod.[46]

Moore is not listening to "such an ecstasy" as Keats hears, but rather remembering a moment from the past; and her own death is not in question. Unlike Keats's "immortal Bird," however, Moore's mockingbird and her young have indeed been "born for death," and though it is not yet their time to die, the "hungry generations" have appeared—in the form of the "piebald cat"—to "tread [them] down" as they never will Keats's bird. Just as Keats is wrenched back to his "sole self" by the sound of his own voice repeating the word "Forlorn!" as if it were "a bell," so Moore is called back to the present by the suddenly "harsh" voice of the mother bird, interrupting her memory of "ecstasy" and forcing her to attend to the emergencies of the present. "Bird Witted" thus justifies its symbolic treatment of the mockingbird by calling attention to the particular exigencies of its situation in a way that does not concern Keats at all; what we hear in the mockingbird's song is the "note" of its own insistent perception of danger, rather than the personal note Keats strikes in the "Ode." The implication seems to be that Keats, for all his display of emotion, has transformed the nightingale into a merely "intellectual" symbol of his own desires, and that in doing so he has indulged in a process very similar to that which works upon the mockingbird itself in "Virginia Britannia."

The mockingbird enters "Virginia Britannia" in a blur of motion so fast that for a moment we are unable even to identify the "terse Virginian" as a mockingbird. But the bird, like the reader, is soon arrested by the command to "Observe," and it comes to a stand "on the round stone- / topped table with lead cupids grouped to / form the pedestal." The mockingbird has begun to slow, to freeze, long before the end of the stanza, however: it is likened to a statue even as it first comes clearly into focus "with head / held half away, and meditative eye as dead / as sculptured marble / eyes." Now, perched on what is explicitly termed a "pedestal" formed by "lead cupids" in a leaden mockery of loving support, it resembles a statue so closely that it is as if it had been turned to "lead" by the sheer force of the "Care" which "has formed" the scene as if for the express purpose of accommodating and subduing the bird—and by the difficult consonants that slow the rhythm of our reading. It is in this posture that the mockingbird enters our memory, so that we are implicated with the poet in the alchemical, "intellectual" transmutation of a living creature into a base material.

"Bird Witted" brings this faintly ominous leaden figure to life again, transforming it into a momentarily animated figure of sound. But Moore's effort to undo the effects of her own "intellectual," Keatsian treatment of the mockingbird by parodic means is doomed to fail—for parody is a mimetic mode, and must employ Keatsian tactics. As in "Virginia Britannia," therefore, the tempo of "Bird Witted" slows dramatically when the sentence arrives in what seems to be the present, when it comes to the "grown bird" and the predicate that places her "delightful note" in the "remote" past. The tempo slows because we are not in the present—or rather because we are in a present which is bound by the Keatsian past: what we are hearing is a "ditt[y] of no tune" like those which play throughout the "Ode on a Grecian Urn"—a "note" played "Not to the sensual ear" but to "the spirit."[47]

We see the mother bird "darting down" to meet the cat, but the engagement is delayed while we are told what impels her to action ("hope . . . of toil"), and when finally she "wages deadly combat, / and half kills" her antagonist, the object of the verb is deferred until the last possible moment—deferred not only by syntax but by typography as well. For in the first three printings of the poem, the letters of the final line are more widely spaced than the rest: the mother bird

> . . . wages deadly combat,
> and half kills
>   with bayonet beak and
>   cruel wings, the
> intellectual cautious-
> l y c r e e p i n g c a t.

The effect is to freeze the scene: the cat is transfixed as it moves toward its prey, and the mother bird is caught as if in mid-air, just on the point of attack, by the "intellectual," "unheard" music of the "Ode on a Grecian Urn." Like Keats's "marble men and maidens," they will remain so, in the memory of art. When we see them again in "Half Deity," the third poem in the sequence, they have been slightly transformed, but they are still fixed in the same attitudes.

Like "Virginia Britannia" and "Bird Witted," "Half Deity" is concerned with the relationship between childhood innocence and adult knowledge, but it explores that relationship more intensively than do the others.[48] It suggests that the passage from innocence to experience occurs when the relationship of observer to observed becomes instead a relation between a pursuer and her prey—when, that is, observation becomes an effort not just to secure visual knowledge of a given object but also to possess that object. Or rather, the passage occurs when the observer becomes consciously aware that she is a pursuer already, and that her pursuit must fail of its object: "Half Deity" implies that observation is never innocent of the desire for possession. The difference between child and adult, therefore, is that the latter has "learned to spare" the object of her desire in a way the child has not—for observation, like imitation, has to be "learned," though it has its origin in an instinctive "curiosity." But the adult "spare[s]" the object only from the physical consequences of the possessive urge. Opting for intellectual rather than merely physical possession, the observer makes the object an object of memory instead of immediate sensory experience; she may therefore seem more innocent than the child who attempts to secure the object physically. We have seen that memory may serve as a warning of imminent danger; but it also poses a threat to the integrity of the object, for it transforms and deadens its objects by subordinating them to patterns already formed.

"A subject and an object," says Emerson in "Experience," "—it takes so much to make the galvanic circuit complete, but magnitude adds nothing. What imports it whether it is Kepler and the sphere, Columbus and America, a reader and his book, or puss with her tail?"[49] Pursuit inevitably becomes self-pursuit, and then "the galvanic circuit" can be made "complete" only in a provisional way, a metaphorical way, and then only with considerable pain. As Emerson writes earlier in the same essay, "souls never touch their objects."[50] But when the soul *is* the object of the soul's pursuit, as it is in "Half Deity"—when the pursuer deliberately puts on the "aspect" of the innocent observer in an effort to repossess and reanimate her own childhood innocence, which is either a memory or a fiction or both—then the closing of the circle inflicts a sharper pain than the one "puss" must feel when she catches up with "her tail" and bites down. For to capture the memory of one's former innocence is to discover, simultaneously, that what one has in memory is what one has lost in fact, and so to discover the full burden of one's guilt. This, I think, is why Moore elected not to include "Half Deity" in late collections of her work: like "Black Earth," it is too explicitly self-revealing, and too deeply disturbing, to suit the public image she had come by then to project so successfully.

"Half Deity" begins by carefully establishing the poet in the posture of innocent observer:

Half Deity

half worm. We all, infant and adult, have
stopped to watch the butterfly—last of the
elves—and learned to spare the wingless worm
that hopefully ascends the tree. . . .

This opening leads us to believe that when the poet stops, a few lines later, "to watch" a "peninsula-tailed" butterfly which "has been / sleeping upright on an elm," she intends only to look at it in order to confirm for herself what others have reported—for "its yellowness, / that of the autumn poplar-leaf, by day / has been observed." We assume that she will otherwise "spare" it her attentions, for, unlike the sea in "A Graveyard," she is evidently not "a collector." We have not yet been given reason to consider that our having "learned to spare" the caterpillar, "the wingless worm / that hopefully ascends the tree," says nothing of our eventual response to the butterfly that caterpillar will become; and so we are not distressed when the poet's apparently matter-of-fact observation gives rise to pursuit, because the poet herself takes no visible part in the chase. So far as we can tell, she is the observer and reporter, not the pursuer.

That role is played by another figure, an "infant" "half deity" who appears without warning a third of the way into the poem. "Disguised in butterfly- / bush Wedgewood [*sic*] blue, Psyche follows" the butterfly from tree to tree—much as the mockingbird "drives the / owl" in "Virginia Britannia"—and the action develops so quickly from this point on that we have no time for surprise at the presence in Moore's work of a figure so obviously and so conventionally poetic, no time to consider that the landscape of "The Old Dominion" has suddenly become so thoroughly Romantic that Moore, like Keats, can all "thoughtlessly" happen upon Psyche in a wood.[51] Perhaps, though, we may explain Psyche's sudden appearance by recalling the strange, offhand comment made earlier, that the butterfly's "yellowness . . . *by day* / has been observed" (emphasis added). The phrase implies that the action of the poem takes place at night, and may in fact be a dream—a typically Romantic mode.

This might also help to account for the specific trees to which Psyche pursues the butterfly. She goes first to a tree whose Latin name, "Micromalus," means "little evil," and whose English name, "the midget / crab," calls to mind not only miniature, inedible versions of forbidden fruit but small, painfully grasping creatures as well; then she goes to "the mimosa," the central symbol of Shelley's "The Sensitive Plant." There the tree inhabits a beautiful garden, and lives in a mysterious affinity with a beautiful lady—at least for a time. For "When Winter had gone and Spring came back / The Sensitive Plant was a leafless wreck."[52] And so Psyche leaves the wrecked mimosa and goes straight "from that, to the flowering pomegranate," the tree whose fruit was forbidden to Persephone, who ate it nonetheless and brought winter into the world.

Keats's "Ode to Psyche" begins with the poet's unexpected discovery, as he wanders "in a forest thoughtlessly," of a sleeping couple whom he recognizes as Cupid and Psyche. But Keats—who feared that "there was nothing original to be written in poetry; that its riches were already exhausted—and all its beauties forestalled"[53]—dismisses "The winged boy" without even troubling to name him, for he has no interest in retelling the ancient legend of Cupid and Psyche's love. All his attention is on Psyche, and he revels in his discovery of a subject whose "riches" have not been "exhausted," whose "beauties" have not been "forestalled": Psyche, "latest born" of the goddesses as Moore's butterfly is "last of the elves," was born "too late for antique vows, / Too, too late for the fond believing lyre." No poet has sung her praises, nor made his name inseparable from hers; she has had

> No voice, no lute, no pipe, no incense sweet
> From chain-swung censer teeming;
> No shrine, no grove, no oracle, no heat
> Of pale-mouth'd prophet dreaming.

The poet begs her to "let" him fill those offices; declaring "I will be thy priest," he promises in the final strophe to build in Psyche's honor

> . . . a fane
> In some untrodden region of my mind,
> Where branched thoughts, new grown with pleasant pain,
> Instead of pines shall murmur in the wind:
> Far, far around shall those dark-cluster'd trees
> Fledge the wild-ridged mountains steep by steep;
> And there by zephyrs, streams, and birds, and bees,
> The moss-lain Dryads shall be lull'd to sleep;
> And in the midst of this wide quietness
> A rosy sanctuary will I dress

With the wreath'd trellis of a working brain,
    With buds, and bells, and stars without a name,
With all the gardener Fancy e'er could feign,
    Who breeding flowers, will never breed the same:
And there shall be for thee all soft delight
    That shadowy thought can win,
A bright torch, and a casement ope at night
    To let the warm Love in!

Keats's "Ode," ostensibly a celebratory gesture occasioned by the poet's discovery of the goddess sleeping in the wood, is transformed by his ambitious desire for originality into an attempt to displace Cupid and possess Psyche for himself. (Compare the similar but far more overt displacement in Whitman's *Song of Myself*: "I turn the bride-groom out of bed and stay with the bride myself, / I tighten her all night to my thighs and lips."[54] What Keats ends by building, therefore, is less "a fane" than what Moore calls in "Half Deity" a "flowering, shrewd-scented tropical / device" whose function is to secure the poet's dominion over Psyche by imprisoning her "In some untrodden region of [his] mind."

Similarly, although Psyche's pursuit of the butterfly in "Half-Deity" seems to spring from a relatively uncomplicated desire "to watch" it, she soon finds herself committed to trapping the elusive creature. She follows it until,

Baffled not by the quick-clouding serene gray
moon, but forced by the hot hot sun to pant,
    she stands on rug-soft grass; though "it is not
    permitted to gaze informally
        on majesty, in such a manner as might
    well happen here." The blind
        all-seeing butterfly, fearing the slight
finger, wanders—as though it were ignorant—
a step further and lights on Zephyr's palm. . . .

Psyche, Zephyr, and the butterfly now form a tableau in which all our attention is directed to the confrontation of observer and observed, pursuer and pursued:

Small unglazed china eyes of butterflies—
    pale tobacco brown—with the large eyes of
    the Nymph on them; gray eyes that now are
        black, for she, with controlled agitated glance

> observes the insect's face
> and all's a-quiver with significance
> as in the scene with cats' eyes on the magpie's eyes
> by Goya. . . .

Psyche only "observes the insect's face" here—but the butterfly, rightly "vexed because curiosity has / been pursuing it," is unable to remain "calm." For if in "Bird Witted" the "delightful note" of a "remote" and untroubled past is recalled as a prelude to danger, "Half Deity" recalls the "deadly combat" of "Bird Witted" in the midst of an apparently innocent confrontation.[55] Psyche's "curiosity" begins to look less innocent, moreover, when we recall that her marriage to Cupid was annulled when she disobeyed the divine injunction against looking upon his face. And "though 'it is not / permitted to gaze informally / on majesty, in such a manner as might / well happen'" again "'here,'" Psyche "'might / well'" find a certain sanction for her curiosity in the reflection that—as Alice says elsewhere—"'A cat may look at a king.'"[56] For that is precisely what does "'happen here.'" The analogy to Goya's "scene with cats' eyes on the magpie's eyes" likens Psyche not to the bird (which would be dubious enough, since the magpie is a thievish bird) but rather to the "intellectual cautious- / l y c r e e p i n g c a t" of "Bird Witted." And earlier poems like "Silence" (where the cat "'takes its prey to privacy— / the mouse's limp tail dangling like a shoelace from its mouth'") and "Peter" (where the cat is naturally inclined "to purloin, to pursue" the "hen") remind us that the cat is most itself in preying upon innocence.

All this may seem to set "Half Deity" at odds with the celebration, in "Bird Witted," of the effort to repel the predator. But we know by now what "Smooth Gnarled Crape Myrtle!" will confirm: that "An aspect may deceive." We must consider, too, the poet's lament in the same poem that "Art is unfortunate. / One may be a blameless / bachelor and it is but a / step to Congreve"; for there is "but a / step" between "Bird Witted" and "Half Deity." We have seen that "Bird Witted" inherits from "Virginia Britannia" the memory, in statuary form, of a living creature—a memory which it reanimates by imitating the intricate aural patterns of Arnaut Daniel's verse. But at the very moment when those aural patterns are most conspicuously displayed, in the fourth stanza where the poet must carry the tune alone, the imitation of Daniel coincides with the silent memory of the "Ode on a Grecian Urn"; and from then on convergent imitations sustain the formal movement of the verse while gradually returning the bird (and the cat with her) to the initial state of immobility. This is not an innocent strategem (if there is such a thing) but a desperately conscious one. "Bird Witted" concentrates upon presenting to the reader the more innocent "aspect" of Moore's poetic enterprise, but it is the peculiar misfortune of an art so completely mimetic that it must imitate whatever comes into its ken. It is, therefore, only by resorting in desperation to Keats, only by forcing both the mockingbird and the cat into conformity with the frozen statuary of the Grecian Urn, that Moore prevents herself from taking a mimetic "step further" with the "intellectual cautious- / l y c r e e p i n g c a t," whose movements the typography has already begun to imitate—prevents herself, that is, from giving the poem an "aspect" as predatory as Psyche's has now become. For, like the poet and the reader in "Virginia Britannia," and like Psyche here, the cat begins by "observing" the "fledgling mocking-birds."

Like the cat, moreover, Psyche is immobilized just when her barely "Controlled agitated glance" reveals the true character of her interest in the butterfly. As her "large . . . gray eyes" darken to "black" with excitement, they become so opaque as to recall the "meditative eye" of the "lead- / gray . . . mocking-bird" of "Virginia Britannia"—an eye seemingly "as dead / as sculptured marble / eyes"; but there is a crucial difference between Psyche's eyes and the bird's. The "Nymph's" eyes, apparently so intensely alive, are in fact "sculptured marble," and so are Zephyr's "mirror eyes" and the "Small unglazed china eyes" of the butterfly itself. The action has been brought to a halt by the sudden assertion—apparently against the Keatsian movement of Psyche's pursuit but actually, as the conclusion of "Bird Witted" attests, in logical confirmation of the end to which that pursuit must lead—of the poet's memory of a "Carved Marble Group by Jean Baptiste Boyer," representing "Psyche trying to capture the butterfly held out on Zephyr's palm."[57]

That memory cannot contain the action for long, however. Reanimated as suddenly as it had been frozen, the butterfly now "springs away, [a] zebra half-deified," and in the next instant the poet takes the irrevocable "step" she had denied herself in "Bird Witted." She thereby reveals the extent to which her own imitation of Keats, parodic though it may be, has entangled her with Psyche. Until now, the poet has preserved her status as observer of the entire episode; but now she suddenly insults the butterfly, calling after it: "Twig-veined, irascible, / fastidious, stubborn undisciplined zebra! Sometimes one is grateful to / a stranger for looking very nice." So intolerable is it that the butterfly should escape that the poet's voice turns markedly childlike, as though by acting the petulant child for a moment (and she is very like Alice just now) she could disguise a deeper, more adult sense of loss and lure the butterfly back.

But "An aspect may deceive," and "looking very nice" is not enough to satisfy the "blind / all-seeing butterfly," which has only wandered onto Zephyr's hand in the first place "*as though* it were ignorant" (emphasis added). It sees, therefore, that it is "free / to leave the breeze's hand" as it would not be to escape the "half-shut" hand Psyche has extended toward it. And so, like Emily Dickinson's "Little Tippler,"

> . . . it flies, drunken with triviality
> or guided by visions of strength, away till
> diminishing like wreckage on the sea,
>   rising and falling easily; mounting
>   the swell and keeping its true course with
>   what swift majesty, indifferent to
>   us, it's gone. . . .[58]

It's "gone," and the poet can only wonder: "Deaf to my / voice, or magnet-nice? as it flutters through / airs now slack, now fresh. It has strict ears," she adds ruefully, "when the / West Wind speaks." The lineation here emphasizes the possessive pronoun ("my / voice"), and the question brings the poet fully into the open. Psyche has served only as a mask—and not a very effective one at that. The poet's interest in the butterfly is as "intellectual," and therefore as predatory, as Psyche's has become—and she, too, is immobilized by the weight of her own desire.

But if the butterfly is finally "indifferent / to" anyone who might take an active interest in it, it has yet been drawn as if by a "magnet" to Zephyr, the Shelleyan "West Wind," for whose words it has such "strict ears," and whose "hand spread out was enough / to tempt the fiery tiger-horse to stand. . . ." Moore's memory of the "Ode to the West Wind" has rescued the poem (and the butterfly) from the impasse to which her imitation of Keats has brought it. As we have seen, what Keats attempts in the "Ode to Psyche" is the attainment of mastery, an ambition which his professed desire to serve the goddess and worship as "priest" at her "fane" cannot conceal; by contrast, Shelley acknowledges the West Wind as *his* master. He seeks not to possess its power for himself but rather to be possessed by it as a prophet is possessed by the divine afflatus. His concern, unlike Keats's, is less for himself than for the "unawakened earth": he seeks to borrow the wind's "power" and make it speak his "words"; he wants it, however, not to glorify himself but rather to "quicken a new birth," to arouse the world from its "Winter" sleep to a revolutionary "Spring."[59]

Moore is not especially concerned with the particular features of the revolution Shelley had in mind, and in fact must have found his doctrines thoroughly incompatible with her own conservative views; but his doctrines are not the issue here. The nature of Moore's interest in Shelley is most clearly indicated by the words of Scofield Thayer, who wrote of Shelley in 1913 that while "many of the poet's ideals now appear scarcely comprehensible, the integrity of his purpose is not the less patent."[60] Thayer's remarks (which Moore transcribed into her reading notebook in November 1928) have a clear bearing on Zephyr's success in attracting the butterfly, though he makes no apparent effort to do so. His "hand" is "spread out," giving assurance of "the integrity of his purpose"—an assurance which the "blind / all-seeing butterfly" recognizes, and by which it distinguishes between the Shelleyan Zephyr and the Keatsian Psyche: Zephyr has "no net" and makes no such attempt as Psyche's to "capture the butterfly" in a "half-shut / hand." Nor is Zephyr more "comprehensible" than Shelley: "many of the poet's ideals now appear scarcely comprehensible," says Thayer—and so, Moore writes, Zephyr's "talk was as strange as my grandmother's muff."

Moore's "talk" is "strange," too; but her struggle to "overcome [her] reluctance to be unoriginal"—which has led her actively to pursue "possible comparisons and coincidences" with other writers—has betrayed her into what she perceives as a loss of "integrity." Significantly, Moore does not imitate Shelley in "Half Deity": rather, she captures the erratic, fluttering movement of the butterfly by parodying the loosely Pindaric form of Keats's "Ode to Psyche." But parody is only another form of imitation, and even in parody Moore is possessed by the Keatsian obsession with originality which she is struggling to "overcome." Inevitably, then, she becomes Psyche, straining after the butterfly which is the emblem of her own soul, and seeing in her inability to capture it the extent to which, unlike the butterfly, she has departed from her own "true course"—seeing, that is, a loss of self, a loss of innocence and "integrity of purpose." "They that have wings must not have weights," she says early in the poem—but she has no wings. On the contrary, she is so weighted down by memory and desire that, like Psyche, she is immobilized, turned to stone. Even the self whose emblem she strains after is only a memory. The closing line, delivered as an artlessly inconsequent throwaway, lodges the entire poem in the past, reminding us that the poet, for all that she "look[s] very nice" "Disguised in butterfly- / bush Wedgewood blue," is not a child but an adult remembering a dream of a childhood long since past: "His talk was as strange as my grandmother's muff."

V

"Such a life as [Shelley's,]" writes Scofield Thayer, "resembles the sepulchral slab in the pavement of an ancient church; the impertinences of name and insignia are worn away by the feet of time, but the crossed arms remain. . . ." The grave thus becomes the image of an inscrutable and anonymous integrity, for Thayer immediately goes on to insist that the incomprehensibility of Shelley's ideals leaves "the integrity of his purpose . . . not the less patent." And so we circle back to "Virginia Britannia," where in the "typical ivied-bower-and-ruined-tower churchyard" of the opening stanza we find that

> A deer-
> track in a church-floor
> brick and Sir George Yeardley's
> coffin tacks and
> tomb remain. . . .

This image is so specific that it bears no obvious relation to Thayer's discussion of Shelley; in the final version, however, the resemblance is much closer. For the identity of the "great sinner" who "lyeth here under the sycamore" is no longer "known": the "impertinences" of Yeardley's "name and insignia" have been "worn away" by revision, leaving only the "deer- / track" and "a fine pavement tomb with engraved top. . . . "

But the original image is more fully informed by Thayer's odd analogy than it seems. Yeardley was the only knighted member of the Jamestown colony, and he received his title in recognition of his work in aiding the community to establish itself.[61] Apparently, then, his "tomb" functions in an ironic capacity as an image of justly rewarded integrity, and thus strikes the keynote not only for "Virginia Britannia" but for "The Old Dominion" as a whole. It is "integrity of purpose" that concerns Moore most deeply as she explores what Thayer calls, in the subtitle of his essay on Shelley, "The Poetic Value of Revolutionary Principles." Like Emerson's nature, the landscape of colonial Virginia "offers all her creatures to [the poet] as a picture-language"[62] which, under Moore's scrutiny, reveals the principles inherent in the original "colonizing" of the New World and the subsequent history of America as a nation which owes its existence to the practical application of revolutionary ideals.

We must bear in mind, however, that "An aspect may deceive." For we find as the poem proceeds that the "picture-language" of "Virginia Britannia" spells out not a linear history of simple integrity but rather a history of principles perverted in the application and from the start. The history of America as this poem tells it is (to borrow a phrase from "Marriage," which in turn derives it from Sir Francis Bacon) a history "'of circular traditions and impostures, / committing many spoils.' . . . " "Virginia Britannia" is an attempt to rectify that history, to set America back on the "true course" of integrity. As we shall see, however, it works by the apparently paradoxical method of "advancing back- / ward in a circle"—a revolutionary method in the strictest etymological sense of the word "revolution," a method which requires that Moore accept the very perversions she is trying to correct and that she accept them not only in principle but in practice as well. Like Whitman, then—a poet for whom she felt a profound distaste[63]—Moore identifies the form of the poem with the form of America itself, which is the form of its history. For those perversions, those "'circular traditions and impostures'" and their "'many spoils,'" are inseparable from the principles to which they give visible expression: they are the history of America. Nowhere is the paradoxical intertwining of principle and perversion, the backward-circling movement of advance, more powerfully evident than in the deliberate use of the word "intimation" to mark the boundary separating the mature poet from the figure of the innocent child and to confess the poet's participation in the circular logic of American history.

The "picture-language" of the Virginia landscape is all the more revealing because it is not entirely the language of nature. As we have seen, the landscape which the poem purports to describe has been "formed" by the "Care" of an anonymous gardener or gardeners, in painstaking and nostalgic imitation of the landscape the colonists had left behind. What remains for us, however, is a monumental and inadvertent parody, "an almost English" landscape dominated not by the "'tame clever / true nightingale'" which "should be here" to suit the tastes of "'one who dresses / in New York but dreams of / London'" (as "Smooth Gnarled Crape Myrtle!" puts it), but rather by the hostile, mimetic, statuesque mockingbird.

The gardeners' efforts to turn Virginia into an earthly Paradise have gone awry, have ended by producing a "Rare unscent- / ed, provident- / ly hot, too sweet, inconsistent flower- / bed" in which "serpentine shadows star- / tle strangers" while the inhabitants remain curiously oblivious. The grotesquely thickened "stem" of "the white wall-rose," however, is itself a sign of danger: for the "wide-spaced great blunt alternating os- / trich-skin warts that were thorns" signify the " 'many spoils' " which have been committed by "the predatory hand" against which, in "Roses Only," the rose's thorns provide the only measure of "proof." Nothing is safe here: the "poor unpoison- / ous terrapin likes to / idle near the sea-top" where it makes easy prey; soon "Terrapin / meat and crested spoon / feed the mistress" of that "everywhere open / shaded house on Indian- / named Virginian / streams, in counties named for English lords!"

The history of "Virginia Britannia," then, is the history not of integrity stoutly maintained but of "tobacco-crop / gains" memorialized on "church tablets," of mixed motives and cross purposes working "on / The Chickahominy"—one of those "Indian- / named Virginian / streams"—to establish "the Negro (opportunely brought) to / strengthen protest against tyranny. . . . " It is a history founded on appropriation:

> . . . Strangler fig, pale fiercely
> unpretentious North American, and Dutch
> trader, and noble
> Roman, in taking what they
> pleased—colonizing as we say—
> were not all intel-
> lect and delicacy. . . .

The Virginia landscape is more than a natural historical record: it is a work of art predicated upon the colonists' (and their descendants') having combined the strength to "tak[e] what they / pleased" with an intense longing "to be unoriginal," to use what they took as the material from which to construct a simulacrum of the English landscape as a permanent monument to England and the past—an enormous mortuary sculpture, as it were. So powerful is that combination of strength and longing that it can assimilate to its grand design even those native elements which, in breaking the silence of the grave, threaten to overwhelm the memory of home with their mockery. Thus the mockingbird—though as it enters the scene, it "drives the / owl from tree to tree and imitates the call / of whippoorwill or / lark or katydid"—falls silent and turns to "lead" under the spell of the gardeners' "Care": it is left frozen in its place, "still standing there alone / on the round stone- / topped table with lead cupids grouped to / form the pedestal."

Of course Moore is among those who have made "Virginia Britannia" what it is by "taking what they / pleased—colonizing as we say. . . . " For the poem which discovers in the landscape the long history of appropriation is itself not only the most recent product of that history, but also a "colonizing" power in its own right.

> . . . The slowmoving glossy
>   saddle-cavalcade
>
> of buckeye brown surprising
> jumpers; the contrasting work-mule and
>   show-mule and witch-cross door and "strong sweet prison"
> are a part of what
>   has come about, in the Black
>   idiom, from advancing back-
> ward in a circle;
>   from taking the Potomac
>   cowbirdlike; and on
> The Chickahominy
> establishing
> the Negro (opportunely brought) to
> strengthen protest against
>   tyranny. . . .

Here Moore registers her own "protest against" the "tyranny" to which Blacks in America have been and continue to be subject;[64] but in "strengthen[ing]" that "protest" with a phrase "opportunely brought" into the poem from "the Black / idiom," she knowingly implicates herself in the very "tyranny" she condemns. The availability of that "idiom" depends, of course, on the institution of slavery, under which "the Negro" was brought to America to sustain the outmoded economy of the South and its "tyrant taste." But Moore uses "the Negro" in a similar way, deliberately appropriating his language to define and sustain the economy of "Virginia Britannia" itself—to enact and "strengthen" the circular logic of its opportunistic history.

Thus Moore is not simply describing a landscape, as she seems to be. Rather, she is extending the method we have seen her use in "Novices" and "Bird Witted," finding in the construction of the landscape itself the technical principles of composition by which she now composes her own imitative reconstruction of a landscape which is already, in her words, "one of America's most undeniable poems."[65] She is not so much writing "Virginia Britannia," then, as rewriting it, and correcting as she goes (much as she does in revising her own poems, including this one); and she is working along the lines laid down almost a century earlier by Emerson, who writes in "The Poet" (1844) that

> . . . poetry was all written before time was, and whenever we are so finely organized that we can penetrate into that region where the air is music, we hear those primal warblings and attempt to write them down, but we lose ever and anon a word or a verse and substitute something of our own, and thus miswrite the poem.[66]

The original settlers of Virginia, forced to "substitute something of [their] own" for the missing "words" of the English original, have "miswrit[ten] the poem" of Jamestown—and, as Emerson tells us a few pages later, "herein is the legitimation of criticism, in the mind's faith that the [poem is] a corrupt version of some text in nature with which [it] ought to be made to tally."[67] Moore's initial response to the colonists' inadvertently parodic miswriting is to counter with a deliberately parodic reconstruction of that parody which both reveals and corrects it. From the outset she intertwines various elements—natural and artificial, domestic and foreign—so thoroughly that all seem equally out of place in the end, and equally at home as well. In the first stanza, for instance, the alternating pattern formed by "the redbird, / the redcoated musketeer, / the trumpet-flower, the cavalier," seems to accommodate "the parson, and the / wild parishioner" without strain; but here Moore has already extended the poem well beyond the temporal and chronological limits of what we call colonial Virginia. In the early seventeenth century "New England was called Northern Virginia," as she points out;[68] and the presence in this closely patterned landscape of "the parson, and the / wild parishioner" points not only to the "deer- / track in a church-floor / brick" but also, and more problematically, to a permanent reminder of just how "unEnglish" this "almost English" scene really is. The pairing is a reminder, too, of just how far America has strayed from its "true course," for it recalls the most celebrated adulterous union in nineteenth-century American fiction—the forest meeting between "The Pastor and His Parishioner" in which Hester Prynne persuades Arthur Dimmesdale to join her in fleeing the oppressive strictures of Puritan Boston.[69]

Following Hawthorne's ironic design (for of course Hester and Dimmesdale are foiled by her devilish, cuckolded husband), Moore binds these figures permanently into the American landscape. And she does so with the same "Care" with which she "has formed, a- / mong" the "unEnglish insect sounds" of stanzas which "should sound like a kind of inexhaustible bumblebee" (as she put it later),[70] "the white wall-rose" with the grotesquely thickened American "stem" whose missing "thorns" are no longer "proof" against "the predatory hand" that governs the landscape. In "Virginia Britannia," however, the "observing" eye does the work of the hand—and "observing" is a very "predatory" activity, as we have had ample occasion to discover.

We cannot gauge the full extent of the eye's rapacity until we consider that it is the poet's simultaneous observance of the forms of the past and of the present which impels her to cast "Virginia Britannia" as a syllabic imitation of the Immortality Ode and, at crucial moments, to complicate that willingness "to be unoriginal" by combining with it the strength to take what she pleases. In doing so—in "colonizing as we say"—Moore reveals the full extent of her unoriginality, of her willingness to let herself be influenced by other writers. For her definition of "colonizing" ("taking what they / pleased") is very nearly identical in phrasing to Eliot's definition of influence. "To be influenced by a writer," says Eliot, "is to have a chance inspiration from him; or to take what one wants."[71] Eliot himself provides Moore with "a chance inspiration" at a crucial moment in "Virginia Britannia," and it is from his most recent work that she takes "what [she] wants." The mockingbird to which we have already devoted so much time may be indigenous to Virginia, but, like virtually everything in "Virginia Britannia," it has been imported, "opportunely brought" in from elsewhere. It comes from Eliot's short poem "Virginia," one of several small landscapes published under the heading "Words for Music" in the *Virginia Quarterly Review* in April 1934:

> Red river, red river,
> Slow flow heat is silence
> No will is still as a river
> Still. Will heat move
> Only through the mocking-bird
> Heard once? . . .[72]

The mockingbird belongs to the immediate present; still, though it "drives the / owl from tree to tree," it cannot overcome the full burden of the past. Having been forcefully appropriated by a poet ever-observant of her contemporaries' work, it is introduced into a scene so rigidly determined by both the English and American past that the bird is struck dumb and cast in lead. For the scene owes its form to Moore's parodic effort to "Observe" the form of the Immortality Ode—an effort which perpetuates, in turn, the awkward attempts of the original colonists to "Observe" the cherished forms of their history.

As Moore's corrective measures take effect, as the present begins apparently to free itself from the bonds of the past, there is a corresponding change in the character of Moore's parody. By the penultimate stanza, parody has become anticipatory as well as reminiscent:

> . . . The song-
> bird wakes too soon, to enjoy
> excellent idleness, destroy-
> ing legitimate
> laziness, the unbought toy
> even in the dark
> risking loud whee whee whee
> of joy, the car-
> away-seed-spotted sparrow perched on
> the dew-drenched juniper
> beside the window-ledge;
> the little hedge-
> sparrow that wakes up seven minutes
> sooner than the lark
>
> they say. . . .

But there is no escape from the past. In the final stanza, the delighted, gently mocking anticipation of Shelley's Skylark shades into a much more straightforwardly honorific imitation of the Immortality Ode, and though the anticipatory note remains, it is muted. For "The clouds that gather round the setting sun / Do take a sober colouring from an eye / That hath kept watch o'er man's mortality," and when the poem encounters a group of stationary figures whom even the flaming sunset "can / not move," Moore resorts directly to Wordsworth. This time, in a final, desperate acknowledgment of her own complicity in and responsibility for the American historical process, she takes liberties not only with Wordsworth's formal patterns, but with his language and, most importantly, with his central symbol as well.

Like "the solid- / pointed star" which "stands for hope" at the end of "The Steeple-Jack," like Zephyr in "Half Deity," the child, receiving an "intimation" which she does not seek, seems to hold out the "hope" of escape from the long history of "colonizing" which the poem has developed. But as Moore writes in "The Hero," hope is not hope "until all ground for hope has / vanished." The child is mother to the woman, a "*historic* metamorphoser" (emphasis added) like the butterfly in "Half Deity"—and so she is doomed to undergo a process of growth which will invert precisely the transformation of "the wingless worm / that hopefully ascends the tree" into a "weightless" butterfly. The child is already "historic," as Psyche is—a figure caught by poetic memory in the attitude from which, like the butterfly from its cocoon, the predatory, "intellectual" adult emerges into history to stand rooted and grasping in "endless imitation" of an innocence which has already receded into the "remote" past and which she knows from the outset to be permanently lost.

Afterword

The posture of the characteristic American is a stasis, like Strether's at the end of *The Ambassadors* or Moore's at the end of "Half Deity." That stasis is produced by the tension between opposing forces of equal power and by an overwhelming sense of loss—and Moore lapses into silence again after November 1936, producing no new poems (and hardly any prose) for the next three and a half years.[1] And when she breaks that silence, in the summer of 1940, the quality of her speech has changed dramatically, and she has redefined her relation to her audience. "What Are Years" reveals the alteration in style and stance very clearly:

> What is our innocence,
> what is our guilt? All are
> naked, none is safe. And whence
> is courage: the unanswered question,
> the resolute doubt,—
> dumbly calling, deafly listening—that
> in misfortune, even death,
> encourages others
> and in its defeat, stirs
>
> the soul to be strong? He
> sees deep and is glad, who
> accedes to mortality
> and in his imprisonment rises
> upon himself as
> the sea in a chasm, struggling to be
> free and unable to be,
> in its surrendering

finds its continuing.

So he who strongly feels,
behaves. The very bird,
grown taller as he sings, steels
his form straight up. Though he is captive,
his mighty singing
says, satisfaction is a lowly
thing, how pure a thing is joy.
This is mortality,
this is eternity.[2]

With its "unanswered" questions about innocence and guilt and courage, its "sea in a chasm" and its singing bird, "What Are Years" is a résumé of themes with which Moore has been preoccupied throughout her career, and of images through which those themes have often found expression. It is also, however, a retreat from the rigorous complexity of her earlier work. The anthropomorphizing of "the sea in a chasm" is exactly the sort of "crude symbolism" against which, as Williams had rightly perceived in 1923, Moore had set herself in poems like "Sojourn in the Whale," and especially in "The Fish" and "A Graveyard."[3] The symbolism here is not crude because it is obvious: it is obvious because it is crude, and it is crude because it is dishonest—because it licenses and covers for the sudden change of grammatical subject at the end of the second stanza which relieves the human actor, the generalized "He" of the poem, of all responsibility for failure in the struggle "to be free." It suggests that that failure is not only natural and therefore inevitable, but also—and precisely because it is natural—positively desirable. In much the same way, the blatantly sentimental reading of the bird's song, which contrasts so startlingly with Moore's treatment of the mockingbird four years earlier, asks us to believe, in effect, that the bird chooses his cage and likes it.

This radically changed style is one aspect of a bid for the attention of an audience which had so far found Moore's poems impenetrable—an audience which Eliot, in his role as editor of Moore's *Selected Poems* in 1935, had consciously (and successfully) sought to warn off by placing the difficult poems of the early 1930s at the beginning of the book.[4] Moore is looking now for a poetry that "encourages others," as she puts it too baldly in the opening stanza of "What Are Years" and few things are quite so encouraging as someone else's admission of "defeat." Her aim is not to explore and criticize and speculate, but quite frankly to persuade (the questions in "What Are Years" are rhetorical, not speculative), and she herself must have been persuaded of the rightness of her change in direction when she learned in November 1940—not long after "What Are Years" was printed in *Kenyon Review*—that *Selected Poems* was being remaindered for a paltry thirty cents a copy.[5] It is hardly insignificant, in this connection, that "What Are Years" is the title poem of the first collection of verse for which Moore herself actively tried to arrange publication.[6]

I do not mean to say that Moore remakes her poetry in a merely cynical attempt to gain popular success. In *What Are Years?*(1941) she speaks out of an urgent sense of what the age demands of its poets; and as Stevens puts it in 1942, the age demands "Of Modern Poetry" that it "be living," that it

> . . . learn the speech of the place.
> It has to face the men of the time and to meet
> The women of the time. It has to think about war
> And it has to find what will suffice. . . .[7]

Perhaps he is thinking of Moore, whom he had met for the first time in 1941;[8] certainly we could do much worse than to describe *What Are Years?* as an attempt to "learn the speech of the place" and to find in that speech "what will suffice" to "encourage others" in time of war: it is no accident that the book ends by calling love "the only *fortress* / strong enough to trust to" (emphasis added).

What Are Years? is arranged very carefully. The title poem announces the book's general themes: mortality, defeat, courage, captivity, endurance, the struggle for freedom. Of the three new poems that follow, the first and the third are concerned with meeting the threat of "extinction"; the middle one is about freedom. None of these poems mentions war in any explicit way. "Rigorists" praises the efforts of a man named Sheldon Jackson to breed Lapland reindeer in Alaska as "a gift preventing / the extinction of the Eskimo," but the implications of Jackson's "battle" are not revealed until the next poem, "Light Is Speech," a sorrowful reproach to France for her ignominious surrender to the German army. "The word France," Moore concludes, "means / enfranchisement; means one who can / 'animate whoever thinks of her.'" That thought in turn animates "He 'Digesteth Harde Yron,'" with its punning suggestion that, pending the arrival of a Sheldon Jackson, the French will simply have to bite the bullet for a while and mount a resistance on their own; the poem begins by listing several ancient species of birds—all "extinct" now—and then goes on to celebrate the ostrich, not as a creature conventionally burying its head in the sand in willful obliviousness, but rather as a "symbol of justice" and the "one remaining rebel" against oppression.

In a mirror image of the way the paper nautilus of the final poem cradles her young, these and the other new poems published in 1940 and 1941 bracket the poems of "The Old Dominion," here reprinted without the collective title and placed in a new order which subsumes their complexities into the volume as a whole, softening and simplifying them. For these new relations change the poems themselves in subtle ways. The mournful conclusion of "Smooth Gnarled Crape Myrtle!" for instance, seems explicitly concerned with events in Europe with which it originally had nothing to do: "And what of / our clasped hands that swear, 'By Peace / Plenty; as / by Wisdom Peace.' Alas!" So, too, "Bird Witted" becomes a poem about the necessity of defending one's children against enemy aggression—though the ferocity of the mother bird is softened considerably by the sentimental rendition of the bird's song in "What Are Years" and by the equally sentimental treatment of maternity in "The Paper Nautilus." Then comes "Virginia Britannia," which, demonstrating the inextricable entwining of American and British interests, makes "Bird Witted" seem in retrospect to argue for the necessity of American intervention in the European conflict.[9] Three new poems take us from here to "The Pangolin," with its celebration of the man who, though "Prey to fear," nonetheless goes forth each day, "mechanicked" for "fighting" so that he becomes "another armored animal" like the pangolin; and finally we come to the fragile "fortress" of the paper nautilus's maternal love.

The problem is that in the newer poems Moore relies on those aspects of what Stevens calls "the speech of the place" which are least adequate to the general conception and the method of *What Are Years?* "In times like these," she said, "we are tempted to disregard anything that has not a direct bearing on freedom; or should I say, an obvious bearing, for what is more persuasive than poetry, though, as Robert Frost says, it works delicately and obliquely."[10] These words were spoken in 1948; but they define the failure of Moore's poetry after 1940. For she is no longer writing for an audience of poets and critics, of people like Eliot and Williams and Pound and Stevens, who can be counted on to work at grasping what she is doing; she is addressing herself to a much larger public composed—as the fate of *Selected Poems* attests—of readers whom she cannot trust to understand her, readers on whom she cannot count at all unless what she writes has "an obvious bearing" on the matter at hand. And for that audience stark, enigmatic poems like "The Fish" will not suffice, nor will poems like "The Jerboa," whose subject-matter, Eliot said, was difficult to ascertain.[11]

And so we get poems like "Light Is Speech," at once slight and heavy-handed, where repetition—which "should be / synonymous with accuracy," as Moore says in "Four Quartz Crystal Clocks," but which all too often accomplishes nothing—hammers the point home. "Yes, light is speech," she affirms. "Free frank / impartial sunlight, moonlight, / starlight, lighthouse light, / are language." In an earlier poem like "Poetry," even a brief catalogue like this one would have brought us to a very different sense of what is meant by the initial claim that "light is speech," but there is no movement of the understanding here. We are simply told that there are different kinds of light, all of which amount to the same thing; and yet the nature of "language" is taken for granted here, and again when Moore goes on to speak in praise of

> . . . Emile Littré,
> philology's determined,
> ardent eight-volume
>   Hippocrates-charmed
> editor. A
> man of fire, a scientist of
> freedoms, was firm Maximilien
>
> Paul Emile Littré. . . .

Moore does not offer to say whether there is any relationship between Littré's philology and his determination; indeed the poem itself, with its awful pun on "frank" speech and its false equation of "France" with "enfranchisement," seems to belie its professed interest in philology. And in fact philology *is* beside the point here: what matters is that unlike the Frenchmen of the present day, who have just surrendered to the advancing Germans, Littré was "determined" and "ardent" and "firm." The value of determination and ardor and firmness has to be affirmed independently of any specific activity; and Moore has to create an illusion of ardor which can be felt even by readers who perceive no philological connection between Littré's ardor and Moore's description of him as a "man of fire."

This is the poetry of nostalgia, in which enthusiasm survives the demise of the subject and increases in inverse proportion to the subject's remoteness. Moore's subjects are receding at an increasingly rapid pace, and this is why she wills herself to "behave," to accept her "imprisonment"; this is why she "steels / [her] form straight up" to sing of what is past or passing, and never of what is to come. But it is agonizing to see her "surrendering" to the imperatives of a nostalgia that reduces the gaiety of the frigate pelican, the fierce protectiveness of the mockingbird, even the false dignity of the nameless, utterly conventional bird of "What Are Years" to the cartoonlike cheerfulness of Woody Woodpecker. "Propriety," she writes in 1944,

> is some such word
> as the chord
> Brahms had heard
> from a bird,
> sung down near the root of the throat;
> it's the little downy woodpecker
> spiralling a tree—
> up up up like mercury. . . . [12]

Like Littré's philology, propriety has been reduced to a "word" of uncertain meaning; and like "Propriety," the work of Moore's later years is an effort to recall and celebrate the world as it was before the war smashed everything. But that world is gone almost beyond recall, and the deliberately fostered illusion of cheerful acceptance cannot mask the undertone of despair. Nor can the apparently modernist texture of the verse conceal Moore's wistful commitment to a civility so narrowly conceived that it amounts to little more than the outworn gentility from which she had struggled to free herself thirty years before. "Art is unfortunate."

Notes

INTRODUCTION

1. Moore, *Selected Poems* (New York and London, 1935).

2. Bernard F. Engle, *Marianne Moore* (New York, 1964); this book appeared before the publication of Moore's *Complete Poems* (New York, 1967; hereinafter *CP*) which superseded *The Collected Poems* (New York, 1951; hereinafter *ColP*). Subsequent commentators have treated *CP* as authoritative: George W. Nitchie, *Marianne Moore: An Introduction to the Poetry* (New York, 1969); Pamela White Hadas, *Marianne Moore: Poet of Affection* (Syracuse, 1977); Bonnie Costello, *Imaginary Possessions: Marianne Moore* (Cambridge, Mass., 1981); and Elizabeth Phillips, *Marianne Moore* (New York, 1983).

3. Laurence Stapleton, *Marianne Moore: The Poet's Advance* (Princeton, 1979).

4. *Poems* (London, 1921) will hereinafter be abbreviated as *P*; *Observations* (New York, 1924; 2d ed., 1925) as *O*; and *Selected Poems* as *SP*.

5. According to a note in Moore's scrap album (Rosenbach Archive), John Warner Moore was ordained on 15 May 1914. There is no full-length biography of Moore; the best sources of biographical information are Winthrop Sargeant's profile, "Humility, Concentration, and Gusto," in *The New Yorker* (16 Feb. 1957), 38–73, and Stapleton's *Marianne Moore: The Poet's Advance.*

6. "Interview with Donald Hall," *A Marianne Moore Reader* (New York, 1961), 253. See chapter 6 for further speculation on the importance of this period to Moore's poetry. *A Marianne Moore Reader* will be designated hereinafter as *MMR.*

7. U.S. Bureau of the Census, *Statistics for Pennsylvania, 1910* (Washington, D.C., 1911), 752.

8. "Poetry," *Others* 5 (July 1919): 5.

9. The phrase is from "In the Days of Prismatic Colour," *Contact* 1 (Jan. 1921): 1–2.

10. William Carlos Williams, *Spring and All,* rpt. in *Imaginations,* ed. Webster Schott (New York, 1970), 101.

11. "The New Euphues" (unsigned editorial), *New York Times* (8 Feb. 1925), sec. 2, p. 6.

12. *SP,* xi.

13. W.H. Auden, "Marianne Moore," in *The Dyer's Hand and Other Essays* (New York, 1968), 296.

14. "When I Buy Pictures," *The Dial* 71 (July 1921): 33; "An Octopus," *The Dial* 77 (Dec. 1924): 475–81.

15. The word "performed" is from Lisa M. Steinman's review of Costello's *Imaginary Possessions,* in *MMN* 6 (Fall and Spring 1982): 47.

16. Ralph Waldo Emerson, "The Transcendentalist," *The Complete Works of Ralph Waldo Emerson* (Boston, 1884), 1:316. The *Complete Works* will hereinafter be referred to as *CW.*

17. Emerson, "The American Scholar," *CW* 1:101.

18. "New York," *The Dial* 71 (Dec. 1921): 637.

19. The phrase is from "When I Buy Pictures."

20. The phrase is from "The Labours of Hercules," *The Dial* 71 (Dec. 1921): 638.

21. See, for instance, her "Interview with Donald Hall" (*MMR,* 260): "I was just trying to be honorable and not to steal things. I've always felt that if a thing had been said in the *best* way, how can you say it better? If I wanted to say something and somebody had said it ideally, then I'd take it but give the person credit for it. That's all there is to it." See also Moore's "A Note on the Notes," *CP,* 262.

22. Thus Stapleton writes: "Marianne Moore's incorporation of phrases or sentences from a widely varied list of authors has an essentially different purpose" from quotation in the work of Eliot and Pound, who quote "to evoke memory, to juxtapose past and present, or to maintain what Pound called the 'subject-rhyme'"; Moore, on the other hand, quotes simply "to avail herself of intersecting perspectives and changing tones of speech" (49). And Costello says: "In any case, Moore's quotations and notes are entirely different from Eliot's. Her borrowings do not extend the meaning of the poem into the worlds they allude to. While in a sense there is no surface immediacy in *The Waste Land,* in Moore's poetry the surface is everything" (185).

23. R.P. Blackmur, "The Method of Marianne Moore," in *Marianne Moore: A Collection of Critical Essays,* ed. Charles Tomlinson (Englewood Cliffs, N.J., 1968), 83. This collection will hereinafter be referred to as "Tomlinson."

24. For a discussion of Moore's influence on *In the American Grain,* see my essay "American Beauty: William Carlos Williams and Marianne Moore," in Dave Oliphant and Thomas Zigal, eds., *WCW & Others* (Austin, Texas, 1985), 49–72.

25. "Part of a Novel, Part of a Poem, Part of a Play," *Poetry* 40 (June 1932): 119–28.

26. "Half Deity," *Direction* 1 (Jan.–Mar. 1935): 74–75; "Smooth Gnarled Crape Myrtle!" *The New English Weekly* (17 Oct. 1935): 13; "Virginia Britannia," *Life and Letters Today* 13 (Dec. 1935): 66–70; "Bird Witted," *The New Republic* 85 (22 Jan. 1936): 311. These poems were printed in *The Pangolin and Other Verse* ([London, 1936], 3–16) under the collective heading "The Old Dominion."

27. "Henry James as a Characteristic American," *Hound and Horn* 7 (Apr.–May 1934): 363–72.

28. Stapleton argues that Moore did her best work in the 1940s; Marie Borroff makes no claim one way or the other, but every poem she discusses in *Language and the Poet: Verbal Artistry in Frost, Stevens, and Moore* (Chicago and London, 1979) postdates 1932. Costello argues that *Selected Poems* represents the peak of Moore's achievement as a poet; Hugh Kenner would make a similar claim (see *A Homemade World: The American Modernist Writers* [New York, 1975]), as would Charles Tomlinson (see his "Introduction: Marianne Moore, Her Critics, and Her Poetry," in Tomlinson).

29. "Rigorists," *Life and Letters Today* 26 (Sept. 1940): 243–45; "What Are Years?" *Kenyon Review* 2 (Summer 1940): 286; "Light Is Speech," *Decision* 1 (Mar. 1941): 26.

30. *The Absentee: A Comedy in Four Acts* (New York, 1962).

31. Moore [with Elizabeth Mayer], tr. Adalbert Stifter, *Rock Crystal: A Christmas Tale* (New York, 1945); *Puss in Boots, The Sleeping Beauty, and Cinderella: A Retelling of Three Classic Fairy Tales Based on the French of Charles Perrault* (New York and London, 1963); *The Fables of La Fontaine* (New York, 1954).

32. "Interview with Donald Hall," *MMR,* 260.

33. *CP,* 131.

34. *CP,* 229.

35. *CP,* 242.

36. *CP,* 210.

37. This poem appears only in the revised edition (1981) of *CP.*

38. Photograph by Esther Bubley, reproduced in *Marianne Moore Newsletter* 3 (Fall 1979): 20. The *Marianne Moore Newsletter* will be referred to hereinafter as *MMN.*

39. *CP,* 117.

CHAPTER 1

1. "The Past Is the Present" was originally published in *Others* (1 [Dec. 1915]: 106) under a title which I abbreviate as "So far as the future is concerned" (the full title is given in the text below).

The poem received its new title—transferred from an abandoned poem beginning "Revived bitterness," published in *Others: An Anthology of the New Verse (1917)*, 74–75—in *Observations* (1924). "Poetry" first appeared in *Others* 5 (July 1919): 5.

The "allusive code" replaces an earlier practice of naming authors directly, as in the following titles: "To William Butler Yeats on Tagore," *The Egoist* 2 (1 May 1915): 77; "To Browning" (later titled "Injudicious Gardening") and "To Bernard Shaw; A Prize Bird" (later just "A Prize Bird"), *The Egoist* 2 (2 Aug. 1915): 126; "George Moore," *Others* 1 (Dec. 1915): 105–6.

2. "Marianne Moore on Ezra Pound, 1909–1915," *MMN* 3 (Fall 1979): 6.

3. *Chimaera* 1 (July 1916): 52.

4. Cf. "A Retrospect," *Literary Essays of Ezra Pound,* ed. T.S. Eliot (New York, 1954), 11–12: "Mr. Yeats . . . has made our poetic idiom a thing pliable, a speech without inversions."

5. [Anon.], *The Literary Digest* 48 (14 Mar. 1914): 450; in Moore, Scrap Album #2, Rosenbach Archive.

6. Tomlinson, 17; emphasis added.

7. Hugh Kenner, *The Pound Era* (Berkeley and Los Angeles, 1971), 192–222 and *passim.*

8. Ibid., 199–210.

9. Moore, "Ezra Pound," facsimile in *MMN* 3 (Fall 1979): 5.

10. Moore's use of Pound's quotation from Boyd is documented in *MMN.* See n. 2. sup.

11. Pound, "The Palette," in *Literary Essays,* 215.

12. Ibid., 218.

13. Moore's notes on Kellogg's Bible talks are preserved in the Rosenbach Archive: R1251/25. See also A.R. Gordon, *The Poets of the Old Testament* (New York, 1900?); George Adam Smith, *The Book of the Twelve Prophets, Commonly Called the Minor,* 2 vols. (New York, 1898); and George Adam Smith, *The Book of Isaiah,* 2 vols. (New York, 1900).

14. For a discussion of Fenollosa's debt to Emerson, see Kenner, *The Pound Era,* 158; earlier in the same book Kenner explains how Richard Chenevix Trench, in an 1857 lecture which gave significant impetus to the compilation of data for the *Oxford English Dictionary* (then called the *New English Dictionary*), supported his argument for historical scholarship by quoting Emerson: "Language is fossil poetry." See *The Pound Era,* 103.

15. Ernest Fenollosa, *The Chinese Written Character as a Medium for Poetry,* in Ezra Pound, *Instigations of Ezra Pound* (rpt. Freeport, N.Y., 1967), 378.

16. Moore, Bible talks, R1252/25. Probable date 4 June 1914.

17. Moore, *Conversation Notebook,* R1250/23, 18.

18. Fenollosa, 367.

19. R1252/25; probable date 4 June 1914.

20. "England," *The Dial* 68 (Apr. 1920): 422–23.

21. Emerson, *CW,* 3:14.

22. Tomlinson, 17.

23. Smith, *The Book of the Twelve . . . ,* 2:129; Moore, *Reading Diary 1907–1915* (R1250/1), page headed "Monday, December 11, 1871." (The notebook had belonged to the poet's grandfather.)

24. Pound, "The Palette," *Literary Essays,* 214.

25. Smith, *The Book of the Twelve . . . ,* 2:138–39.

26. Pound, *The Spirit of Romance,* 5.

27. Moore, Bible talks, R1252/25, 9 Dec. 1914.

28. Ibid., 27 Dec. 1914.

29. Smith, *The Book of the Twelve . . . ,* 1:12.

30. Moore, Bible talks, R1252/25, 10 June 1914.

31. Ezra Pound, "A Few Don'ts by an Imagiste," *Poetry* (Mar. 1913); reprinted in *Literary Essays* as part of "A Retrospect."

32. Kenner, *The Pound Era,* 173.

33. "Interview with Donald Hall," *MMR,* 260.

34. Howard Nemerov, ed., *Poets on Poetry* (New York, 1966), 9.

35. "Interview with Donald Hall," *MMR,* 260.

36. Stapleton, 5.

37. Moore, "Diligence Is to Magic as Progress Is to Flight," *The Egoist* 2 (1 Oct. 1915): 158.

38. The conversation, which seems to have taken place sometime in or before October 1915, is

reported in Moore's *Conversation Notebook,* R1250/23, 17. See also my "Scarecrows and Curios," *MMN* 1 (Fall 1977): 13–15.

39. Moore, *Unfinished Poems* (Philadelphia, 1972), 59.

40. "Diligence Is to Magic as Progress Is to Flight."

41. Moore, "To a Steamroller," *The Egoist* 2 (1 Oct. 1915): 158.

42. Elizabeth Bishop, "Efforts of Affection: A Memoir of Marianne Moore," *The Collected Prose,* ed. Robert Giroux (New York, 1984), 137.

43. Norman T. Gates, "Richard Aldington and Marianne Moore," *MMN* 1 (Spring 1977): 17.

44. Ellen Williams, *Harriet Monroe and the Poetry Renaissance: The First Ten Years of "Poetry," 1912–1922* (Urbana, Ill., and London, 1977), 154.

45. In all, seventeen of Moore's poems appeared in 1915—a very good year for a beginner.

46. Stapleton, 6–7 and 234, n. 13.

47. "Interview with Donald Hall," *MMR,* 255.

48. Stapleton, 235–36, n. 32.

49. *P,* 24.

50. "Sojourn in the Whale," *Others: An Anthology of the New Verse (1917),* 78; Stapleton (6–7) established the link between Moore's letter and the poem.

51. "New York," *The Dial* 71 (Dec. 1921): 637.

52. Ivan Turgenev, *The Diary of a Superfluous Man,* trans. Constance Garnett (New York and London, 1906), 35.

53. Ibid., 44. Moore transcribed the passage into her *Reading Notebook 1907–1915* (R1250/1); it appears on the fifth page of "MEMORANDA," and it is heavily marked in Moore's hand.

54. Turgenev, 15.

55. Ibid., 16.

56. *Reading Notebook 1907–1915* (R1250/1), page headed "Cash Account. June."

57. Smith, *The Book of the Twelve . . . ,* 2:131.

58. Nathaniel Hawthorne, "The Custom-House," *The Centenary Edition of the Works of Nathaniel Hawthorne* (Columbus, Ohio, 1962), 1:36.

59. Harriet Monroe, et al., "A Symposium on Marianne Moore," *Poetry* 19 (Jan. 1922): 208–16. See also Louis Untermeyer, *American Poetry Since 1900* (New York, 1923), 346 ff.

60. "Critics and Connoisseurs," *Others* 3 (July 1916): 4.

61. Ford Madox Hueffer, "Impressionism—Some Speculations," Part II, *Poetry* 2 (Sept. 1913): 217.

62. Ibid.

63. George Santayana, "The Elements and Function of Poetry," in *Interpretations of Poetry and Religion* (1900; rpt. New York, 1911), 261–62.

64. Kenner, *The Pound Era* (Berkeley and Los Angeles, 1971), 80.

65. *O,* 23.

66. "Those Various Scalpels," *Contact* 1 (Jan. 1921): 1–2; reprinted from the Bryn Mawr College *Lantern,* where it appeared in 1918.

67. Tomlinson, 57.

68. See T.S. Eliot [signed "T.S. Apteryx"], "Observations," *The Egoist* 5 (May 1918): 69–70.

69. Smith, *The Book of the Twelve . . . ,* 1:27–28.

70. Untermeyer, 367.

71. Tomlinson, 73.

72. From an early MS of "Picking and Choosing" in the Rosenbach Archive.

73. Adolphus Alfred Jack, *Poetry and Prose: Being Essays on Modern English Poetry* (New York, 1912); quoted by Clark S. Northrup, in "A New Study of Poetry," *The Dial* 52 (16 June 1912): 465.

74. Northrup, "A New Study of Poetry," 465; Review of Thomas Hardy in "Current Poetry," *The Literary Digest* 48 (6 June 1914): 1370; "Current Poetry," *The Literary Digest* 48 (9 May 1914): 1129.

75. Jack, quoted by Northrup in "A New Study of Poetry," 465.

76. See, for instance, John Hall Wheelock, "To the Dreamers," quoted in "Current Poetry," *The Literary Digest* 48 (21 Mar. 1914): 641; a week earlier the same magazine had expressed its preference for the verse of Harriet Monroe over *Des Imagistes* (see "Current Poetry," *The Literary Digest* 48 [14 Mar. 1914]: 561; this is the review Moore pasted into her scrap album). See also Arthur

Davison Ficke's sonnet "Poetry," which leads off the inaugural issue of *Poetry* in 1912: *Poetry* 1 (Oct. 1912): 1.

77. William Morton Payne, unsigned lead article, "New Lamps for Old," *The Dial* 56 (16 Mar. 1914): 232; attributed to Payne by Nicholas Joost, *Years of Transition: "The Dial" 1912–1920* (Barre, Mass., 1967), 32.

78. *O,* 96.

79. T.S. Eliot, "The Borderline of Prose," *The New Statesman* 9 (19 May 1917): 15; see chapter 4 for a detailed account of Moore's increasing interest in Eliot's work.

80. Moore, *Unfinished Poems* (Philadelphia, 1972), 73.

81. "Radical," *Others* 5 (Mar. 1919): 15; Moore dropped the poem from her "canon" after 1925.

82. Quoted in "On Raw Material," *MMN* 1 (Fall 1977): 11.

83. William Wordsworth, "Preface to the Second Edition of . . . 'Lyrical Ballads,'" *The Poetical Works of William Wordsworth,* ed. E. de Selincourt (Oxford, England, 1952), 3:385–86.

84. *The Egoist* 5 (Apr. 1918): 55.

85. Moore, Notebook, R1250/24, 35.

86. *The Dial* 71 (July 1921): 34; the original title, "A Graveyard," was shortened to "A Grave" in 1924.

87. *O,* 96.

88. Tomlinson, 17.

89. *Others* 1 (Dec. 1915): 105; the poem is reprinted here in its entirety.

90. *O,* 2d ed., 31.

91. Tomlinson, 73.

92. Guy Davenport, "Marianne Moore," in *The Geography of the Imagination* (San Francisco, 1981), 115.

93. Moore, "Humility, Concentration, and Gusto," *Predilections,* 13.

94. *CP,* 36.

CHAPTER 2

1. There has been relatively little discussion of Moore's treatment of poetic form. Hugh Kenner's discussion (*HMW,* 91–118) remains the best; next is Roy Fuller's "An Artifice of Versification," in *Owls and Artificers: Oxford Lectures on Poetry* (La Salle, Ill., 1971), 46–68. See also Margaret Holley, "The Model Stanza: The Organic Origin of Moore's Syllabic Verse," *Twentieth Century Literature* 30 (Summer/Fall 1984): 181–91. Holley argues that for each of Moore's syllabic poems it is possible to locate the "model stanza" after which the rest of the poem is patterned.

2. Emerson, "The Poet," *CW,* 3:15.

3. Moore, "England," *The Dial* 68 (Apr. 1920): 422.

4. "Interview with Donald Hall," *MMR,* 259.

5. Moore, "A Note on Poetry," in William Rose Benet and Norman Holmes Pearson, eds., *The Oxford Anthology of American Literature* (New York, 1938), 1339.

6. Moore, "When I Buy Pictures," *The Dial* 71 (July 1921): 33; idem, "People's Surroundings," *The Dial* 72 (June 1922): 589.

7. "Roses Only," in *Others: An Anthology of the New Verse (1917),* ed. Alfred Kreymborg (New York: Alfred A. Knopf, 1917), 80–81.

8. Moore's phrase works its way into Eliot's account of Ben Jonson's poetic reputation: "For some generations the reputation of Jonson has been carried rather as a liability than as an asset in the balance sheet of English literature" (T.S. Eliot, *The Sacred Wood* [1920; rpt. 1928], 104; hereinafter *SW*). "Ben Jonson" appeared in 1919, more than a year after Eliot had reviewed the *Others* anthology in which "Roses Only" was first published.

9. Emerson, "The Transcendentalist," *CW,* 1:312; emphasis added.

10. Ibid.

11. Ibid., 312–13.

12. In *The Oxford Book of English Verse 1250–1900,* ed. Sir Anthony Quiller-Couch (Oxford, England, 1906), 186—where Moore might well have seen it—the "Bridal Song" is attributed to either Fletcher or Shakespeare.

13. Emerson, *CW,* 1:317.

14. Robert Herrick, "To the Virgins, to make much of Time," *The Oxford Book of English Verse 1250–1900,* 266–67.

15. William Carlos Williams, *Spring and All,* in *Imaginations,* ed. Webster Schott (New York, 1970), 102.

16. Emerson, *CW,* 1:334.

17. Tomlinson, 49.

18. Emerson, *CW,* 1:316.

19. (London) *Times Literary Supplement,* 21 July 1921, 471.

20. Emerson, *CW,* 1:323; see also his insistence that "Everything real is self-existent" (316).

21. *Others: An Anthology of the New Verse (1917),* ed. Alfred Kreymborg (New York, 1917), 83–84.

22. Emerson, "Hamatreya," *CW,* 9:35. Lisa Steinman calls Moore's lines "a possible echo of Emerson" ("Moore, Emerson, and Kreymborg: The Use of Lists in 'The Monkeys,'" *MMN* 4 [Spring 1980]: 7), but I see no reason to be so tentative about it, especially in view of Moore's reliance on Emerson in "Roses Only."

23. Emerson, *CW,* 1:323.

24. *O,* 40.

25. Emerson, *CW,* 1:327.

26. William Blake, "The Sick Rose," *The Illuminated Blake,* annotated by David V. Erdman (New York, 1974), 81.

27. Emerson, *CW,* 1:316.

28. *HMW,* 100.

29. *The Egoist* 5 (Aug. 1918): 95.

30. MSS in the Rosenbach Archive show Moore trying out a number of possibilities; nor was she satisfied with the solution quoted here.

31. *Others for 1919: An Anthology of the New Verse,* ed. Alfred Kreymborg (New York, 1920), 125–26.

32. *O,* 42.

33. *The Dial* 71 (July 1921): 34.

34. *CP,* 100.

35. Tomlinson, 54.

36. *SP,* 31.

37. *Hound and Horn* 7 (Oct.-Dec. 1933): 32; *CP,* 23. As Pamela White Hadas points out in *Marianne Moore: Poet of Affection* (Syracuse, 1977), the phrase first appeared in Moore's poem "Ennui," published in the Bryn Mawr student magazine *Tipyn O'Bob* in 1909 (Hadas, 137–38).

38. Compare Williams's "The Yachts" (1935): Moore's influence shows itself near the end of the poem, where suddenly "It is a sea of faces about them in agony, in despair / until the horror of the race dawns staggering the mind; / the whole sea become an entanglement of watery bodies . . ." (Williams, *Selected Poems,* ed. Randall Jarrell [New York, 1963], 72).

39. In the MS and in the first published version of "The Fish," only the "wedge" was made of "iron"; the "edge / Of the cliff" was simply that. The change is crucial, for it reinforces the suggestion that we have to do with something other than "the natural object" here, and it establishes an equivalence between the destroying object and the object being destroyed.

40. See "In This Age of Hard Trying Nonchalance Is Good And—," in *Others: An Anthology of the New Verse (1917),* 79; and "Radical," *Others* 5 (Mar. 1919): 15.

41. MS of "The Fish," Rosenbach Archive.

42. *Tell Me, Tell Me: Granite, Steel, and Other Topics* (New York, 1966), 5–6.

43. "Interview with Donald Hall," *MMR,* 261.

44. *CP,* 136.

45. "Interview with Donald Hall," *MMR,* 261.

46. Here I invert Kenner's argument (*HMW,* 99) that "The voice shaping sentences is anxious to be understood; these stanzas are cut and laminated in severe corrective to that anxiety. . . ." It seems to me that, on the contrary, the speaker would prefer not even to understand *herself,* and that the pattern forces a kind of attention to what is and is not being said that the speaker would rather withhold.

47. "Interview with Donald Hall," *MMR,* 263.

48. "Black Earth," *The Egoist* 5 (Apr. 1918): 55–56.
49. T.S. Eliot, *The Complete Poems and Plays . . . 1909–1950* (New York, 1971), 30.
50. MS of "Black Earth," Rosenbach Archive.
51. Henry James, Preface to *The Portrait of a Lady* (New York, 1908), 1:xi.
52. James, *The Portrait of a Lady,* 1:287–88.
53. Ibid., 2:57.
54. *Contact* 1 (Jan. 1921): 2.
55. Emerson, "The Transcendentalist," *CW,* 1:317.
56. Nathaniel Hawthorne, "The Artist of the Beautiful," in *The Complete Novels and Selected Tales,* ed. Norman Holmes Pearson (New York, 1937), 1156.
57. The Prince Rupert's drop is a fragile glass bauble, formed by dropping molten glass into cold water, whereupon the glass takes the shape of a tadpole. It thus bears a certain structural resemblance to the elephant, which is perceived as "Black earth preceded by a tendril." The analogy suggests, moreover, what the elephant has to fear: the peculiar feature of the Prince Rupert's drop is that while the thick end can withstand considerable pressure, the frail "tendril" at the other end holds the thing together: pinch it off, and the drop explodes into dust. See Moore's "Pedantic Literalist" (*The Egoist* 3 [Aug. 1916]: 95), where she begins a train of insults by comparing the pedant of the title to a "Prince Rupert's drop, a paper muslin ghost. . . ." And compare Charles Leonard Moore, "Essays and Essayists" (*The Dial* 59 [15 July 1915]: 45): "All other literary kinds [except the essay] are fenced about with restrictions: they have laws and methods which they cannot overstep; a circle is drawn about them to keep out the evil influence which would tear them to pieces; they must retain their form, like a Prince Rupert drop, which if it be pinched in the tail shatters into fragments." It is worth noting, in this connection, that Moore writes of "the strange experience of beauty" that "it tears one to pieces" ("Marriage," 1923).
58. "Interview with Donald Hall," *MMR,* 263.
59. The first of these unusual rhyme-pairs is from "Critics and Connoisseurs"; the second is from "Black Earth"; and the third is from "My Apish Cousins" (only in the version of 1917).
60. Moore, "The Sacred Wood," *The Dial* 70 (Mar. 1921): 336.
61. Marie Borroff's essay on "The Uses of Syntax" in what she calls "Marianne Moore's Promotional Prose" begins with an epigraph made by arranging "an advertisement published . . . in the 28 June 1930 issue of *The Illustrated London News*" so that, "If the hand of the illusionist has been successful, it . . . not only looks but sounds like a stanza from a poem by Marianne Moore" (*Language and the Poet: Verbal Artistry in Frost, Stevens, and Moore* [Chicago and London, 1979], 80). Significantly, Borroff tries only one stanza, whereas I have tried to demonstrate that what counts —what distinguishes Moore's verse from prose no matter how it is arranged—is the replication of syllable-count and rhyme-scheme in stanza after stanza; had Borroff persisted, her illusion would have collapsed of its own weight.
62. Williams, *Spring and All,* 146.
63. "Interview with Donald Hall," *MMR,* 258.
64. The original version of "In the Days of Prismatic Colour" was published in the Bryn Mawr College *Lantern,* no. 27 (1919), 35; the revised version appeared in *Contact* 1 (Jan. 1921): 2.
65. Herman Melville, *Billy Budd, Sailor (An Inside Narrative),* ed. Harrison Hayford and Merton M. Sealts, Jr. (Chicago and London, 1962), 128: "The symmetry of form attainable in pure fiction cannot so readily be achieved in a narrative essentially having less to do with fable than with fact. Truth uncompromisingly told will always have its ragged edges; hence the conclusion of such a narration is apt to be less finished than an architectural finial." Melville's concern for "the ragged edges" of truth dovetails nicely with E.H. Kellogg's passionate rhetorical question about Christ: "Is X [Christ] Apollo Belvedere in a long vista'd corridor or any cold or academic thing?" (Bible talks, R1252/25, c. 3 Feb. 1915.)
66. The notion of woman's culpability advanced here squares oddly, I know, with the overtly feminist intensities of poems like "Sojourn in the Whale," "Marriage," "Sea Unicorns and Land Unicorns," and "Silence" (see chapter 4 for a discussion of "Silence"; for an account of "Sea Unicorns and Land Unicorns," see my "American Beauty: William Carlos Williams and Marianne Moore," in Oliphant and Zigal, eds., *WCW & Others,* pp. 66–71). It seems to me better to let the apparent contradiction stand than to try to explain it away by saying, for instance, that "In the Days of Prismatic Colour" parodies the Marvellian position from which it seems to take off.
67. *Others* 1 (Dec. 1915): 105; see also chapter 1.

68. "An Egyptian Pulled Glass Bottle in the Shape of a Fish" was first published in *Observations* (20), but *MMN* prints a version of the poem that dates from 1915. The same article quotes statements by the Icelandic sculptor Einar Jonsson, whose work inspired the whole of the original version (and part of the final one as well), to the effect that "nothing is more dangerous to art than tradition. . . . Schools of art are impossible, and there ought not to exist forerunners or followers in art." See "Not of Any School," *MMN* 2 (Spring 1978): 9–12.

69. Cf. "The Steeple-Jack," in which the water is "etched / with waves as formal as the scales / on a fish" (*Poetry* 40 [June 1932]: 119).

CHAPTER 3

1. "Picking and Choosing" and "England" appeared in *The Dial* 68 (Apr. 1920): 421–23.

2. Margaret Holley mentions Moore's "five-year foray (1920–25) into free verse," but does not indicate the extent, the consistency, or the importance of this period; nor does she indicate that Moore had really abandoned syllabics during these years (Holley, "The Model Stanza: The Organic Origin of Moore's Syllabic Verse," *Twentieth Century Literature* 30 [Summer/Fall 1984]: 181).

3. Moore told Eliot in 1934 that *Observations* was arranged chronologically. TL unsigned, 2 July 1934; Rosenbach Archive.

4. The only other exception to this rule is "An Egyptian Pulled Glass Bottle in the Shape of a Fish," first published in *Observations* (20) in the four-line stanzas of the original draft (1915).

5. Thayer, unsigned "Comment," *The Dial* 78 (Feb. 1925): 174–80; idem, "Comment," *The Dial* 78 (Mar. 1925): 265–68.

6. Herbert S. Gorman, "Miss Moore's Art Is Not a Democratic One," *New York Times Book Review* (1 Feb. 1925): 5; "The New Euphues" (unsigned editorial), *New York Times* (8 Feb. 1925), sec. 2, p. 6; Edwin Seaver, "A Literalist of the Imagination," *The Nation* 120 (18 Mar. 1925): 297–98; Wilbert Snow, in *New York Herald-Tribune Books* (17 May 1925): 3; Joseph Auslander, in *New York World* (18 Jan. 1925): 8; Margaret Widdemer, *New York Evening Post Literary Review* (8 Aug. 1925): 4; Yvor Winters, "Holiday and Day of Wrath," *Poetry* 26 (Apr. 1925): 39–44.

7. "Interview with Donald Hall," *MMR*, 265.

8. Stapleton, 31.

9. The syllabic MS of "A Graveyard"—called "A Graveyard in the Middle of the Sea"—is in the Rosenbach Archive; the syllabic version of "When I Buy Pictures" is in *P*, 17. See also Bonnie Costello, "'To a Snail': A Lesson in Compression," *MMN* 3 (Fall 1979): 11–15. There is a syllabic version of "Like a Bulrush" in *Others: An Anthology of the New Verse (1917)*, 76; the free-verse text is in *O*, 38. See chapter 1 for an account of the different versions of "Poetry."

10. Moore, "Feeling and Precision," *Predilections* (New York, 1955), 3.

11. MS of "Picking and Choosing," Rosenbach Archive.

12. *P*, 17.

13. Moore, unsigned "Comment," *The Dial* 79 (Aug. 1925): 177.

14. Moore's *Poems* was compiled by H.D. and Winifred Ellerman (Bryher). It is usually said that they worked without Moore's knowledge; but the most that can be said is that while Moore did not actively collaborate in producing the volume, she probably gave tacit consent. Laurence Stapleton quotes a letter from Moore to H.D. which shows no surprise at the fact of the book's publication; on the contrary, Moore is surprised only by how well she comes off. See Stapleton, 28.

15. *P*, 17.

16. Quoted by H.D. in "Marianne Moore," *The Egoist* 3 (Aug. 1916): 118.

17. Henry David Thoreau, *Walden; or, Life in the Woods, Writings* (Boston, 1897), 3:128–29.

18. "A Graveyard," *The Dial* 71 (July 1921): 34.

19. Stapleton, 235–36.

20. Henry James, Preface to *The American*, in *The Art of the Novel*, ed. R.P. Blackmur (New York, 1934), 33.

21. James, *The American Scene*, ed. Leon Edel (Bloomington, Ind., 1968), 77.

22. Pound, "A Pact," in *Personae* (New York, 1971), 89.

23. *Others* ceased publication after July 1919, *The Egoist* after December 1919.

24. *O*, 98.

CHAPTER 4

1. Moore, "A Note on T.S. Eliot's Book," *Poetry* 12 (Apr. 1918): 36–37.
2. Moore, "The Sacred Wood," *The Dial* 70 (Mar. 1921): 336.
3. Ibid., 339.
4. "English Literature Since 1914" appears in *MMN* 4 (Fall 1980): 12–21.
5. Ibid., 13–14.
6. Ibid., 15.
7. Ibid., 13.
8. *O,* 97.
9. Emerson, "The Transcendentalist," *CW,* 1:323.
10. T.S. Eliot, "In Memory," *The Little Review* 5 (Aug. 1918): 44; emphasis added.
11. Ibid., 45.
12. Ibid.
13. Tomlinson, 17.
14. *Letters of Ezra Pound 1907–1941,* ed. D.D. Paige (New York, 1950), 141–44.
15. MS of "Picking and Choosing," Rosenbach Archive. Compare to the "XY" of "So far as the future is concerned."
16. "People's Surroundings," *The Dial* 72 (June 1922): 588–90.
17. *MMN* 4 (Fall 1980): 21.
18. Williams to Moore, 21 March 1921: quoted by Costello, *Imaginary Possessions,* 161. Williams is responding to Moore's review of *Kora in Hell.* The complete text of his letter is in the *Selected Letters* (1957; rpt. New York, 1984), 52–53.
19. I am well aware that this reading seems wildly unlikely as a judgment on Pound, and that it is much more plausible as a comment on Williams. But it would be inconsistent with Moore's practice to take a phrase formerly applied to Pound ("natural promptness") and use it to allude instead to Williams.
20. Grace Schulman, "Conversation with Marianne Moore," in *Contemporary Poetry: A Retrospective from the "Quarterly Review of Literature,"* ed. T. Weiss and Renée Weiss (Princeton, 1975), 434.
21. *O,* 101; the phrase comes from France's *Honeybee,* and was copied into Moore's *Reading Diary 1916–1921* (152) on 26 November 1920.
22. Wallace Stevens, *Harmonium* (New York, 1923), 100; "Sunday Morning" appeared in *Poetry* in 1915.
23. Moore, "The Sacred Wood," *The Dial* 70 (Mar. 1921): 339; *MMN* 4 (Fall 1980): 21.
24. *MMN* 4 (Fall 1980): 21.
25. *O,* 100.
26. Tomlinson, 18.
27. *O,* 101, 98.
28. *Contact* 1 (Jan. 1921): 1–2.
29. *O,* 101.
30. *SW,* 52.
31. Ibid., 51–52.
32. Yeats, *The Collected Poems* (New York, 1956), 78; *SW,* 49.
33. *SW,* 49.
34. Emerson, "The Poet," *CW,* 3:40.
35. *SW,* 50.
36. Ibid.
37. Ibid.
38. Ibid.
39. *The Waste Land* was first published in *The Criterion* in October 1922; its first American appearance was in *The Dial* 73 (Nov. 1922): 473–85. Moore's "Novices" was published in *The Dial* 74 (Feb. 1923): 183–84.
40. T.S. Eliot, *The Complete Poems and Plays . . . 1909–1950* (New York, 1971), 50.
41. Ibid., 46–47.

42. The original sources for these quotations were composed in English, Italian, and French.
43. Moore's comment on W.H. Hudson in "English Literature since 1914," *MMN* 4 (Fall 1980): 14.
44. *Secession* no. 5 (July 1923), 12.
45. *SW,* 52.
46. *O,* 102.
47. Ibid.
48. George Adam Smith, *The Book of Isaiah* (New York, 1896), 2:282; Moore, *Reading Diary 1916–1921,* 128.
49. From "An Egyptian Pulled Glass Bottle in the Shape of a Fish" (*O,* 20).
50. The following entry in Moore's *Reading Diary 1916–1921* (62) was probably made in the fall of 1919:

> Swinburne's Letters. ed by Mrs Disney Leith
> Putnam Introduction
> .....and as there is no beach or shore of any kind, you can imagine how the sea swings to and fro—between the cliffs, foams and swells beats and baffles itself against the steep faces of rock. I should guess it must be unique in England. Seen from above and on horseback it was very queer, dark grey swollen water, caught as it were in a trap, and [heaving] with rage against both sides at once, edged with *long panting lines of incessant foam* that swung & lapped along the deep steep cliffs without breaking and had not room to move at ease. [Emphasis added.]

51. *SW,* 149.
52. Ibid.
53. Moore, "The Sacred Wood," *The Dial* 70 (Mar. 1921): 336–37.
54. *MMN* 4 (Fall 1980): 14.
55. *O,* 102.
56. Pound, "E.P. Ode pour l'election de son sepulchre," *Personae* (New York, 1971), 187; see Eliot, *The Complete Poems and Plays . . . 1909–1950,* 37.
57. Pound, *Literary Essays,* 7.
58. Ibid., 9.
59. Moore, "The Accented Syllable," *The Egoist* 3 (Oct. 1916): 151.
60. Ibid., 152.
61. Ibid.
62. Ibid.
63. Edgar Allan Poe, "The Philosophy of Composition," in *The Works of Edgar Allan Poe,* ed. Edmund Clarence Stedman and George Edward Woodberry (Chicago and New York, 1903), 6:43–45; Moore refers to Poe's essay in her *Reading Diary 1916–1921,* 4 (13 Apr. 1916).
64. Moore, "Translator's Preface," *The Fables of La Fontaine,* trans. Marianne Moore (New York, 1954), x.
65. "Silence," *The Dial* 77 (Oct. 1924): 290.
66. *O,* 104.
67. *O,* 105.
68. *O,* 52.
69. *SW,* 48; emphasis added.
70. *O,* 105.
71. Robert Frost, "Mending Wall," in *The Poetry of Robert Frost,* ed. Edward Connery Latham (New York, 1966), 33. "Mending Wall" is the first poem in *North of Boston* (1915), to which Moore responds enthusiastically in an unpublished poem called "To Our Imported Grasshopper, 'North of Boston'" (*Unfinished Poems,* 57). The opening lines of Moore's homage to Frost read: "As I unfolded its wings, / In examining it for the first time, / I forgot the war. . . ."
72. Nathaniel Hawthorne, "The Custom-House," *Centenary Ed.*, 1:44.

CHAPTER 5

1. Emerson, "The Poet," *CW,* 3:40–41.
2. Ibid., 40.

3. "An Octopus," *The Dial* 77 (Dec. 1924): 475–81.
4. "Sea Unicorns and Land Unicorns," *The Dial* 77 (Nov. 1924): 411–13.
5. Moore's final note to the poem reads: "Quoted descriptions of scenery and of animals, of which the source is not given, have been taken from government pamphlets on our national parks" (*O,* 107).

For a fully documented account of Moore's trip to Mt. Rainier and of the composition of "An Octopus," see Patricia C. Willis, "The Road to Paradise: First Notes on Marianne Moore's 'An Octopus,'" *Twentieth Century Literature* 30 (Summer/Fall 1984): 242–66.

6. John Milton, *Poetical Works: Paradise Lost, Paradise Regained, and Samson Agonistes,* ed. Merritt Y. Hughes (New York, 1933). Willis points out several Miltonic echoes (260–63).
7. *The Complete Poetry and Selected Prose of John Donne,* ed. Charles M. Coffin (New York, 1952), 97–98.
8. In *The Complete Tales and Poems of Edgar Allan Poe* (New York, 1975), 882:

> *March 22d.*—The darkness had materially increased, relieved only by the glare of the water thrown back from the white curtain before us. . . . And now we rushed into the embraces of the cataract, where a chasm threw itself open to receive us. But there arose in our pathway a shrouded human figure, very far larger in its proportions than any dweller among men. And the hue of the skin of the figure was of the perfect whiteness of the snow.

9. Henry James, *The Golden Bowl* (New York, 1909), 1:13.
10. Ibid., 22; it was the South Pole Pym was heading for.
11. James, Preface to *The Golden Bowl,* vi–vii.
12. Laurence Stapleton, "Neatness of Finish!" *MMN* 1 (Fall 1977): 16. Williams's *Kora in Hell* (1920) is reprinted in *Imaginations,* ed. Webster Schott (New York, 1970).
13. *Imaginations,* 71.
14. Ibid.
15. Ibid., 72.
16. Quoted by Stapleton in *The Poet's Advance,* 36.
17. *HMW,* 96; Costello, 66–67. Kenner calls perception "a moral act" in Moore, though not a religious one. He sees Moore's concentration on visual detail as being in effect a refutation of Ruskin's willingness to "impersonate Isaiah"—that is, a deliberate turning away from prophecy. Costello argues that the two components of Ruskinian perception—(1) "the earnest and intense saying of natural facts," which precedes and requires (2) "the ordering of those facts by the human intellect"—"tend to pull apart in [Moore's] verse" (68).

Costello reports that Moore transcribed this passage into a reading notebook and later used it in an article for *The Dial.*

18. "So far as the future is concerned" reverts to Habakkuk; "Poetry" measures itself against the prophetic intensity of Blake; and "Novices" concludes with a mimetic tribute to Isaiah.
19. "English Literature since 1914," *MMN* 4 (Fall 1980): 14: "Hudson is given over to precise seeing. He has predominently [*sic*] the scientific attitude of mind in conjunction with spiritual vision."
20. *O,* 106.
21. *O,* 107.
22. Emerson, "The Poet," *CW,* 3:23, 30.
23. Emerson, "Experience," *CW,* 3:76–77.
24. "Sea Unicorns and Land Unicorns," *The Dial* 77 (Nov. 1924): 411–13.
25. Williams, *Imaginations,* 73.
26. Emerson, "Experience," *CW,* 3:53–54.
27. As Costello points out (259n.), "The pamphlet of *National Parks Rules and Regulations* includes an aerial photograph of Mt. Rainier that makes it look like an octopus, and the prose caption calls it 'an octopus of ice.'"
28. Costello, too, remarks on the near-incomprehensibility of the poem's opening images, and the paragraph just concluded is indebted to her discussion (82–83). But she does not offer to account for the difficulties she describes, nor does she seem to recognize the centrality of the Adamic "power" which "we are still devoid of." Her long reading of the poem fails because it limits itself to treating "An Octopus" as a descriptive poem, and does not ask what function the "description" might serve.
29. *O,* 107.

30. John Winthrop, *The History of New England from 1630 to 1639* (Boston: Little, Brown and Company, 1853), 1: 97.
31. Ibid., 11: 280–81.
32. Johnathan Edwards, *Images or Shadows of Divine Things*, rpr. in George McMichael, ed., *Anthology of American Literature* (New York, 1980), 1: 248.
33. Moore, "The Camperdown Elm," *CP*, 242.
34. Moore, "The Jerboa," *Hound and Horn* 6 (Oct.–Dec. 1932): 108–13.
35. Emerson, *Nature, CW*, 1:14.
36. Ibid., 16.
37. Ibid., 31.
38. Emerson, "The Poet," *CW*, 3:40.
39. See, for instance, James's rendition of the shadows in the opening paragraph of *Portrait of a Lady* ([New York, 1908], 1:1), a paragraph whose method is typical of that employed throughout the novel. First we see "shadows"; then we see that the "shadows are straight and angular"; then we discover that they are being cast by specific individuals; and finally we discover the persons involved.
40. The line is from "Sea Unicorns and Land Unicorns."
41. Tomlinson, 48, 52.
42. Ibid., 49.
43. Ibid., 52–53.

CHAPTER 6

1. "Part of a Novel, Part of a Poem, Part of a Play," *Poetry* 40 (June 1932): 119–28.
2. Wallace Stevens, "A Poet That Matters," *Life and Letters Today* 13 (Dec. 1935): 61–65.
3. M.M. to J.W.M., TLS, 26 June 1932; Rosenbach Archive.
4. Scofield Thayer, as quoted by William Wasserstrom in *The Time of "The Dial"* (Syracuse, 1963), 113.
5. Nicholas Joost, *Scofield Thayer and "The Dial": An Illustrated History* (Carbondale, Ill., 1964), 251–52.
6. Wasserstrom, 115.
7. Ibid., 132.
8. "Interview with Donald Hall," *MMR*, 267.
9. Moore, "Brooklyn from Clinton Hill," *MMR*, 182.
10. "Interview with Donald Hall," *MMR*, 256.
11. "Brooklyn from Clinton Hill," *MMR*, 192.
12. "Interview with Donald Hall," *MMR*, 254.
13. Moore, unsigned "Comment," *The Dial* 85 (July 1928): 89–90.
14. Moore, *Reading Diary 1924–1930* (R1250/5), 155.
15. Ibid., R1250/5, 126.
16. Quoted by T. Sturge Moore, *Albert Dürer* (London, 1905), 151.
17. Ibid., 152.
18. Moore, "Comment," *The Dial* 85 (July 1928): 89–90; see R1250/5, 159.
19. *SP*, x.
20. From an early draft of "The Steeple-Jack" in the Rosenbach Archive.
21. Moore, "If a Man Die," *Hound and Horn* 5 (Jan.–Mar. 1932): 319.
22. Moore, "Comment," *The Dial* 85 (July 1928): 89.
23. Ibid., 90.
24. Erwin Panofsky, *The Life and Art of Albrecht Dürer* (Princeton, 1955), 123.
25. Moore, "Comment," *The Dial* 85 (July 1928): 89.
26. M.M. to Barbara Kurz, TLS, 25 April 1961; facsimile in *MMN* 1 (Fall 1977): 7.
27. Moore, "Comment," *The Dial* 85 (July 1928): 89.
28. Panofsky, 38.
29. The terms *cosmic* and *local* are from a letter by M.M. to J.W.M., written before she had found Williams's misplaced letter in the postcard drawer. TLS, 19 June 1932; Rosenbach Archive.
30. A. Kingsley Weatherhead (*The Edge of the Image: Marianne Moore, William Carlos Wil-*

liams, and Some Other Poets [Seattle and London, 1967], 59) makes this analogy but does not pursue it.

31. Botanical information is derived from Donald Wyman, *Wyman's Gardening Encyclopedia* (New York, 1977); his advice on the spiderwort is on p. 249.

32. Moore, "If a Man Die," 319.

33. Nathaniel Hawthorne, "Rappaccini's Daughter," *The Works of Nathaniel Hawthorne* (Boston and New York, 1882), 2:107–48.

34. See Williams, "Marianne Moore": Tomlinson, 57.

35. In the *Dictionary of Symbols and Imagery* ([Amsterdam and London, 1974], 204) Ad de Vries quotes Walter Scott: "Fox-glove and nightshade, side by side, / Emblems of punishment and pride." See Wyman on the Salpiglossis (978).

36. Moore, *Reading Diary 1930–1943* (R1250/6), 57.

37. Emerson, "The American Scholar," *CW,* 1:86; the passage Moore quotes in "The Student" is on 95–96.

38. Emerson, *Nature, CW,* 1:31.

39. Emerson, "The American Scholar," *CW,* 1:101.

40. Ibid., 88.

41. *CP,* 100.

42. Donald Attwater, *The Penguin Dictionary of Saints* (Harmondsworth, England, 1965), 43–44.

43. In the Rosenbach Archive.

44. Edmund Burke—*not* Kenneth—is praised in "Picking and Choosing" as "a psychologist"; he is quoted in "Silence" and in the revised version of "The Student" (1941; *CP,* 101).

45. My discussion of Coolidge is indebted to Robert K. Murray, *The Politics of Normalcy: Governmental Theory and Practice in the Harding-Coolidge Era* (New York, 1973).

46. Notes to *What Are Years?* (New York, 1941), 49; see also R1250/6, 35–36, for Moore's transcription from Eberleis. The entry was probably made in November 1931.

47. See Moore's review of the *Letters of Emily Dickinson,* in *Poetry* 41 (Jan. 1933): 223.

48. Hawthorne, *The Scarlet Letter, Centenary Ed.*, 1:243.

49. Ibid., 41.

50. Ibid., 44.

51. Ibid., 38.

52. *Poetry* 37 (May 1931): 106–9.

53. George Washington, "First Inaugural Address," in *An American Primer,* ed. Daniel J. Boorstin (New York, 1968), 191.

54. Hawthorne, "Fancy's Showbox," *Works,* 1:256.

55. Hawthorne, *Works,* 1:17.

56. M.M. to J.W.M., 28 August 1932; Rosenbach Archive.

57. Moore, "Comment," *The Dial* 85 (July 1928): 89.

58. M.M. to Barbara Kurz, 25 April 1961: *MMN* 1 (Fall 1977): 7.

59. Ibid.

60. "Brooklyn from Clinton Hill," *MMR,* 183, 184.

61. "Letter to Barbara Kurz," *MMN* 1 (Fall 1977): 6.

62. "The Frigate Pelican," *The Criterion* 13 (July 1934): 558.

63. Emily Dickinson, #1129 in *The Complete Poems of Emily Dickinson,* ed. Thomas H. Johnson (Boston, 1960).

CHAPTER 7

1. The *OED* offers "gay science" as a nineteenth-century translation of the Provençal *gai saber*; see the entry for *gay.*

2. "The Jerboa," *Hound and Horn* 6 (Oct.–Dec. 1932): 108–13.

3. "Camellia Sabina," in *Active Anthology,* ed. Ezra Pound (London, 1933), 189–91.

4. William Cullen Bryant, "To a Waterfowl," in F.O. Matthiesson, ed., *The Oxford Book of American Verse* (New York, 1950), 54–55.

5. Moore, "Henry James as a Characteristic American," *Hound and Horn* 7 (Apr.–May 1934): 363, 371.

6. "Half Deity," *Direction* 1 (Jan.–Mar. 1935): 74–75; "Smooth Gnarled Crape Myrtle!" *The New English Weekly* 8 (17 Oct. 1935): 13; "Virginia Britannia," *Life and Letters Today* 13 (Dec. 1935): 66–70; "Bird Witted," *The New Republic* 85 (22 Jan. 1936): 311. "The Old Dominion" sequence appears in *The Pangolin and Other Verse* (London, 1936), 3–16.

7. Moore, "Henry James as a Characteristic American," 366–67.

8. Ibid., 363.

9. Witness what James E. Breslin calls Williams's "*baptism in filth*" in "The Wanderer" (1914) and his constant motif of descent. See Breslin, *William Carlos Williams: An American Artist* (New York and London, 1970), 23.

10. Moore, "Humility, Concentration, and Gusto," *Predilections* (New York, 1955), 13.

11. "Virginia Britannia," *Life and Letters Today* 13 (Dec. 1935): 70.

12. Costello, *Imaginary Possessions,* 105.

13. Moore, untitled lecture. Typescript headed "Sarah Lawrence College, May 1, 1940," in the Rosenbach Archives. Referred to hereafter as the "Sarah Lawrence lecture."

14. *ColP,* 113.

15. Hector St. John de Crèvecœur, "What Is an American?" (Letter III), *Letters of an American Farmer* (London, 1912), 53.

16. Marie Borroff, *Language and the Poet: Verbal Artistry in Frost, Stevens, and Moore* (Chicago and London, 1979), 130–31.

17. William Wordsworth, "Ode: Intimations of Immortality," *Complete Poetical Works* (London, 1891), 360.

18. Donald Wesling, *Wordsworth and the Adequacy of Landscape* (New York, 1970), 7.

19. Moore, "England," *The Dial* 68 (Apr. 1920): 422–23.

20. Henry James, *Hawthorne* (New York, 1880), 42–43.

21. Ibid., 43.

22. William Bradford, *Bradford's History "Of Plimoth Plantation"* (Boston, 1896), 95–96.

23. Washington Irving, "The Author's Account of Himself," *The Sketch-Book of Geoffrey Crayon, Gent., Irving's Works* (New York, 1880), 2:14–15.

24. Irving, "Rip Van Winkle," *Irving's Works,* 2:58–59.

25. Thomas Cole, "Essay on American Scenery," in *American Art 1700–1960: Sources and Documents,* ed. John W. McCoubrey (Englewood Cliffs, N.J., 1965), 101.

26. James Fenimore Cooper, *The Pioneers; or, Sources of the Susquehanna; Works of James Fenimore Cooper* (New York and London, 1897), 4:31: "The composite order . . . was an order composed of many others, and was intended to be the most useful of all, for it admitted into its construction such alterations as convenience or circumstances might require."

For discussion of *The Course of Empire,* see McCoubrey, *American Tradition in Painting* (New York, 1963), xx.

27. Cooper, *The Last of the Mohicans; or, a Narrative of 1757, Works,* 2:144; emphasis added.

28. Moore, Sarah Lawrence lecture, 1.

29. Thomas Gray, *Elegy Written in a Country Churchyard,* in *The Oxford Book of English Verse 1250–1918,* ed. Sir Arthur Quiller-Couch (New York, 1940), 531.

30. Williams, "The American Background" (1934), *Selected Essays* (New York, 1954), 134.

31. Williams, *In the American Grain* (1925; rpt. New York, 1952), 216. For a fuller account of Moore's early response to *In the American Grain,* see my "American Beauty: William Carlos Williams and Marianne Moore," in Oliphant and Zigal, *WCW & Others,* 66–71.

32. Edgar Allan Poe, "The Raven," in *The Works of Edgar Allan Poe,* 10:9. Williams, *In the American Grain,* 218.

33. *The Advancement of Learning* (1605) appeared two years before Jamestown was settled; *The New Organon* appeared in 1620, the year the *Mayflower* reached the New World. See Moore, "Sir Francis Bacon," *The Dial* 76 (Apr. 1924): 84–91.

34. Moore's note in *What Are Years?* (New York, 1941), 51: "Sir Francis Bacon: 'If a boy be bird-witted.'"

35. Kenner, "Meditation and Enactment," Tomlinson, 162.

36. Ibid.

37. Ibid.

38. Ibid.

39. Wallace Stevens, "Of Modern Poetry" (1942), *Collected Poems* (New York, 1954), 240.

40. Kenner, "Meditation and Enactment," 163.

41. Ezra Pound, *ABC of Reading* (1934; rpt. New York, 1960), 53.

42. Ibid.

43. Moore, "The Cantos," *Poetry* 39 (Oct. 1931): 38–40; emphasis added.

44. Moore, "The Jerboa," *Hound and Horn* 6 (Oct.–Dec. 1932): 113; "The Plumet Basilisk," *Hound and Horn* (Oct.–Dec. 1933): 32; "The Frigate Pelican," *Criterion* 13 (July 1934): 558; "The Pangolin," *The Pangolin and Other Verse,* 18.

45. John Keats, "Ode to a Nightingale," *The Complete Poetical Works and Letters of John Keats,* ed. Horace S. Scudder (Boston and New York, 1899), 145.

46. Keats, "Ode to a Nightingale," 144.

47. Keats, "Ode on a Grecian Urn," *The Complete Poetical Works and Letters,* 135.

48. "Half Deity" has been almost completely ignored. Costello does not mention the poem at all; nor does Borroff; nor Hall (*The Cage and the Animal* [New York, 1970]). Nitchie mentions but does not discuss it in *Marianne Moore: An Introduction to the Poetry* ([New York, 1969], 110). Engle, who lists it among the poems which "we may assume that Miss Moore does not wish . . . to be considered representative" because she omits it from *The Collected Poems,* describes it as "a long poem on insects that has many fine passages" (*Marianne Moore* [New York, 1964], 117). Hadas gives it a cursory glance in *Marianne Moore: Poet of Affection* ([Syracuse, 1977], 181–82). Stapleton (105) gives a brief summary of the poem's plot and says, "one may see that [Moore] did not quite succeed in working through the parallel between the child's approach to the butterfly and its rebuff when the butterfly succumbs to Zephyr's enchantment." I disagree, as my argument will show.

49. Ralph Waldo Emerson, "Experience," *CW,* 3:81.

50. Ibid., 52.

51. Keats, "Ode to Psyche," in *Complete Poetical Works,* 142–44.

52. Percy Bysshe Shelley, "The Sensitive Plant," *Complete Poetical Works,* ed. Thomas Hutchinson (New York, 1933), 589–96; the lines quoted appear on 596.

53. Letter quoted by W. Jackson Bate in *The Burden of the Past and the English Poet* (New York, 1972), 5.

54. Walt Whitman, *Song of Myself,* in *Complete Poetry and Selected Prose and Letters* (London, 1967), 62.

55. This is true only for the order in which the poems appear in *The Pangolin* . . . ; if we consider them in the order of composition, it is rather the case that the "deadly combat" of "Bird Witted" recalls and explodes the apparent innocence of the confrontation here.

56. Lewis Carroll, *Alice's Adventures in Wonderland* (1936; rpt. New York, 1976), 92.

57. Moore, notes to *The Pangolin* . . . , 23.

58. #XX in *Poems by Emily Dickinson,* ed. Mable Loomis Todd and T.W. Higginson (Boston, 1893), 34. As Dickinson said in a letter to Higginson dated 25 April 1862, she had "For Poets . . . Keats—and Mr and Mrs Browning" (Thomas H. Johnson, ed., *Emily Dickinson: Selected Letters* [Cambridge, Mass., 1971], 172).

59. Shelley, "Ode to the West Wind," *Complete Poetical Works,* 578–79.

60. Moore copied these phrases from Thayer's essay, "Shelley: or the Poetic Value of Revolutionary Principles," which had appeared in the *Harvard Monthly* in April 1913; see Rosenbach 1250/5, 165–66 (6 Nov. 1928).

61. Moore, Travel and Museum Notes, Rosenbach 1251/19, n.p.

62. Emerson, "The Poet," *CW,* 3:18.

63. Elizabeth Bishop writes, in her posthumously published memoir "Efforts of Affection: A Memoir of Marianne Moore" (*The Collected Prose,* ed. Robert Giroux [New York, 1984], 143: " . . . on one occasion, when we were walking in Brooklyn . . . I noticed we were on a street associated with the *Brooklyn Eagle,* and I said fatuously, 'Marianne, isn't it odd to think of you and Walt Whitman walking this same street over and over?' She exclaimed in her mock-ferocious tone, 'E*liz*abeth, don't speak to me about that man!' So I never did again."

64. See "The Labours of Hercules," "The Hero," and "The Jerboa" for additional instances of Moore's "protest" against the treatment of blacks.

65. Moore, Sarah Lawrence lecture, 1.

66. Emerson, "The Poet," *CW,* 3:13–14.
67. Ibid., 29.
68. Moore, Sarah Lawrence lecture, 1.
69. Nathaniel Hawthorne, *The Scarlet Letter, Centenary Ed.*, 1:189–98. This is the title of chapter 17.
70. Moore, Sarah Lawrence lecture, 1.
71. T.S. Eliot, "In Memory," *The Little Review* 5 (Aug. 1918): 44. See chapter 4 for a discussion of this essay and its importance to Moore.
72. T.S. Eliot, "Virginia," *Virginia Quarterly Review* 10 (Apr. 1934): 200. The same issue contains an article on three eighteenth-century Virginia gardens and another on slavery in Virginia.

AFTERWORD

1. In 1937 Moore published two reviews and one short story ("The Farm Show," *Life and Letters Today* 16 [Spring 1937]: 57–60); in 1938 she answered an enquiry from the editors of *Twentieth Century Verse* (12 [Oct. 1938]: 114) and produced "A Note on Poetry" accompanying a selection of her work in *The Oxford Anthology of American Literature* (ed. William Rose Benet and Norman Holmes Pearson [New York, 1938], 1319); in 1939 she produced nothing at all.
2. *What Are Years?* (New York, 1941), 1.
3. Williams, *Spring and All,* in *Imaginations,* ed. Webster Schott, 100–101.
4. T.S.E. to M.M., TLS 20 June 1934; Rosenbach Archive.
5. Stapleton, 110–11.
6. Ibid., 110. Stapleton does not link this (for Moore) extraordinary effort to the "failure" of *Selected Poems.*
7. *The Collected Poems of Wallace Stevens* (New York, 1954), 140.
8. "Interview with Donald Hall," *MMR,* 269.
9. It is in the war-time context of *What Are Years?* that Moore first revises the final stanza of "Virginia Britannia" to admit "the town's assertiveness"; she retains the seventeen-line stanzas of the original version until 1951.
10. "Humility, Concentration, and Gusto," *Predilections,* 12.
11. *SP,* xi.
12. *ColP,* 147.

Index